BLACK KNIGHT

BLACK KNIGHT

The Ronnie Knight Story

by
Ronnie Knight
with
Barrie Tracey

CENTURY
London   Sydney   Auckland   Johannesburg

Copyright © Mason Publications 1990

Published in Great Britain in 1990 by Century
An imprint of Random Century Ltd
20 Vauxhall Bridge Road, London SW1V 2SA

Random Century Australia (Pty) Ltd
20 Alfred Street, Milson Point, Sydney, NSW 2061, Australia

Random Century New Zealand Ltd
PO Box 40–086, 32–34 View Road, Glenfield, Auckland 10, New Zealand

Random Century South Africa (Pty) Ltd
PO Box 337, Bergvlei 2012, South Africa

Ronnie Knight's right to be identified as the author of this work has been
asserted by him in accordance with the Copyright, Designs and
Patents Act, 1988

Set in 11 on 13pt Times by
Speedset Ltd, Ellesmere Port, South Wirral

Printed and bound in Great Britain by
Mackays of Chatham

British Library Cataloguing in Publication Data

Knight, Ronnie
  Black Knight : the Ronnie Knight story.
  1. Great Britain. Armed robbery. Biographies
  I. Title   II. Tracey, Barrie
  364.1552092

ISBN 0–7126–3945–4

Preface

Sometimes I take a sideways glance in the mirror and I say to myself: 'Ronnie Knight, old son, you must have a double somewhere out there.'

He is the one everybody keeps reading about. The villain they call 'Britain's Most Wanted Man'. He is the notorious, dangerous drug baron. The infamous King of the Costa del Criminals. He is the Ronnie Knight wanted by the Old Bill in connection with two of Britain's biggest armed robberies, involving the little matter of £32m or so. Everybody knows about this Cockney playboy character. Millions of words have been written and broadcast about him. He gets the sort of close attention usually reserved for your film stars and Royalty.

The unflattering profile of my spitting image has been reflected in years of Press, television and radio publicity. They have charged, tried and sentenced their fictional Ronnie Knight . . . and howl for his blood.

As I gaze into my mirror it seems unreal that this ruthless gangster everybody is hearing about all the time is . . . me! The real Ronnie Knight. Talk about a nasty shock to the system!

During my life I have done a few things about which I am definitely not proud. I have never expected to be nominated for the Good Citizen of the Year Award. An angel I am not. But if I was guilty of half the wickedness attributed to me I would cut my throat and hope to die.

The mass media has created an image of me, as a mixture of The Scarlet Pimpernel, Al Capone, Don Juan and a Mafia Godfather, credited with pulling off feats that would leave Superman gasping for breath!

It's a funny feeling seeing your picture large as life in newspapers carrying tales that are nearly always fantasy, usually ridiculous and just as often impossible. They say I flit in and out of England like a migrating swallow, swooping in whenever the mood takes me by flying the 1,200 miles from my home in Spain aboard a little light aircraft. Without so much as a blush they diligently report how I touch down on some secret airfield and swan into old London town to conduct some suspect business and get together with my old mates. And hey-presto, the stories go, before you can say 'Jolly Jack Flash' I'm zooming back to what they call my sunshine sanctuary down in Benalmadena, Malaga . . . where I'm sitting right now hoping to put the record straight.

In all these high-flying fantasies about me jetting around like an Arab prince there's never any mention about the three or four landings a small plane would have to make on the way. Or about air traffic control. Or customs. Or the police.

Same as the old chestnut about me nipping the sixty-odd miles into Gibraltar every time I fancy a pint and a game of darts.

Several publications printed pictures claiming you-know-who was behind the wheel of a Rolls Royce shooting over the border. Since the driver looked about as much like me as does Frankie Bruno, they got round it by saying that this was 'Knight in a heavy disguise'.

I ask you!

The latest pork pies hot off the presses claim that I've bought a little palace in Morocco and that I am lining up getaways in Central and South America, in case I get extradited from Spain. On top of all that I am condemned as a callous crook, bank robber and mastermind criminal. Worst of all I have been branded as an evil drug baron, lording it over an army of heavy henchmen like I was the worst person in the world. Not so long ago I was accused of organizing acid-house parties. Now that was a new one on me. Because I could not tell you the difference between an acid house and a public house.

Those who paint me as the villainous Black Knight count on the belief that I'm in no position to hit back. For reasons I intend to reveal later they could be in for a rude awakening! But as matters stand they see me as fair game. The 'Screw Ronnie Knight' season is open all year round.

Now I know how Prince Charles, Diana, Fergie and the rest of the Royals must sometimes feel! They have to take it all lying down, because their hands are tied, too.

I have been imprisoned in my own home for weeks on end by reporters and cameramen poking their long lenses into my private life. They have rattled my rooftop with whirring helicopters, frightening the fur off all the pets in the neighbourhood and causing a fortune in damage.

Before anybody starts accusing me of hypocritical whitewashing let me hold up my hands and confess that I have seen and heard things that would make your hair curl! Occasionally I have found it necessary to bang a few heads together. However, I can tell you without fear of contradiction, that the recipients of my attentions were invariably nasty little toe-rags, conmen who would nick the sugar right out of your tea, or charmers who used to go round beating up women and kids.

I moved in interesting social circles, from the down-to-earth world of the East End to the High Society glamour of showbusiness. For more than twenty years I was married to famous actress Barbara Windsor, whose success in the hilarious 'Carry On' movies made her one of Britain's most popular and successful actresses.

My West End club, The Artistes and Repertoire, was the hottest place in town; a popular meeting-place for famous stars, successful businessmen, lawyers . . . and assorted members of the Old Bill. It was also the regular haunt of colourful characters like Ronnie and Reggie Kray, the Richardsons and a rogues' gallery of wrongdoers who were largely responsible for the rising crime figures of that era.

Brutality and death were never far away. I was surrounded by gangland violence. On the worst day of my life my little brother David died bleeding in my arms after the poor kid had been stabbed through the heart in a bar-room brawl. Later I tried to kill the rat who killed my David. Somebody else beat me to it, but I wasted six months of my life in prison before a jury found me not guilty. I will never stop blaming myself for my brother's death.

Apart from my close encounters with the law I admit that I was also never totally honest with our favourite friend, the good old Taxman. If he ever got wind of some of the back-pocket enterprises in which Ronnie Knight had a hand, then I suspect I would be in his bad books. I just hope he never gets to hear about what I got up to.

To my dying shame I must also concede that my record as a husband and father is not one of which I can be proud, as I will explain later.

But I am not the bank robbing, evil bastard so graphically and frequently reported. Blowing up safes, hurting innocent people and planning big robberies are way out of my league.

So, you might ask yourself, how come Ronnie Knight has earned notoriety as 'Britain's Most Wanted Man'?

He would not be named as one of the so-called 'Famous Five' sought in connection with the infamous £7m Security Express raid unless he was a member of the gang? Would he? And what about the £25m Brinks-Mat gold bullion haul, the celebrated 'Crime of the Century' at Heathrow Airport? Surely he must have had a slice of the action, the story goes. The case against me appears formidable.

Scotland Yard has a warrant out for my arrest in connection with the Security Express job. I am suspected of handling stolen goods, which I take to mean laundering some of the 'hot' stolen cash. I am a friend of Freddie Foreman, dubbed the former henchman of the Kray Twins. He was recently kicked out of Spain and is currently awaiting trial. I am no stranger to the other three of 'The Five', Clifford Saxe, who used to run The Fox pub in my old East London stamping grounds, John Mason and Ron Everitt. They all used to be regulars at the A and R. All four have homes close to me on the Costa del Sol. But I've never done any business with them.

Even more incriminating, two of my brothers were convicted for the Security Express raid. Big brother Jimmy got eight years and Johnny is still serving a twenty-two stretch.

Only a fool would pretend that it does not look a bit on the dodgy side. So how have I landed up to my neck in trouble?

It all goes back to my early days in the East End. I grew up, started work and took my first tottering steps into the adult world with pals who turned out criminals, like the Kray twins. While they all pursued their chosen callings I concentrated on my own ambitions. I graduated to become a leading face on the London social scene as a big-spending club-owner. Sports celebrities frequented the place, like soccer manager Malcolm Allison, who I recall claimed he had a percentage holding in the club at one time. Pop stars Freddie Mercury and Queen dropped by. So did famous actors and singers. All sorts rubbed shoulders, swapped jokes and had a good time. The way I looked at things, mixing with the rock stars didn't make me a Mick Jagger. Entertaining actors didn't mean I was busting a gut to do Hamlet. And having friends amongst the lawless fraternity was not evidence that I was a crook.

In those days I was doing very nicely for a former East End delinquent.

Not a lot of people know this. But like Cockney actor Michael Caine I started out life in the fish business in a manner of speaking. He was a porter at Billingsgate market humping around baskets of cod and rock salmon. I was a rag-and-bone man exchanging goldfish for old woollies. Never be ashamed of your humble beginnings, I always say.

Once I had made it to the top of the pile I was eternally grateful for my good fortune. I kept telling myself it was all too good to last.

Damn right it was. Suddenly I am 'Britain's Most Wanted Man'. It's splashed all over the front pages that Ronnie Knight has done a runner to the Costa del Sol where he has bought this luxury £250,000 mountainside hideaway. Where did all his money come from? Hint-bloody-hint. Could it possibly be his ill-gotten spoils? Later the Old Bill issued a warrant for my arrest and one for my wife Sue. Since then we have been living with the daily threat of being kicked out of Spain hanging over us.

With all the bad publicity I have had it is understandable that most people believe that all I've ever done is lead a life of villainy, with a record as long as your arm. My only form is a couple of teenage probations and a fifteen month sentence, when I was in my mid-20s, for buying a few hundred feet of cloth that fell out the back of a van. Those prison gates clanging behind me was the worst sound I'd ever heard – something I never want to hear again.

So there you have it. There are two sides to the much ballyhooed story about Ronnie Knight. You have seen and heard the fictional version. The reality is another story.

The verdict is yours.

1

'Hopalong Ronnie' and 'Bootie Knight'. That was what they used to call me when I was a kid. I got the nicknames on account of contracting a bone-rotting disease that nibbled its way into me right thigh and put me in hospital for almost three years. When I came out I'd got a withered-up little leg, three inches shorter than my good one. Stuck on the end of the gammy limb was an ugly-looking boot built up to help me walk without toppling over. What I learned from that spot of bother was that people can be bloody cruel. They can be nasty. Even to a scraggy little nipper with a limp. The pasting I took over being crippled and the misery that went with it was what I remember most about my childhood in the East End.

But I've never forgotten all the different smells associated with close-knit life in a hustling and bustling inner city: the crowded streets, butcher's, grocer's and factories all huddled together. With some people it's seeing or hearing that becomes highly developed. With me, for reasons I cannot account for, it was the weird and wafting aromas that imprinted themselves in my memory.

One smell that always gets my nostalgic juices gurgling is the heavy, earthy pong of sawdust.

To this day I've got a highly sensitive sniffer. Since those early days it has graduated to become especially partial to a whiff of sexy, feminine perfume.

All my life I've been a sucker for men's fancy deodorants, too. I've got a cabinet full of the stuff, enough to float a little cruiser. Must be a couple of dozen and I ain't ashamed to admit that I give myself a good all-over dousing when I get dressed up.

Ronald John Knight made his entrance into this funny old world early one bright and crisp morning on the 20th of January, 1934. I was the third son of Jim and Nellie Knight, a well-known and respected couple in the neighbourhood. They already had two lads, my big brother Jimmy who was nine and Billy, aged five. Natural enough my

10

mum was hoping for a little girl to complete the family circle, so to speak. But it was just as well for domestic reasons that I turned out to be another boy. We lived in a tiny two-up-two-down terrace in Downham Road, just off of Pitford Street, Hoxton. There wasn't no room for a girl!

The area was one of the roughest and toughest places gracing the fair borough of Hackney E.8. Our street was a little architectural jewel long since demolished, along with most of the neighbourhood.

Whenever I think of those early days I can sniff it, the pungent pong of the wood chippings, wafting across from Jinkinson's saw mill just over the road. First thing of a morning they'd start up the whining saw, there would be a screeching and a screaming of the metal pulverizing the timber. Then that warming, slightly burned aroma of the shavings. Me dad worked for the mill, driving a lorry all round the East End delivering the stuff to pubs and butchers' shops. He was always covered head to toe in the dusty powder. Sometimes, with a strong sun behind him, he looked like a ghost walking in the door.

At nights we kids used to climb over the fence and lark about in the soft, warm shavings, like nippers playing in the sand at the seaside. It was lovely, jumping up and down and rolling in that spongy, smelly playstuff.

The only event that impressed me when war broke out in 1939 was seeing the beaming look of happiness on me old mum's face when she told us that we were forsaking the splendour of Downham Road for a far fancier address a couple of miles away. We moved lock, stock and modest bits and pieces to 113 Hindle House, Arcola Street, Stroke Newington. To see me mum's face when she shepherded us kids through the front door for the first time you would have thought she had inherited a stately home. Bless the old dear, I reckon it must have been one of the happiest days of her life. Compared to what we had left behind, our new abode was a little palace. What matter that it was on the fourth floor, there was no lift and getting our furniture up the stairs was a job and a half?

We settled in nicely. It was like a little bit of paradise with hot and cold running water, heating, and three bedrooms, which we needed on account that Johnny had come along two years after me.

A hard fact you soon learn in life is that nothing is perfect. Our elevation into high-rise bliss was soon shattered. Mum and dad got into trouble because we'd got our little white mongrel terrier 'Gel-Gel' all safely tucked up with us. Apparently some nosy-parker neighbours blew the whistle and complained that there was an illicit canine pattering around the block. Gawd, did we all love that little bit of fur and bone! One of the family she was, getting on a bit but a lovely little thing, no trouble to nobody.

We were all broken-hearted when the men from the council said pets were banned and didn't we know that we were bloody well breaking the precious rules. 'Gel-Gel' had got to go, the flint-hearted council men told me mum. It was either the dog or us who would be booted out. That put the frighteners on us, as was the intention of the housing department bureaucrats who had all the sensitivity of a team of slaughtermen on piecework. But we all loved our little gel so much that for a time it was touch and go. We tried keeping her under wraps, out of the way of the neighbours, but in the end we got the ultimatum. Either 'Gel-Gel' vacated the premises or 'your tenancy will be terminated forthwith'.

Fortunately one of our old friends from down the road offered to have her, so she went to a nice home.

The fact that we was in the middle of the Second World War, the biggest Blitzkreig in history, surrounded by death and destruction and human wretchedness, meant nothing to me. It was completely normal; we didn't know anything else. When I look back, like I often do, I can never get over how we all just lived through it without trembling in mortal fear that we would never see tomorrow. Course it was the same for everybody, but just the memory of it now brings me out in goosepimples.

Being on the fourth floor with no lift was no picnic. But it had its advantages. It meant we got quite a bird's-eye view of the air-raids. We used to try to spot the doodlebugs zooming in. They were aiming at Simpsons just over the road where they made all the military uniforms. Never even occurred to me that one of them might go off course and crash into our block of flats.

'Here, Nell, take the kids down to the shelter,' me dad used to say when the sirens started. Then he would turn over in bed and try to get a good night's kip. Jim Knight wasn't one to let the Jerries interfere with his sleeping arrangements. What was good for my dad seemed all right by me. So I used to plead with my mum to let me stay with him. But like a clucking hen she'd gather us lads together and herd us down to the street shelter – with a clip around the ear if we made a fuss.

Like most East Enders we were a close family unit, especially when our only sister Patsy came along. Then our tragic baby brother David . . .

12

Mum was the one who kept everything together, looking after the house, the kids and making sure we always had a pair of boots, all from her half-crown a week in the clothing club. Come birthdays and Christmases there would always be something extra. A little present. A few bob. In spite of the hard times, she always managed to make it special. Gawd knows how she and millions of mothers like her managed to cope in those bad old days. When you grow up you don't never forget things like what your old mum used to do for you.

The old man was also typical of the time and place. After finishing work it was straight round the pub for him. He wasn't no drunkard nor nothing, but he surely liked his spot of beer. While he was down the boozer his dinner was baking up in the oven. When he hadn't reached home by a certain time at night it was all right by us. My mum used to remove the burnt offering, put the plate on the table and give us the nod. We were always hungry so we used to wolf it down before you could say your prayers. It was all the better with the gravy dried up and the spuds extra browned and crispy. If there was a bit of meat we used to save it till the last. Yeah, we were glad when our dad stayed on drinking. Me mum knew that when he came home he'd be too knackered to bother about his grub. That's the way it was in them days. No doubt about it.

For me the carnage in war-blasted London didn't mean a dicky. I never bothered about the fires, the bombs, the horrors and the daily death count of innocent people blown to smithereens.

What really upset me, left me with a cold, clammy feeling inside the pit of my belly every morning, was having to go to the local Shackleton School. Now that was real hell.

On the first day my mum dragged me there it took about half a second for me to calculate that I hated the place. I didn't like the gloomy building. I couldn't stand the teachers. Having to sit at a desk all day listening to them droning on drove me crazy. Whenever I could I sneaked out, hid in the lavs and tried to play truant. No indignity was too great to avoid the misery of books and blackboards. At night when the bombers came over I used to kneel down, close my eyes and pray like hell that they'd drop some near the school so I wouldn't have to go next day. In my happiest dreams I saw the school buildings going up in an inferno after a direct hit. But they never got near it.

All I was interested in was sport. Fun and games and the he-man stuff. Learning readin', writin' and sums seemed cissy stuff. Since I was going to be a famous soccer player what did I need all that brain-aching rubbish for?

When the London blitz was at its worst, the skies hummed with the constant drone of the big bombers carrying their wicked weapons that screamed and howled and burned and destroyed. So, nearly all us young kids were evacuated out of London, into the wilds of the countryside. Gawd, those wide, open spaces really frightened me at first. All the fields and trees and hedges, with hardly a decent street in sight. The animals, huge horses and cows and hundreds of sheep all over the place. I can still remember the earthy smells of that time way out in the sticks, just as I recall the pong of the city sawdust. The thing I could not get over was the painful quiet. Blimey, you could hear yourself thinking out loud. It used to make my ears itch, it was so peaceful.

They sent me to a little farm, somewhere in Cambridgeshire, though I'm blowed if I can even recall the name of the place or of the farming family they put me with. I cannot say the family was all that pleased to take in this spindly, East End urchin who turned up at the local station with a label round his neck with his name and address scrawled on it. I felt a real outcast, like a mongrel puppy that nobody buys sitting in a pet-shop window. All I wanted was to go back home with me old lady where, despite the raids, I felt safe and secure.

But this family took me in. All the countryfolk did it during the heavy bombing. They may not have fancied having sniffle-faced kids sharing their table, but it was all part of the war-time spirit I kept hearing them talking about. They treated me all right. I did a few odd jobs on the farm, cleaning out the pig-pens and pulling up weeds. It was strange for a city boy to be working on the land. But I grew to like it. I developed quite a taste for the open air life – and it stimulated an interest in growing things that I would otherwise probably never have had. In return for my daily chores the family made sure I never went hungry – and kept me nice and clean.

Carbolic-smelling, soapy bathnights is what I remember most. They used to stick a bleeding zinc tub slap bang in the middle of the parlour. They'd fill it with water, then make me strip off right in front of everybody and dump me in. You wasted nothing in them days, so they made me share my bath with their young daughter, who was about seven years old like me. I used to go mad, because I was that embarrassed. The little girl didn't care a bit, but I didn't know where to put myself. I reckon that early experience is one of the reasons why I'm so shy! Every scrub-night for the year or so I was there it was the same story. I would sulk and struggle and make a fuss, and they would scold me for being a stupid nuisance. All the time I was trying to cover up my little private parts while the little girl smiled and didn't give a fig leaf.

Was I glad when I went back to the East End and once again got into a lather with me brothers!

One day when I was about nine and figuring on whether I'd go to the Arsenal or Spurs a bloody big bomb fell across the road and left a massive crater. Half a dozen horses got killed. Although I loved animals it didn't mean a candle to me. Life came cheap. Animals or human. It was happening all the time all around us. They didn't mess around in those days. The dead horses were dragged into the hole. The grave was thinly covered over and we were delighted because the levelled ground gave us somewhere to play a decent game of soccer.

What I didn't know then was that those rotting carcasses were going to cripple me for life.

A few weeks later I fell down on the makeshift pitch and cut my right thigh on a sharp brick or something. It didn't seem nothing to make a fuss about, but when I got home my mum pulled up my little short trousers and put a plaster on it. When I went out to play I felt a right girlie. So I tore off the plaster and didn't give it another thought. Three nights later I'm lying in our bed with me brothers Jimmy and Billy beside me and I'm crying out with pain. My leg felt like it was on fire. I was in agony.

When my mum saw my state, burning worse than a furnace and with me leg swollen up like a balloon, she ran out for the doctor. The doc took one look at the cause of my grief, called an ambulance and had me carted off to Hackney's Kingsland Road Hospital. I'd picked up a germ from the rotting horses. Something called osteomyelitis, a disease that rots the marrow in your bones, turning them into putrefying pus. Did it stink! That's one smell I never want to experience again. Not ever.

That was the start of three years in hospital, four or five operations that was to leave me with a long, gaping scar on my thigh.

Being a lad of creative mind I was later to use the disability to my advantage by casually indicating to impressionable young ladies that it was either (a) my war wound, which I did not like to talk about or (b) the result of a sword duel.

When I lay in the kids' ward whiffing the disinfectant and methy smells I was heartbroken. I kept thinking about my soccer heroes like Stan Matthews, Mortenson, Finney and Len Shackleton. They were sporting legends. Did this cruel injury mean that the name Ronnie Knight would never be up there with them?

The plaster started at my waist and went right down to the end of my foot with only me toes sticking out the end like forlorn little chipolatas. I did feel sorry for myself. After six months they took me into the country to a hospital in Carshalton, Surrey. It was lovely there. Nice and bright and cheerful. They used to wheel me in my bed out into the nice sunshine.

I've always found that life often provides its little compensations when you are down on your luck. For me the big bonus that made all the suffering worthwhile was that my little mind wasn't being needlessly bogged down with the rigours of school. No teacher. No books. No boring stuff like that. I could read enough to cope with the *Dandy* and the *Beano*. For what did I need to learn any more?

One day into the ward comes a boy about my age who also had something wrong with his leg. He was the first chocolate I had ever seen. He told me he came from Jamaica or something like that. That boy really fascinated me, I tell you. Not because he was all black and shiny with funny, wirewool hair. No, what really impressed me about him was how he could catch butterflies in his hand. We would be lying there in the sun. A butterfly would come a-fluttering by. This ebony-black right hand would snake out like a cobra's tongue – and he had got it trapped in his fist. Never failed. He never hurt them, though. Soon as he had them he'd let out a scream of delight, show a mouthful of teeth big and white as piano keys and set the colourful creatures free. How he did it so easy really used to piss me off. When he wasn't looking I tried to catch one myself. But by the time I closed my fist the little beauties were settling on a flower fifty yards away. I never did catch one. It really got me down that the chocolate kid was faster on the draw than me.

My mum used to visit me whenever she could. In those days hospitals weren't too keen on parents visiting their kids, with some crap about it being bad psychology. The logic was that it was better for long-term young patients to be totally isolated from family. Whatever genius dreamed that up ought to have been cast away on a desert island inhabited by hungry cannibals.

I was almost thirteen when they let me out. There was a reception committee on parade to greet me when I got back to our flat in Arcola Street. Neighbours were gawping out of windows, standing on the balconies staring and muttering things like it was good to see me back and what a terrible time I must have had.

The war had ended soon after I'd gone to hospital, but it didn't seem all that different. And here I was a puny little kid, withered right leg with what looked like a deformed clog on the end. Blimey, was I in for some stick.

'Booty Knight'. That was the name that stuck like bricks to mortar. After that it was only time before the local sport became dreaming up new nicknames to delight me.

So it was that I teetered precariously into the mysteries of teenagerdom. 'Hoppy Ronnie', the local gammy cripple, thick in the head and absolutely useless in an arse-kicking contest! The boys taunted me. The girls teased and humiliated. Gawd, how it tormented my already dented pride. I was often driven to tears. Since I was a scrawny little devil there wasn't much I could do in the way of thumping a few noses. I had to grimace and bear it, marking the card of those who were the real sadists, as opposed to those indulging in your normal childlike torment.

Later, as my physique blossomed and my courage mounted I was to discover the therapeutic value of a well-timed whack. I directed that at those, both past and present, who laboured under the misapprehension that taking the mickey out of those less fortunate was the fun sport of the week. It amazed me to see how the biggest and most mouthy of the bullies deflated like a burst bubble when they got a poke on the end of the nose.

I also learned another lesson that was to figure largely in my life: good mates are important. A group, or a gang. Belonging. A few good pals from the block 'minded' me. If anyone took too many liberties, my mates would sort them out. In the early days that helped a lot, since I could not even regain my pride by excelling at sport, the only activity which I had been good at. You can't nip neatly down the wing and slam in a goal when you are dragging a club foot behind you.

Still, it wasn't all doom and gloom. The bright spot was that they had no place for me in the overcrowded classrooms at the despised Shackleton penitentiary. I couldn't believe my good fortune. I'd got off studying during my three years in hospital, now I looked like getting away with more time off. Perhaps this was God's way of squaring things with me. He was doing me a favour, I thought. But after my mum kicked up a ruckus, they did take me back. Returning to school was a black day.

I had received no education at all in the hospital, which was another little idiosyncrasy of the time. I was years behind with everything. Not that the thought seemed to occur to any of the teachers at the school. My little minders got me through. When we had any questions in class, adding up or English, my mates used to slide their books over and let me copy out the answers.

It was easy at first, 'cos the teachers didn't seem to care overmuch. But then they wised up and started trying to hammer my brains a bit more. Then, thank heaven, we had a new teacher and it was lovely. He didn't know a thing about my aversion to all matters related to learning. They had forgot to tell him. He must have thought I was trying to be teacher's pet. I volunteered for everything going. Collecting the milk bottles, sharpening pencils, cleaning up, running errands. Anything to get away from my horrible little desk. It took him ages to cotton on, before he suddenly realized that I was hardly ever there for the lessons.

Whenever I could manage it I played truant. I gave the baker and milkman a hand. I did odd jobs and hung around Harry's Coffee Bar. He was an old ex-boxer was Harry Chamberlain. I looked up to him. He had done all right by himself, with his boxing and his little business. It proved you could make your way in the world without having to waste precious time on studying.

Me mum didn't see things that way, though. What with her and the truant catcher they soon had me back doing hard labour. And this time they put me in a class with a real bossy teacher, whose name I wiped out of my mind the day I left school. This master took my allergy to studying very personally indeed. Like that every time I shirked, skipped lessons or tried being smarty-arsed was an act of defiance directed straight at him. He reaped his revenge in several interesting ways. His favourite was to use the wicked edge of the ruler. 'Hands on head,' he'd order, slicing me deftly on the nut. 'Hands out,' he barked, swiping my palm with the downward stroke and clobbering my knuckles on the upward journey.

He did not believe in missing a trick.

'Knight,' he hissed in my ear. 'You are going to regret being a lazy, indolent and stupid boy.'

Now I really despised Mr Whatsisname. Real, deep down, gut-wrenching hate. I'd have cheerfully locked him in a safe and thrown away the key. But wherever he may be now, I'll say this: you were absolutely bloody right. Not getting a decent education and being so cocky about avoiding learning is one of the biggest regrets of my life. Maybe I've not done so bad, all things carefully considered. But there have been many times when I've remembered that ticking off and wished to God I'd got down to me books. You cannot go on reading the *Beano* for the rest of your life.

But that's using good old hindsight, a knack at which we are all brilliant. At that time, when I was constantly getting my proverbials chewed off for being the class clown, all I thought about was leaving the dreaded school and becoming a proper man. Me and my mates 'Poochy' Massey, Albert Lennard and Sid Smith, that's what we talked about night and day. Getting out in the world, strutting your stuff and not having teachers nagging at your earlobes all the time.

It was a tough neighbourhood we lived in. You had to learn to be street-wise. By the time I had almost recovered from me gammy leg, I knew how to look after myself. I had discovered that you didn't have to be particularly big or strong. You just had to have a bit of bottle and never back down.

I got into a few scrapes and punch-ups, nothing serious mind. But every rumpus I got into I hoped and prayed would end in me getting my nose broken. You see, apart from me crippled leg I had this great big beak of a hooter. When I stood sideways it stuck up like a rhino's horn. I was ashamed of it. Even before 'Booty' it had been 'Beaky'. So it is no wonder that I have always been over-sensitive about my appearance.

Still, my old mum loved me for all my faults and failings, didn't she? All I wanted was to get out into the big wide world and make a princely fifty bob a week so I could swagger back home and give Nellie a bit of money.

Manhood stood beckoning down on the street corner. I couldn't wait.

2

Baker and Sellsman's, a little upholstery firm, was the place where I presented myself to begin my first day's honest labour. I was fourteen years of age and confident with it. All I wondered was how long it would be before I became the gaffer.

The first few days knocked the shine off my grandiose aspirations. I started out as the 'spring boy', which I soon learned was a polite way of saying general dogsbody. I stationed myself underneath a little loft where the craftsmen were working. When they wanted something, a 'number six' spring, bit of cloth or a cuppa it was my little legs what did the running about. They had me shooting up and down the yard like a washerwoman's elbow.

Still, at the end of a memorably boring week I got my first pay packet. Inside was a couple of crispy sovs and near enough ten bob in change. Cor. I felt like a millionaire.

'Look what I got here,' I excitedly yelled to me mum. 'How much have I got to give you for me keep and that?'

Ten bob, she tells me. Same as your brothers. And don't go spending all your wages. Put a little bit by for a rainy day, she advised.

With two quid in my pocket I was Jack the Lad. Soon I was drifting up to the Tottenham Royal on Friday and Saturday nights. These weekend dances were the social and cultural highlight of the week. After five and a half days slogging away you had a bath, put on the gear and put on the style.

Everyone used to go there, including my best mate Poochy, a nickname he got 'cos he had this blond hair and cheeky little 'poochy' face. I've known him all me life. We still get together now and then and I have never once called him by his real name. Would you believe it, I can't even remember. George I think it is.

We was like the Four Musketeers, with Siddy and Albert, parading round the Royal, posing all over the place and giving the girls the once over. Mind you I was red-faced and innocent in those days.

Twanging a girl's bra-strap in a dark alley was the height of sexual derring-do . . . though by the time we'd got round to bragging about the exploits it was real sizzling stuff. You know, 'she couldn't keep her hands off, gasping for it, a real little nympho'. Just the usual sort of exaggeration young blokes have always indulged in. I don't know why they do it, but they always do.

Ever since my leg had got better and I'd been able to afford a pair of decent shoes, I'd been obsessed by clothes. I became a super-smart dresser, spending every penny I had on all the stylish gear. Mind you after I had paid me keep and other odds and ends I didn't have a lot left for your really nice suits and coats. Since it was very important to me that I looked the complete goods I had to discover a way of overcoming my cash-flow problem, seeing how it was more of a trickle.

So I began helping myself to my big brother Jimmy's outfits. He was really special in the classy gear stakes, was my Jimmy. And since we were about the same size I'd help myself to his coats, trousers, shirts and shoes and hit the town looking like I'd stepped out of Harrods display window.

The deceptive little ruse had a number of very serious disadvantages, one being that I lived in mortal terror of staining, creasing or otherwise spoiling Jimmy's gear. That's why I would sometimes be standing as though surrounded by a force field, sipping my half of whatever, with the head bent forward at 90 degrees so as to minimize any spillage accident.

Parading in Jimmy's outfits also meant that through necessity I became a sort of Cinderella-feller. I had to make sure I got home before my Jimmy of an early morn so that I could safely tuck away the suit. That little ruse kept him blissfully unaware of the game I was up to. Thus it often happened that I missed out on a series of Big Chances. I would often spend all night chatting up a likely bird, giving her the full benefit of my company and undoubted talents on the dance floor before suggesting we took a little stroll round the back. Then, just when I sensed a bit of stocking top was in the offing, I would have to forsake the fruits of my labours to ensure that Jimmy didn't discover my secret.

Many a time it was touch and go, especially when I was really worked up and I seemed to be on a certain winner, but in the end discretion always ruled over me passion. There would always be another girl the next week. But if Jimmy found out he might disrobe me and I couldn't turn up looking like a dog's dinner. Everybody had got used to seeing me dressed up. I had a reputation to uphold. I could not let myself down. I would have died of shame.

It was about this time in my mid-teens development that I had my first brush with the law, a little escapade that got me off on the wrong foot at a tender age. That's how things happen. A silly mistake and you're on the road to trouble.

I was with some boys out of Stoke Newington. We were out on the town one night doing nothing particular when someone suggested we went for a little joyride. Wild horses wouldn't have dragged the truth out of me then, but the thought of actually nicking a car gave me a dull, throbbing ache in the pit of my stomach. Not that anyone would ever have noticed as I stood around nonchalantly while this right little rascal, who had assumed the role of boss, picked out a sporty looking Jag. He opened it up in a twinkling and soon has us roaring around. He had snatched the motor with such skill and ease that I thought to myself that if he had not done it many a time before then I was a suitable candidate for the priesthood.

For a couple of hours we swanned around the streets on an interesting little sightseeing tour, waving at passing acquaintances like we was Royalty and almost forgetting that we were riding in what might be termed a stolen vehicle. Suddenly this budding getaway artist pulls into the kerb and stops the Jag. It was right outside his house in some little back street. He clambers out. 'I gotta go now and have me tea, otherwise me old lady'll give me what for,' he said, nipping down the road like a scalded greyhound.

Me and the other two looked at each other.

We were miles from home. 'We can't drive, can you?' They looked pleadingly at me, sensing that I was the natural successor as the leader of our little group.

Instead of owning up that I didn't know a clutch from a big end I puffed myself up and said sure I could handle it. No trouble at all for Ronnie Knight. What a bleeding idiot.

A few minutes later I'm stop-starting down the road like a rubber kangaroo, weaving from side to side and jumping on my brakes every time I saw another car a mile away. Who should suddenly pull up alongside me as I sat there cussing and trying to restart the motor but a couple of London's finest boys in blue. It was a quick case of 'Hello, hello . . . and what do we have here then? Could it be Mr Stirling Moss hisself?'

Then we were taken for a drive. Straight down to the local nick. A sergeant well-versed in the art advised us of the error of our ways by bollocking us rotten then charging us with taking and driving away. I hardly heard a word of his lecture on account that I had other worrying thoughts on my mind. I knew that the coppers had sent a car round to break the glad tidings to me mum – and I was dreading her turning up at the station to take me home. I was in for a real pounding. Didn't I know it!

For once me mum was too upset to wallop me one. She was particularly upset because a while earlier my brothers had been in a spot of bother. I think my poor old lady was getting really brassed off with her little boys bringing home trouble all the time. She was weary of the worry and aggravation. 'Course she was. It was all our fault.

'Wait 'till your dad gets hold of you,' she warned with more than a hint of menace.

I was really frightened at the thought of getting home to the old man. I'd had a few wallops from him. He used to give it to us with his belt. I'd tried all the duckin' and dodgin' but he always managed to land it. On the arse if he could, but anywhere if you squirmed around. He always wore that workman's belt, even at nights when he put his evening suit on. I used to ask him why he always had the belt on, believing that if he took it off it might somehow disappear and save me from further punishment. But he glared at me and told me: 'I've had this belt on every day of my life. If I start leaving it off now I'll go getting a cold in me belly.'

So I got a belting like usual. Not a real beating, but enough to make sitting down a pain in the bum for a good few days.

When we appeared in court I gaped open-mouthed as the cops had me down as a hard little rascal who had jumped behind the wheel and led the other lads astray. Not a word about the real expert who had set it all up. It was all down to me, according to the coppers. Well, there was nothing I could do about it. I mean to say, I could not tell them the truth. That would have been grassing. And that you do not do. Under any circumstances.

The beaks gave me twelve month's probation and a warning to steer clear of trouble in future.

Being on probation didn't seem so bad. Bit of a conversation point down at the Royal and other social gatherings. Having a 'record' gave me a reputation, a touch of notoriety. I thought it did me no harm at all.

We pulled a few little tricks out on the streets. Of course we did. Like any kids. But we never nicked anything serious. Only maybe a few sweets from the front counter of the corner shop. A bottle of pop.

A carrot or two. Nothing heavy. Never cigarettes on account I never smoked. It was all innocent fun, with our world revolving around the Royal. We were attracted to it like moths to a candle. It was all we lived for.

Our little firm, out of Stoke Newington, had an occasional run in with a visiting mob, like The Angel lot or The Dalston Boys. We'd bump into each other, have a knockabout. A bit of blood would get spilled. But they weren't what you could describe as vicious punch-ups. Just friendly little set-tos. In the end one side would win. We'd turn round, walk away and arrange to meet next week for another one. It was like fixing a football fixture.

There was one particular young firm, however, that we did not engage in the weekly fisticuff sessions. A couple of boys called Ronnie and Reggie. The Kray Twins. We became really good mates in those early days, developing a relationship that lasted until just before they was put away. The Twins figured larger and later in my life, as you will soon discover.

The main activity of all us young bloods was perfecting the pose and chatting up the birds, an art that I was beginning to study with a new-found enthusiasm for learning. Mind you, I was still an absolute beginner. Sex and all its frightening mysteries was beyond my wildest comprehension. For all my Mr Smoothy cool, a pair of firm young boobs pointed in my direction made my throat crackly dry. A seductive, wriggling bottom was enough to send me scarpering for cover.

I was still working as a spring boy down at the upholstery firm. However, when I related the story of how I made so much dosh I could lash out on the top gear, it leaned more towards me having my own little furniture firm with a string of workers doing the necessary. Maybe I was not strictly honest. But it was better for my image.

After only a few months I decided to put settees and armchairs firmly behind me. My old man had got out of the sawdust lark. He was driving a lorry for a scaffolding firm near our block of flats and soon managed to get me signed on. They put me on erecting straight away. Tough work. But by the time I was seventeen I had learned the job inside out, had put on a few muscles here and there and could hold my own with anybody. It was hard going, but the money was good. I was picking up £30 a week and that put me in the big time.

During the Coronation in 1952 we were building all the stands along the route. It was flat out, back-breaking work round the clock. I had hands like old leather gloves. At the end of it I was worth a few hundred quid, a fact about which I delighted in bragging to me mate Poochy, who had found his calling in the rag trade.

Albert, bless him, had filtered into the sawdust business. His theory was that he was set up for life, since so long as there were pubs they'd always need the shavings. Siddy was doing all right in his old man's haulage business.

At the time I was well on the way to achieving my dream of becoming a top-class soccer player. I was turning out regularly for Tottenham Juniors and just waiting for my big break to get into the senior side. Then one day all my childhood dreams of being a soccer hero, scoring for England and having me picture in the papers were all shattered.

The boss of the scaffolders called me in and gave me an ultimatum. 'You cannot keep taking Saturdays off to play friggin' football,' he warned me. 'What's it to be? Scaffolding or soccer – 'cos you cannot keep having weekends off.'

I pointed out to him in no uncertain terms that it was The Spurs I was playing for. Not the bleedin' Boys Brigade. The Spurs. I educated him about how I was improving my technique with every passing week and how those in the know were predicting that I would become a big soccer star.

The gaffer indicated that he didn't give a toss if I was about to be named captain of England. The job came first. Which was it to be? It was make-your-mind-up time. So I had to pack in my budding football career. Broke my little heart, it really did. I was sure I could have made the grade, but it came down to a question of pounds, shillings and pence. There was no money in professional soccer at that time. Lots of kudos and glamour. But short on the green stuff.

Tommy Harmar, he was my hero, one of the Spurs greatest. Yet he was on only twelve quid a week. I could earn more than that in one day. So scaffolding won. As the boss pointed out, good jobs like I'd got didn't grow on trees.

As it turned out I didn't stick to scaffolding for much longer after that. My Billy told me he was doing very nicely indeed from his big scrap yard on Hackney Downs. I had a quiet word in his ear, enquiring if he had a suitable opening for a bright young feller like me. Billy was buying and selling virtually any commodity you could mention. Rags, papers, tin, steel, copper, old wood. The lot. Everything had a price, he used to say. And so long as you sold it for a lot more than it cost then everything was tickety-boo.

The role Billy had in mind for my apprenticeship wasn't exactly what I'd bargained for. I'd rather fancied myself in an executive position. Sitting behind a desk and spending a few hours a day wheeler-dealing on the old dog and bone and picking up a nice pay packet without having to get my hands dirty. Instead my job was to go rag and boning. Fortunately I didn't have to walk the streets leading a horse and cart like Steptoe and Son. No, I had a broken down lorry. But I was still out there working as a rag-and-bone man, swapping balloons and goldfish for tatty old odds and ends.

What we wanted more than anything was good quality woollies. They brought the best money. So if the punters brought a bundle of woollies we'd give them a fish. If kids carried the stuff out we used to tell 'em that if they got some more they could have two fishes. Amazing how they all loved those golden scales swimming round and round in jam jars. Nobody ever wanted the balloons, unless all the fish was gone.

Every business, big and small, has its pitfalls. In that particular trade you could sometimes get conned rotten. Unscrupulous little urchins would give you a big bag stuffed with woollies on top and while you was weighing it they would run off with their pair of goldies. Too late I'd find out that underneath a couple of threadbare sweaters was useless old rubbish. Oh, the dirty tricks the sneaky little devils used to get up to.

I remember once a kid brought this super big bale of stuff. I thought it couldn't be all woollies because I could not be that lucky. But I checked every piece and it was all the genuine article. Full of gratitude, I gave the lad a couple of fish and threw in a balloon as well. He hops down the street happy as a pig in muck. I'm pleased with myself 'cos I've made a nice few bob. A few hundred yards on I suddenly hear this woman's voice screeching blue murder.

'Stop, stop!' she cried.

So I stops. She comes panting up like an old carthorse and starts rummaging through the lorry.

'You bloody idiot, you just took some stuff off my lad . . . He nicked it out the drawers. It's all my old man's best stuff you silly bugger.'

She was screaming like she was being interfered with, so I had to give it her all back. Otherwise the next thing you knew she would have been calling the police and you could have got into trouble. When I asked her for the fish back she gave me a mouthful, going on about how we should be prosecuted for encouraging kids to commit misdeeds. She was a real bagful. I pitied her poor old man. Fancy waking up to that every morning. I shuddered at the thought.

Unpleasant encounters of that kind tended to give me the high sort of profile I tried so hard to avoid. The last thing I wanted was for anyone to see or hear me. Usually I hid quietly in the back while old Albert did the pitchin', hollering them immortal words: 'Any old rags, any old bones. A goldfish for your woollies.'

Just sitting there listening made me cringe, it did. My biggest dread was that I would meet someone I knew, especially from down the Royal or one of my other stamping grounds where I was more renowned for my sartorial elegance than collecting old rags. I did not advertise the fact that I went around spending me days blowing up balloons. On the contrary. Every time I thought I recognized a face I'd dive in the back of the van and stay put till they had passed. It got so bad that in the end I would only work the streets miles and miles away where I thought nobody knew me. Even then I laid low. The money was good, but the humiliation I had to suffer did not bear thinking about. The indignity nearly done for me!

We also did a bit of scaffolding foreigners, alongside my Jimmy who had his own business up in Kingsway by the old *Hackney Gazette* building. Jimmy had married Maisie Jinkinson from the sawdust firm. She was a right grafter who helped him in his yard.

My other brothers were courting pretty seriously. Despite all my natural, boyish charm I wasn't exactly what you'd call an experienced ladies' man. I'd had a few moments – and quick moments at that, I'm sad to admit – but the only girl I'd really got properly involved with was June Billingham. She lived on the third floor of the block and I'd known her since I was five. June was always a good-looking girl and as she began to bloom and blossom she attracted a posse of boys hanging round hoping to get off with her. I managed to scare away most of the competition, but there was this determined little trier called Donald Leech, who was always poking his oar in. For a while it was touch and go between me and Leechy, because he was a persistent little sod who did not scare off easily. In the end it was June who made her preference by choosing me. As I recall Donald Leech took his rebuff pretty well.

Years later he gave me a real shock. I was in court on some minor matter or other when this geezer walks straight up to me and enquires: 'How you doing Ron, old boy?' and goes rabbiting on about the old days. I didn't know him from Adam . . . till he reminded me he was my old adversary in romance, Don Leech. Well, how was I supposed to recognize him? He'd got a flippin' wig on – and I deduced he was a barrister of some note.

But going back to my wooing of June: I suppose I was advantageously placed to win her affections, since I lived on the next floor. It all started off nice and innocent, like. You know, groping around in the bus shelter and the landing when we were just inquisitive kids. June came from a big family. There must have been twelve or fourteen of them, though it seemed like a regiment.

'Course, June's parents never liked me. If it had been their wishes Leechy would have won hands down. Nearly all the neighbours had got the Knight brothers marked as right little bastards. If we played hookey or got into a little spot of bother they called us terrible boys and bust a gut to scurry down to the appropriate authorities. Most of the mothers had fainting fits if they found their darling little daughters was mixing with one of us. June's parents were no exception. They didn't like me and they made no bones about it.

Me and June were about seventeen when she told me I was going to be a daddy. We had innocently and awkwardly resolved the mysteries of sex one night on the steps between the third and fourth floors. It was the first time for the both of us. And like most of life's introductory offers it was a memorable, if not entirely satisfactory, experience. However, once we had broken the barriers, I dedicated myself to the pursuit of perfection like I was practising for the Olympics. Since in those days I was as worldly about contraception as I was about splitting the atom, it wasn't really surprising that the inevitable happened. June was a couple of months gone when she mentioned it. Although I was a mere stripling I do recall that I took it exceptionally calmly, as if I half expected it. I think I was subconsciously making sure that Donald Leech was put out of the running once and for all. Well, I had certainly done it now.

In those days you were considered a very naughty boy if you didn't do the right thing by the girl. But that didn't apply because we had been talking about getting married, so there was no fuss or scandal. Naturally I got the evil eye from June's mum. She seemed grateful and relieved that I was going to do the decent thing and after we set the date she came dangerously close to treating me with a degree of civility. We had a nice little white wedding round at the local parish. June was only a few months gone so her condition didn't show. All our families and friends were there and we had a traditional type of East End knees-up.

June and me were happy enough. We moved in with her mother, 'cos her dad wasn't about any more for some reason or another. It was all right. Her mum did all the washing and cooking. I had it all done

28

for me, really. I was eighteen. An old married man and about to experience the joy of parenthood.

After a few months hunting around we found a flat at Highbury, near the Arsenal football ground. It was like the top floor in a private house. Just a little sitting-room, a bedroom and the sink and cooker on the landing. It wasn't up to much, but at least we were on our own. I had worn out my welcome with the mother-in-law.

I carried on the rag-and-bone calling, making a good bit of money. At the end of a hard day tramping the street I'd go home and have me dinner, get changed and go out. June was never a drinker. She wasn't interested in going down the boozer, so I was out all the time with my mates. They still hadn't got hitched and were fancy-free. I acted like I was, too. Down at the Green Man, our local, they used to have concerts and talent nights. Deep down I always fancied myself as a bit of a crooner. I wasn't too bad a singer and for a bit of a laugh we'd go round the talent contests like at the Pegasus in Green Lane, Stoke Newington, and all over South London.

There was one serious impediment jeopardizing my desire to become a singer. This being the fact that I only plucked up the nerve to get up on stage after I'd had a few stiff worry-killers. Sometimes I had too many and forgot the bleedin' words, which didn't impress the judges too much. My favourite tunes were the old Al Martino hits, songs like 'I could have danced all night' and my favourite 'Who are We?' After I'd won a few contests and picked up a tenner a time for my trouble I began to have visions of a career in showbiz. 'Ronnie Knight' up in lights over some dance hall began to have a certain attraction. It sure as hell would beat ragging and boning, I reckoned.

I got a second prize at a Butlin's holiday camp in Skegness, beaten by a guy who just got up there and mimed. One of the judges was the comedian Charlie Drake. When I met him years later I told him how he probably ruined my career.

That wasn't true though. I did have an offer to turn professional with Cyril Stapleton, who was the leader of one of the biggest bands around at the time. It was all fixed. I had a preliminary audition and all I had to do was sing with the band to clinch it. But when the crunch came I bottled out. I just didn't turn up. The thought of standing up there in front of a paying audience scared the pants off me. Since I had to get virtually pickled pink to perform as an amateur how did I reckon I'd manage in front of hundreds of paying punters? And what if I had to appear on telly with millions goggling at me waiting for me to cock it all up? The prospect terrified me. If I'd taken it on I'd probably have ended up as a lush or nervous wreck. Most probably both.

Now again, on cosy nights by the fire the thought occurs to me that had I persevered I might just possibly have got over the stage fright bit and made singing my career.

There is absolutely no doubt that had I made my career in showbusiness it might have saved me a whole lot of discord that was about to follow.

3

She was just about the sexiest, most desirable woman I'd ever met. I fancied her so much my front teeth ached. There she stood, all beaming smiles and coy glances. Unless I was very much mistaken she was giving me the old come-on-and-get-me signals. I couldn't believe me luck. I transmitted back on full power.

Barbara Windsor was young, around twenty, beautiful and a fast-rising star, making her name in musicals like Lionel Bart's *Fings Ain't What They Used T' Be* and other big West End shows. She had also become a big hit on the Jack Jackson telly show and from where I came from she was a celebrity.

Barbara was only four foot ten and a bit inches tall, with a lovely, infectious giggle and dazzling personality. There was a couple of other fascinating things about Barb that attracted my full attention. Together they measured 38 inches. Any man who denied lusting after those voluptuous boobs was either a liar . . . or bent as a spaniel's hind leg.

Those far-from-hidden assets were later to become saucily exploited in the famous 'Carry On' films but at that memorable meeting my thoughts were fixed firmly on the more immediate prospects coming my way. I was as lusty as any other 23-year-old and meeting Barbara under such promising circumstances was like a gift from the gods.

Funny how things turn out. Only a little while earlier I had been reading about her little fling with Bing Crosby's son Gary, who was trying the almost impossible trick of following in his father's famous voice tracks. Jesus, I thought, that was a hard act to follow. Gary (so the story went) had gone ga-ga over Barbara and was booking suites at the Dorchester for romantic little tête-à-têtes.

She had also thrown a big party at a posh club in Knightsbridge to announce that she was engaged to another singer, a good-looking guy called Cliff Lawrence, who was about my age, but was described politely as being somewhat highly strung. I remembered that well, because apparently Barbara's parents didn't take too kindly to her choice of a prospective mate on account that the said Cliff spent more time in the dole queue than exercising his tonsils.

I gathered the folks were keener on having a Crosby for a son-in-law than an out-of-work hopeful, especially after Bing himself had gone backstage to chat to Barb when she was appearing in cabaret at the famous Winston's night-club. But by the time I got to meet her she was unattached – and, I fervently hoped, available.

From the famous Hollywood Crosbys to your East End Knights. That was one hell of a change in scenario. But being of fatalistic nature I was not going to let precedence stand in my way. Freely I will admit that at first I was a bit awestruck just at being with her. Well, she was a star, wasn't she? On the telly and all that. But I played it so cool no one would have guessed. I was going great guns, until I almost blew it by asking her for her autograph, a slip-up that I hastily covered with a nonchalant flick of the head and knowing smile.

I deserved an Oscar for my low-key performance, keeping all casual, oozing just enough of the Knight charm to give her a taster of the good things to come. The fact that I was glibly chatting up this blonde bombshell while I'd got a wife and baby indoors never entered my head. It did not cramp my style one little bit.

I'd first bumped into Barbara a couple of months earlier down at the Pegasus, where her uncle Ron Ellis was the singer/compère. I used to do a bit of warbling at the boozer and I reckon Barb must have first clocked me down there one night. Now fate had guided our paths to this salt beef bar on the corner in Stamford Hill. I was passing the time of day with this nice Yiddisher boy called Neil, who was a film extra or stunt-man or something, when Barb pops in for a quick bite of the kosher. Our brief encounter was renewed.

Deep down I knew that something had clicked between us the moment that her eyes met mine. You can always tell, can't you? That old black magic starts weaving its wicked spell and the full orchestra fiddles away in the background. Yes, Barbara was keen on me. No doubt about it. But she didn't exactly jump into my arms. Neil gave me her phone number. Every day I called she kept saying she was working. Too busy to see me and all that.

I was persistent, gave her the full charm treatment down the phone. But after a few weeks constantly getting the cold shoulder treatment I became dispirited. The glorious memory of that heaving bosom was beginning to fade into the land of never-never. I had already decided to give up the impossible dream and seek pastures new, when I thought I'd give her one last try. This time, she was different. She was quieter, more attentive and interested. Then, right out of the blue, she said: 'Why don't you come on over and pick me up?'

Batman couldn't have made it any quicker.

Out to dinner we went. Some posh place up West. It was Ronnie Knight at his finest: attentive, complimentary, witty and the perfect gent. We had a lovely night out, culminating in a kiss and a cuddle in my motor after I took her back to her smart pad in Stamford Hill, where she lived with her old mum Rosie and step-father Len. She told me her real John had done a bunk from home when she was only twelve. I imagined how terrible that must have been and I felt sad about it.

We had a long, intimate chat about our lives, our hopes and aspirations. I've got to be honest. I wasn't absolutely truthful to Barbara that first night, nor for any of the nights that were to follow after that. When she'd asked me about myself I'd forgotten to mention one or two minor matters. Like, for instance, that back indoors I had a little wife. And a baby daughter. Or that June had already hinted to me she thought there was another little Knight on the way. These were areas of my life that I faithfully continued to omit from all of our conversations as Barb and I got to know each other. The truth was that despite my lifestyle I was still going back home to her indoors every night after work.

June and me weren't really hitting it off. Our marriage wasn't up to much. Not surprising, all considered. I was no prize husband. Some might criticize me for being a bit selfish. Still, young men don't think, do they? To me indoors had become just a base. I'd have me tea, get changed and go out round the clubs all night, getting home in the early hours, having a quick kip . . . then out to work. Some days I was almost dead on my feet. It got so June was seldom there even when I went home. She used to spend all her time with her mother and the family. It suited me.

Anyway, that was the secret side of Ronnie Knight I discreetly kept from Barbara. The reason I didn't level with her was simple. I was scared she would dump me if she knew the truth. Very soon my irresistible wooing swept Barbara off her feet . . . right into the chintzy bedroom of her flat.

Barbara fell for me in a big way. No doubt about it. She kept telling everybody she was in love, extolling my attributes like I was entered for the Prince Charming Stakes and going on about how I was quietly masterful and had wowed her with my earthy sex-appeal. I was never quite sure what she meant by that, but since it seemed to be doing the trick, whatever it was, why should I go upsetting the applecart?

There was one area in which I did assert myself: the matter of Barb's dress sense, which bordered on the skimpy, leaning towards displaying the goods. I was very firm. I let it be known that in my book nice girls did not go around flaunting their bum and boobs like a tart looking for a bit of trade. I honestly did not like it – and I still do not. Somewhat to my surprise, Barb took it all in and dramatically changed her ways, asking me to help choose smart blouses and skirts and more acceptable evening wear. She was tickled pink at my interest in her clothes and appearance and was proudly announcing that Ronnie Knight had given her something she had desperately needed . . . a touch of class.

I thought to myself: this little set-up is just too perfect.

At first I got on reasonably well with Rosie. She was not exactly thrilled to death that me and Barb conducted our discreet little affair at the flat, avoiding the need for sneaking off to hotels or anything like that. It was all very comfortable.

The really big problem nagging away at me like a toothful of toffee was keeping my double-life secret. Sometimes Barbara's curiosity got the better of her and she would throw in a teaser about family background. I stalled as best I could.

When she asked where I lived I told her I had just taken a tiny little bachelor pad that wasn't up to much. I explained I didn't want her to see the place until I'd tarted it up. Barbara had already swallowed the line that I'd left June ages ago and had nothing to do with her any more. Undoubtedly I was extremely bloody convincing because Barb never so much as questioned my circumstances.

But as our love affair blossomed and flourished my double life became so complicated that sometimes I felt I was in danger of disappearing up my own backside. After a night of heavy passion with Barbara I'd toddle off home in the early hours to June. On the rare occasions Barbara quizzed me about her indoors I'd lie through my pearly whites swearing that June and I were through. Finished. Yesterday's news. I promised Barb I was completely faithful to her. As far as I was concerned other woman didn't exist, I told her. I was so convincing I almost had myself believing it.

'Course it couldn't last. I had to get copped out and when I did, God help me.

It was her good old Uncle Ron down at the Pegasus that dropped me in it, about five months after me and Barb had got it together. Ron found out that not only was I still with June, but that she was in the family way again. Now there was a tasty tit-bit of gossip if ever there was one. I will never know why Ron went and grassed me, 'cos we'd always been good mates and I thought we got on well. Anyway, he tells his sister Rosie and that was as good as putting it on the BBC. My two-timing little game was about to be exposed . . . to my considerable and undeniable discomfort.

When Rosie had first started giving me funny, little sideways glances I couldn't work out what was wrong. I'd just catch her staring at me, then looking away when I turned to her. She hadn't let on to Barbara at that stage, though how she managed to hold her tongue for so long continued to be a source of amazement to me. It was no secret that she was no fan of Ronnie Knight. She made it clear that in her opinion her little Barbara was wasting herself on the likes of me.

Rosie favoured a little Yiddisher boy who lived at the bottom of the flats, a geezer called John Bloom. That was him, the one that went on to become a washing machine millionaire. Next in line on Rosie's list of prospective husbands was a market trader called David Starr, who was doing very nicely with his stalls down Leather Lane, flogging toffees and chocolates so fast they was working overtime at the factories.

Rosie certainly spotted their potential in those early days – just like Bloomy, David Starr went on to fame and fortune in the millionaire bracket. She deserved full credit for her perception did Rosie. And looking back, if I am completely honest, I cannot argue that she had got me pretty well weighed up, too.

If we had words Rosie could turn a cruel tongue. She would slag me off calling me a 'no-good, no hope wheeler-dealer'. Thank God old Rosie never got wind of the days I had tramped round the streets totting for old scrap and woollies. Had she known about that I would never have heard the last of it.

Fair do's to Barbara. She never criticized or looked down on me 'cos I was not exactly in the big league, businesswise. She did not push me to become a tycoon. She was a doll about my method of earning a living. But Rosie just could not take to me. She could not find it within herself to look on me as a prospective son-in-law. I was left with the nagging thought that she just did not like me. Any lingering doubts I had about Rosie's true feelings were shattered the day she asked me: 'How much do you want to leave my Barbara alone?'

Talk about cut to the quick! I was too choked to retort with a witty riposte. Rather sulkily I told Barbara what her dear old lady had gone and done and Barbara went absolutely start raving mad at Rosie, telling her she was a wicked old woman who had done a terrible thing in even thinking that she could buy me off.

What I did not know at the time, of course, was that Rosie knew all about my little secret: that June was busting out all over again and I was responsible for the coming harvest. I have never been absolutely sure why Rosie kept the big secret from Barbara for so long. Maybe it was simply because she knew it would hurt her.

Finally she could contain herself no longer. She let the cat out the bag about me still being with June and her being somewhat pregnant again. Barbara's reaction took me back to those bad old days during the war. The bombings were all relatively peaceful compared to the verbal blitz my Barbara unleashed on me. She got me in the bedroom and locked the door. Then she went berserk and let me have it with all barrels blazing. She screamed and shouted. She called me names I'd never heard before.

I'll tell you, that girl had a real talent for swearing, a vocabulary of vulgarities so rich that I wished I could have remembered the choicer passages so that I could have looked them up at a more opportune moment. She told me to do things with myself that frankly were impossible. That slagging off was an education in the art of inflicting serious internal injury without leaving a bruise. No sooner had the barrage subsided than the floodgates opened. It transpired that I was a no-good liar, two-timing, cheating conniving rat who deserved a certain interesting demise, the method of which brought tears to my eyes just thinking about it. Barb was at pains to point out that I had promised most faithfully that I was away from her indoors, that I had had nothing to do with her from the day I met Barbara.

Now the truth was out. Not only was I still with June. But far from having nothing to do with her she was expecting again! Yeah, I thought forlornly to myself, get out of that one.

In life there are times you can bluff your way out of a tricky situation. There are times when you can smooth over the troubled waters with a double-dose of the old charm. Occasionally the best form of defence is a full-frontal attack. At that particular moment as I sat there listening to Barbara sobbing away and giving up a silent prayer for help from above, none of the well tried and tested manoeuvres seemed to fit the bill. As a final resort I considered that a cover-up story might work.

I set the imagination going to dream up a plausible tale that would calm Barbara down and give me a little light relief from the earache. A good line struck me. I could claim that it was all the work of some troublemaker spreading malicious rumours just to cause me a bit of grief. But with June several months pregnant (and waddling past the Pegasus every day) I realized that Barb might spot the flaw in that line.

For once in my life I was stuck for words. I had little choice but to sit there taking the colourful verbals, hearing how sewer rats would run a mile to avoid me and how I was the dirtiest deceiver in the history of mankind.

Barbara finally calmed down long enough to inform me that we were all washed up. If she ever clapped eyes on me again it would be too soon, she sobbed. So I thought to myself: 'This time, I think she means it, Ronnie. She'll never see you again. It's all up.'

There was nothing for it. I slunk out with a hurt look on my face and my tail between my legs.

There was only one place to go – back to her indoors.

June wasn't in the mood to console me in my darkest hour, either. To be fair and decent I could hardly expect any understanding from my wife that my mistress was upset because she'd just found I'd been a bit economical with the truth over my marital arrangements. The irony was that despite June's delicate condition it really was all over between us. There was nothing left, at least on my part. June had been my first girl. I had really loved her and had wanted to get married. Now it was all gone. She was like a stranger.

It seems ridiculous, but I never really knew how June felt about it all. We didn't seem to have two words to say to each other. Perhaps the truth is that I just didn't care.

It was Barb I wanted all right. I couldn't get the girl out of my mind. During the next week I was on the blower so much that my left ear felt like a braised lamb chop. I knew that Rosie was out working as a machinist and that my Barbara was all alone in the flat. She must have known it was me ringing all the time. She never answered. You never can tell with women, can you? I mean they are so unpredictable. Just when I'd finally accepted that me and Barbara were yesterday's news, guess what happens?

'All right then. Let's talk it over,' she murmurs.

A few hours later after a nice little meal we are back in her flat, all cosy and lovey-dovey.

I'm telling Barb how sorry I am for lying. It was only because I'd been scared of losing her. I swear blind that it really is all over with me and June and I don't ever anybody else but my lovely Barbara.

'You are the only girl for me,' I kept promising. 'Give me another chance. I'll never let you down again.'

I must have been extremely convincing, because despite my hitherto ropy record Barbara went for it. I reckon she really must have loved me and knowing that I was a bit of a rascal she gave me the benefit of the doubt.

One complication I carefully concealed from Barb was the fact that I still hadn't managed to find myself a little place of my own. When I left Barb that night after a blissful session of making-up I got in my motor and drove back to June indoors.

If June had known I was knocking off Barbara on a regular basis she would likely have kicked me out. If Barbara had even suspected that I was still two-timing her she would undoubtedly have killed me.

During this extremely trying period of my complicated life there were times when I honestly feared that my frayed old nerves would get the better of me. To this day I don't know why I kept carrying on like that, flitting between them both like a busy little honey bee on piece work. Why didn't I move out somewhere else? The only reason I can think of is that I couldn't bear the thought of being on my own. I'd always been part of a big family, with lots of people around me all the time. I didn't fancy going home to an empty place. I suppose that's the top and bottom of it.

On the other hand I knew that, if I did get somewhere, Barbara would move in with me fast as lightning.

Rosie was still a bit strict and Barb had made no secret of the fact that she would have welcomed the freedom and privacy of a place of our own. Although that's what I desperately wanted, I could not bear the thought of telling June that it was all over, packing up and walking out on her. I thought she probably still loved me. Even after everything. My whole East End background wouldn't let me do it. I could not cast June off like an old glove. It wasn't in me.

So I got settled in a somewhat bizarre and complicated routine. After working down the scrap yard or doing a bit of wheeler-dealing, I'd go home to June, have something to eat, get changed and go out. Then I'd pick Barbara up. I'd take her to the theatre or night-club where she was performing. Then it would be out on the town with the lads. In the early hours I'd collect Barb after her cabaret, having a few drinks if she was a bit late. I suppose I got a bit of a reputation as a stage door Johnny, but it never bothered me. Often we'd go on to some big showbiz party. There was the regulars, like Danny La Rue, Ronnie Corbett, Lance Percival, Ronnie Fraser, Kenny Williams and all the others from Winston's Club.

I remember one night Danny threw a really big bash at his beautiful Hampstead pad. It was like some swish scene out of a movie. Danny had knocked all the downstairs rooms into what resembled a great big club. A real star-spangled affair it was. You know who was knocking out a tune on the old piano? Noel Coward, that's who. Tinkling away on the ivories for all he was worth. Talk about a room with a view! Then that Russian ballet bloke Rudolf Nureyev ponces around. A lovely walker, no doubt about it. Moved like he was on castors. Over in the corner I spotted Roger Moore and noticed that Dottie Squires was not with him. He was a handsome hound in those days was Roger. He had done the swashbuckling 'Ivanhoe' and 'Saint' series on the telly and he drew the girls like horseflies to a cowpat.

I was always very impressed, meeting these big stars. Although Barbara was only a kid she was quite a celebrity. I suppose it was inevitable that certain people wondered what me, a nobody, was doing in such illustrious company. But it never bothered me. We always had a lovely time. I enjoyed the music, the drinking and the dancing.

And when it was all over, Barb and I would go back to her place to say our romantic good nights. Then, just as the milkmen were airing the streets, off I would quietly slip back to June.

Looking back on those frantic days and nights that seemed to merge into one long merry-go-round, I think I must have been a bit loony. The miracle is how I managed to get away with it for so long. Why didn't I do the decent thing, leave June and set up a nice little love-nest with Barbara? That would have been the sane and sensible (not to mention decent) thing to do.

But I sure enough did not. In fact I cannot remember giving it serious consideration. My attitude was that I was getting by very nicely under the existing arrangement and I could see no reason to alter courses in mid-voyage, so to speak.

On the business front it was all going lovely. Having put me Steptoe days firmly behind me, thank the lord, I had branched out into a wider spectrum of wheeler-dealing. You know, a bit of this, a taste of that. I was prepared to consider any interesting proposition that would have the knock-on effect of broadening the scope of my business interests. That is how I came to learn how to operate an industrial sewing machine during one entrepreneurial venture into knocking out oven-mitts and ironing-board covers on the cheap. This is how it all came about.

Peter Gibson was the sort of character you never forget. You might hate him. He might drive you to tearing your hair out by the roots. He was unreliable. You were safer betting on a three-legged donkey in the Derby than counting on Pete. For all that I loved him. He was a one-off. Among his many talents was the fact that he was a master tailor. He could run you up a decent looking suit out of a dustbin liner. Pete was always dreaming up brilliant schemes like how to make a million in a year or two. His latest get-rich-quick sensation was turning out a couple of life's most basic requirements: oven mitts and ironing-board covers.

It took a while for him to convince me of the potential in this particular enterprise. But as the night wore on, Pete became increasingly persuasive and I began to glimpse the future in his vision. So, I put in a grand or two of the necessary and we launched our business. Off we went down to Commercial Road to have a look around a small factory that was up for grabs. We had a good nose around, it seemed to be ideal for our purposes, so we rented it. My job was to go into Woolworths, buy a pair of mitts and an ironing cover. I returned to the factory where Peter, who knew everything there was to know about the sewing game, carefully took them apart. My next little task was to use them as patterns to carefully cut out cloth which Pete and his missus Betty expertly sewed around the foam. When we had got a few hundred in the bag we would go up the West End armed with a couple of suitcases and Pete would play the pitching game. He would find a little corner on a busy thoroughfare, throw open his case and begin a sensational spiel that had the mitts and covers flying out like hot cakes on a Polar trek. That was another of Pete's attributes. He could sell a blow-up doll to a sheikh! I never knew how he did it. Me, I could not have given them away with a free Hoover.

Despite the intervention of the 'Ello, 'ello, what have we got 'ere and if you don't be moving along smartish I'll book you double-quick' brigade, our off-beat venture became a sweet little earner. Indeed, it was such a good business that other pitchers, hawkers and market traders were soon round asking us from whence we obtained our highly desirable merchandise. That is precisely how business empires are built. You spot an opening in the market-place, move in and before you know it you hit the jackpot.

I couldn't cut out fast enough and Pete and his missus could not stitch speedily enough to meet the growing demand. I even turned to doing a bit of machining myself, but we just could not cope. The pitchers were there first thing in the morning with their empty cases begging for the stuff. So we put an ad in the local paper and wound up with fifteen girls working for us. We were churning out the goods like a Chinese co-operative. Everything ticked over like a well-oiled little sewing machine for about six months. We were cleaning up very nicely indeed.

Then Pete's other great talent began to predominate. I am talking about his ability to behave as though the clock had never been invented. Many a morning I would wander down to Commercial Road to see how my investment was flourishing, only to find a dozen girls queuing up at the factory door waiting for Peter to arrive with the key. Of a cold and frosty day I felt it my duty to invite the young ladies over to a nearby caff where we would fortify ourselves with a coffee and round or two of toast.

It was definitely not good for business hanging around until lunchtime for Pete to put in an appearance. Since the girls were on piecework they were also somewhat pissed off with the opening-up arrangements. Then he would turn up with a smile on his face and cheery word for all. He did not have a care in the world, that man. One day he was so late I thought he had died, so I smashed the door down. No sooner was the deed accomplished than Pete turns up grinning like a football pools millionaire.

'Hello, boy,' he chirped, deftly stepping over the horizontal door.

'I had to break it down because you weren't here to open again, Pete,' I informed him.

'Yeah, I sort of deduced that, boy. Right then, let's get to work. Another day, another dollar.'

'Might I suggest that you hand one of the keys over to the girl foreman,' I suggested, 'so as to eliminate the necessity for breaking down the bleedin' door every now and again?'

'Oh, no, boy. Can't do that,' he said. 'These days you just cannot trust people.'

We staggered on for about a year. Although it meant a few hundred a week in the old back pocket, it was the hardest money I had ever earned. The day we closed up shop added ten years to my life expectancy.

Down at the scrapyard I was doing very nicely, thank you, though pressure of business necessitated the gamble of me chancing my arm virtually every day. Anything that came along I took it. Copper, lead, steel, iron. Anything. Well, you couldn't keep stopping and asking where every little nut and bolt came from. Not when you was up to your eyes. You had to trust to people's basic honesty.

All things considered and by keeping the old hooter to the grindstone I was making a nice living. In a thrusting week me and my Billy could take maybe three grand between us. That was a helluva lot of money in them days. My carefully considered philosophy was easy come easy go. I took the view that what I spent today I could easily make again tomorrow. Only the finest was good enough for Ronnie Knight and those in his company. The best restaurants, clubbing and cabareting at the top places in town. It was a non-stop carousel of fun and frivolity. I worked hard all day and whooped it up for most of the night.

But then, I was young and foolish, wasn't I? My biggest passion was always clothes. I'd think nothing of lashing out a couple of hundred on a suit, with matching crocodile shoes, expensive shirts and silk socks.

Yeah, I dipped my beak into The Good Life all right. And bless me if I didn't like the taste. I blew all my money every week. I never thought about tomorrow. That was always the time when another deal would come up and I'd make a good few more sovs to keep up the big-spending lifestyle. Now that I'd got everything sorted out with Barbara the only worry that rattled around inside my head was that something terrible would happen and I would run out of cash. Every night I used to say a little prayer that during the next day I'd make enough money to see me through another night. The dread that I might fail nagged away at me so much sometimes that I could barely snatch a decent kip.

Life's little graph is bound to have its ups and downs. You cannot reasonably expect it to be plain sailing all the way. If you have highs, then a gentle downward curve is as inevitable as night follows day. Unknown to me the Great Graph Writer in the sky was about to ink me in for a downward nosedive that made Niagara Falls look like a dripping tap.

While my financial fortunes had been bringing my ship home on a regular basis I had on occasion been sailing perilously close to the wind. There had been times when I had mentally questioned the origin of certain materials offered to me, but being so busy I had given my trusted clients the benefit of the doubt. One serious error of judgement, concerning the matter of an assortment of scaffolding

42

gear, had resulted in my second spell of probation. After that I became a bit more cautious and vowed to enforce a little more discretion.

Greed is the devil. You are doing all right, making a tidy bit by your honest labours. Nothing to worry about. All your receipts nicely in order so you can show them to the Old Bill when they turned you over. Life's simple that way. Until greed gets you in its grasping little grip. I will never know what madness came over me. But when I was offered this vanload of lovely cloth that they made suits out of I just could not say no. There was about £3,000 worth and I could see a tidy profit in the deal. Unknown to me the Old Bill was well aware of events in the pipeline. So much so that they had the van under surveillance and immediately the material was nicked they pulled in the gang responsible. While all this was going on I was applying myself to how I could best spend my profits from the deal. A million thoughts sprang to mind, but I decided to wait until the crispy notes were safely tucked away before making a final decision.

I was having a quiet drink in Hackney Downs, reading the morning papers and minding my own business, when into the corner of my eye came the image of a shifty-looking character, who attracted my attention because he was so small. Came just above your ankles, he did. I was about to swap a few niceties with him when he tells me his name is Mr Hopkins. He adds that he is a copper. And informs me that he is about to arrest me. Grinning at this little, weedy runt I says: 'Do me a favour. Go play games somewhere will you, short-arse. Only as you might detect I'm busy.'

Suddenly I was surrounded by coppers. They leaped out the woodwork. Before I know it I am bundled outside into a car and I'm down at Islington nick.

It was the first time I'd been in a cell and I wished I wasn't there.

What was my mum going to say? And me dad? And Jesus Christ. And Barbara.

I regretted everything then. What had I wanted to do this for when I had my own nice little business, the scaffolding and the yard, earning a lovely living and not a worry in the world?

The rozzers said someone had to come and bail me out for £100. The one that came was my dear old mum. She was furious, especially as my brothers had of late both been away for offences of a somewhat similar nature. When my mum got me home Jimmy and Johnny were waiting for me like a couple of alligators at feeding time. They gave me what for. They was pastin' me for upsetting our mum and dad by

43

getting into trouble, telling me I was no good and should know a damm sight better. They didn't have a kind word to say.

'You bastards,' I yelled back. 'You're always in fucking trouble and now you're bollocking me for doing the same.'

They didn't let up. 'Yeah, well, our mum's had enough heartache and trouble with us two, without you bringing her more aggravation,' they retorted.

When they'd done my mother had her turn.

Gawd, did she clonk me! 'I'm sorry mum,' I cried. 'I'll never do this again. Never. Not in a million years.'

While I was waiting for my dad to come home for his go I wasn't thinking about his belt. What was really gnawing at my guts was how I was going to tell Barbara that so soon after clearing up the little misunderstanding over June I was about to stand trial on a receiving charge. When I got round to phoning Barbara she was a very worried lady. Just before I'd been lifted I'd told her I was on my way round to her place after buying some papers. I was 24 hours late and Barbara was in a state. When I told her that I had been nicked on some ridiculous receiving stitch-up she went halfway barmy. Hello, I thought, Vesuvius is about to erupt again. Poor little Barb was so upset and ashamed that I couldn't bear to see her suffering. I had to comfort her at any cost, even if it meant that I had to bend the truth an inch or two.

'Don't get upset, luv,' I soothed. 'It's all a silly misunderstanding. I was just in this pub passing the time of day when the Old Bill drops by to pick up a couple of people. I only got dragged in because I happened to be standing next to them. I was just an innocent bystander. In the wrong place at the wrong time. These unfortunate things happen in life and we must not let them get us down.

After I had faithfully assured her beyond any shadow of doubt that it was all a mistake Barb struggled to pull herself together. First, she said she was so happy that I hadn't got anything to do with the nasty business. Next she wanted to know what was going to happen. For example, when was I going to see a solicitor to sue for wrongful arrest?

My little heart skipped half a dozen beats and I felt the blood draining out of my face before I managed to catch my breath and regain my composure. No, no, I don't think so, I told her. After all the police were just doing their jobs and made an understandable little cock-up. I could hardly have a go at them for carrying out their public duty. Now could I? Since they could not touch me because I never had nothing to do with it, wouldn't it be best all round to let things settle down all nice and natural like?

My Barb gave a great big sigh of relief. I didn't mind telling the big porkies if it made her feel better. It was a small price to pay. Anyway, I wasn't too worried about it. After the initial shock I had calmed down and concluded that I had over-reacted. It was nothing much to get excited about. Just a bit of receiving.

If I did a guilty with mitigating I would be down for another nice bit of probation. Back on Mr Hooper's naughty boy books. There would be no fuss or bother. Just a little court appearance where I'd admit to my sins and promise to change me ways in future. It was all so piffling that it wouldn't even make the papers. Barbara would never know. With that load off my mind Barbara and I just carried on . . . I forgot all about the trifling matter.

It was about that time that I first began to realize that Barb was only really happy in her own environment, on the showbiz scene, in theatres and clubs, mixing with other actors, comics and singers. I got on with some of her pals really well, especially the likes of little Kenny Williams, Danny La Rue, Sid James and the rest of the 'Carry On' crew. But I was an outsider and at times I really felt it. It wasn't my cuppa tea. I did have those early aspirations of becoming another Al Martino. Barb kept on telling me that if she had been behind me I'd have been a big star. I just didn't have that extra bit of push. In my heart I knew what the trouble was: lack of confidence. I was too shy.

After a few drinks I'd get up and belt out a few tunes. But like I said I could never have plucked up the courage to sing in a proper night-club. Even today I cannot play golf on a crowded course 'cos I cannot bear people looking at me while I swing a club. I suppose it's a dread of making a right prat of myself.

A bloody fine entertainer I'd have made.

With Barbara it was different. She'd been doing a turn since she was a little toddler. When she was in the spotlight, the centre of attraction, she was in her element.

It takes all sorts to make a world.

They had theirs. I had mine.

We were all happy.

*

Fifteen months. Fifteen friggin' months.

And I had counted on another spot of probation. Just shows how

45

wrong you can be sometimes. The most careful calculations can go cock-eyed. When the judge announced his sentence on the receiving charge I died. I died, I tell you. Me whole twenty-four years flashed before me. Even when the geezer in front of me went down for eighteen months I was still counting on being back on Mr Hooper's weekly get-togethers.

Blimey, I'd only had a couple of little offences before. It didn't seem fair that they would send me down like the others. They had got a bit of form. They were professionals. It was only a second time for me.

Fifteen months. Even with good behaviour it would be a least 365 days. June had already gone bonkers and told me our marriage was all over. All things considered that came as no real surprise. Me mum and dad had had their say. So had me brothers – both of who knew what I was about to sample on account that they had already been guests of Her Majesty on similar offences. Not that it prevented them telling me what a bastard I was for breaking me mum's heart with me bad ways.

It was no good kidding Barbara now that I was just an innocent bystander. When she had found out the inevitable she had been wonderful. I had been anticipating a taste of grievous bodily harm. I got softness and sympathy. All she kept asking me was why I had lied to her. I'd explained that I didn't want her worrying her pretty little head over my problems. She must have believed me because she said no more after that. They really are funny creatures are women.

But honest to God I had never dreamed that I would be going away. Away I was going though. First stop Brixton Prison.

4

The first thing they do is strip you off.

They leave you standing there like an idiot. They sneer at you like you've got a nasty disease. Then they throw you into a bath.

Next, it's down to the stores for the prison uniform. For a dresser like me, climbing into that coarse, uncomfortable outfit was worse than being flogged.

I thought to myself: Jesus Christ, what am I doing in here?

One of the screws led me along the passage. Like a little lamb to the slaughter. We come to a barred and locked gate. 'I got one for number four,' he yells.

Up three flights of steel stairs, along the landing and into the cell. The keys crunch, crunch in the lock . . . then jingle-jangle as the warder clip-clops away.

When you first arrive they put you in a cell on your own. Suddenly I noticed how cold it was. The feeling of loneliness is indescribable. You feel hopeless and helpless. And very sorry for yourself. So sorry you could cry. In all my years this was definitely the worst thing that had ever happened to me.

So I sat there, head in me hands, telling myself what a bleedin' wally I'd been. What the hell did I want to go and get myself in here for? Never again, I said. You just cannot beat the Old Bill can you? You can't beat them no matter how smart you are. I thought I was flash, too clever by half. Well, this is where it has got you, old know-it-all Knighty. Well and truly up to your neck in it and serves you bloody well right. I didn't half give myself some stick. A right little lecture.

What was I doing getting mixed up with dirty business and receiving when I had a very nice legit life that brought me in fair and just rewards for an honest day's labour? There I was, the envy of practically every bloke in Britain with Barbara in me bed, enjoying a High Society social whirl. And I'm not satisfied. I'm a greedy sod, that's what I am.

I reckon every prisoner goes through his full-of-remorse period. It's only natural when you think about it. It don't last too long. In the end you have to get used to it and face the facts. It's no good crying your eyes out. You get ulcers. Then heart attacks. You end up dead. It is also a wise decision to forget trying to be a hard nut in the slammer. Because sure as hell you cannot beat the prison system. The screws are gods in there. You have to accept that as a con you have all the rights and privileges of a piece of dog dirt. Trying to show everybody what a tough character you are by taking on the boys with the batons is a recipe for a sore head – and lonely little holidays in solitary.

All these options considered, Ronnie Knight decided to play it straight. Keep me distinctive hooter clean and hope that being a good boy would get me a full remission. After due deliberation I had concluded that I doubted that I was going to enjoy doing my little bit of porridge.

Inside I learned a few little tricks to help me survive. Like making the best of things, pretending it's all a nightmare and that you will wake up soon . . . and dreaming of what the future holds.

'Course, that was in Brixton, the remand prison. All in all it wasn't so bad there.

Now Wandsworth, my next port of call, was a different proposition altogether. Not so much another nick as another planet, inhabited by creatures of a different species . . . on both sides of the bars. They send you there to get a short, sharp shock. And credit where it's due, that is precisely what you get. In that joint anything terrible that has happened before suddenly becomes a trip down memory lane. You look back on the previous bad times with a degree of fondness. In Wandsworth your soul is exposed.

You realize that all those promises you had earlier made to yourself about never doing anything silly again had not been made in strictly serious vein. You might have been kidding yourself, or at a particularly low ebb. Now you renew the vows. This time you mean them. You never want to land in this place again. What a mixture of human garbage there was in there. From the whining little toe-rags to your real heavies who must have had bone where their brains should be.

One right nutter refused to wear the prison shoes. He said they were unbecoming and kept tossing them outside his cell. He got a belt round the ear for his trouble. Then down for a few days strictly private. But it didn't seem to bother him none. Took it like he was going on a little holiday. Others took exception to the food, which I admit was hardly *haute cuisine*, and would find interesting ways of disposing of it.

Yet again there were those who objected to all things in general and spent their miserable existences in a combination of conflict and confusion, aggressive with both warders and inmates alike. They were the real misfits. They seemed to hate life and everything and everyone in it.

But keeping out of trouble paid off. After a few months I was transferred to Eastchurch open prison, somewhere out in the wilds of Kent, surrounded by fields and trees. It whisked me back to my evacuee time at the end of the war. Once I settled in I thought to myself that it was a bit of all right. After the rigours of Wandsworth it was like a nice little bed and breakfast. I reckoned I could serve out the rest of my time peaceful and without undue suffering.

Another lesson I had learned about prison life was to use every little crumb and sliver of microscopic advantage you could muster. That explains why Ronnie 'Booty' Knight suddenly developed a pronounced limp in his damaged right leg. A close examination by those inquisitive enough to enquire revealed a very deep, eight-inch scar gracing my right thigh which I must confess looked very painful indeed. Just thinking about it could bring tears to my eyes.

With a wound like that it was obvious that I could not be assigned to heavy labour, such as toiling on the land or breaking up rocks. Other duties that required lifting heavy implements or long periods of standing were also considered unsuitable for my condition. So it was that Ronnie Knight found himself up to his elbows in vegetables, rapidly and justifiably promoted to Head Kitchen Boy.

The job carried a certain amount of status and envy. In every respect the role (although something I would have died doing on the outside) was a very sweet little number. Fellow captives were soon currying favour with me in the hope that portions coming their way would be somewhat more generous than those dished out to less well connected cons.

For example, there was many a time that I would inform the kitchen squad screws that certain ingredients provided to feed the prison populace were not up to human consumption. A cabbage might be rotten or a cut of meat developing an interesting aroma. When I pointed out these matters I was invariably told to 'Go on . . . get it in the pot.' The trick then was to ensure that the slightly off offerings were designated to those cons who were not in the Ronnie

Knight appreciation society. When my boys came in I would just give them a certain look that directed them immediately to fodder that was at least uncontaminated, if not exactly three-star fare.

My gammy leg solved another problem. None of the vigilant screws batted an eyelid as I'd limp out of the kitchen, complaining that the old wound was playing me up rotten, when the real handicap was trying to walk with a dozen purloined steaks down me trousers.

On the other hand running the kitchen gave me a genuine interest. It was where I learned to cook, even making bread and cakes. I became quite proud of my culinary skills. I did not take kindly to unfair or unwarranted criticism of my nice little meals, especially considering the handicaps I was working under. After all I did not get the finest of raw products with which to create tasty dishes. But I did my best – and anybody who wasn't happy was in for a whacking!

Undoubtedly I could stick it out in relative comfort until the day of freedom dawned.

Someone, though, had other ideas. Someone who obviously didn't like me. They set out to make Ronnie Knight's life a misery. One day the Governor called me up to a little tête-à-tête. Instead of complimenting me on my kitchen prowess (as I had sincerely hoped), he was saying how he'd had a certain anonymous letter. This scurrilous note apparently went into fine details about how I'd taken over as the prison supermarket manager in general and the tobacco baron in particular. The undercover informers claimed that I was going round selling cigarettes and trading in other bits and pieces that help to make a prisoner's life a mite more tolerable. Little odds and ends like a bit of cheese, marmalade, dried tea, milk and margarine. Sometimes it would be like Christmas and there would be a big lump of beef or ham up for auction, nearly all nicked from the kitchen.

What you needed to bid for these little goodies was tobacco. It was the only currency with which you could trade. The sneaky grasses squealed that I was on the make and doing very nicely out of it, too, particularly with my influence in the food department. The implication was that I had heavied myself into the position of Mr Big. Numero Uno. King of the Cons.

It wasn't true. I had done a bit of dealing here and there to keep myself out of mischief and to provide a few little necessities of life, but I wasn't in the big league. What I suspected was that the real baccy dealers feared I had aspirations of taking over their territory and decided to stitch me up. A very nice professional job they made of it.

They got me nailed to rights with planted evidence, grasses and a malicious whispering campaign. The upshot was that before you could say 'a packet of Woodbines' I was out of my kitchen whites, out of Eastchurch . . . and back in lovely Wandsworth.

And me a non-smoker.

My brief sojourn in the countryside had softened me. It somehow made it even worse being back in the hell hole.

There must have been a thousand or more doing time. And it seemed that more than half of them was queer. Wise men learned to sleep with one eye open, your back to the wall and a prayer on your lips. The cells were crowded out like smelly cattle sheds. But by far the worst of all the indignities in the pen is the lack of privacy. You cannot so much as scratch your arse without prodding somebody with your elbow. Terrible it is. Terrible.

You get a lot of time on your hands. You think a lot about what you done and why you were daft enough to do it. During the long, lonely nights I relived every minute of my misspent life. If I'd had longer legs I'd have given my own backside a good kicking ten times a day for all my foolishness. Every morning at six o'clock I renewed the promise to myself that never again would I end up in jail. You will see why I developed this particular aversion after drinking in the following little ritual.

The crack of dawn was slopping out time. A charming little daily ceremony that had my sensitive stomach cartwheeling through its morning acrobatics, twisting and turning like a snake down a ferret hole. Holy Jesus, the ammonia stink of piss and excrement was terrible. It made me sick. Me, who had this extra-sensitive snifter used for carefully selecting all your expensive fancy sprays and perfumes. Me, with the taste for the finer things in life.

I had done wrong to end up here in the first place. I knew it. Maybe I deserved it. But gawd, was I paying! What surprised me was that most of the prisoners didn't give a toss. They pissed and shat in their pots and dished it out like they were serving the morning porridge. I just could not do it. Not to save my life. Not in those smelly little tin pots. Not even if it meant I had to spend all night biting me lips holding it in. I always waited till the morning when I could go to the loo and do it properly. At least as near properly as you can inside.

The toilet block had been thoughtfully designed to ensure that all persons and all things could be seen at all times. There were no hiding places. It was open-plan, which was all very well for houses and offices, but not exactly ideal for lavatories. There were little bat-wing doors leading to the toilet bowls, so everybody could see you, sitting there with your trousers round your ankles and a grimace on your reddened face. Every little grunt echoed like thunder. While you were trying to do your business, somebody would burst in without so much as a by your leave. They carried their swimming pots and emptied them down the sluice like they was throwing out the tea leaves.

'Hello, mate,' they'd chatter as you sat there trying to cover yourself, save a bit of pride and uncurl your constricting bowels.

'Do me a favour and piss off quick,' I'd snarl.

They'd shrug, look hurt and storm off like they'd just been whacked when they had been intent on performing a good deed.

If I live to see England win the World Cup again I'll never get used to that sort of thing. Every time I think of the indignity of it I want to throw up. The only consolation I had during those terrible months was that Barbara stood by me. An angel she was. Even when I was out in Eastchurch she didn't complain about having to take two-hour taxi rides to come down and visit.

All the time I was getting messages from June that she wanted to come to see me so that we could sort things out. But I was not interested. I was having none of it. Our marriage was all over. Washed up. Finished. On top of that I didn't want Barbara to know that June had been to the prison. She would have gone nuts. For all her sweetness and light Barb was one jealous lady. It took very little to rouse her. One spark on the touchpaper and it was standing back out of harm's way.

I didn't want to run the risk of upsetting an already delicately balanced situation. I worried that if Barb even thought I was making up with June she would give me the elbow. It was dreaming about Barbara that kept me going. I was scared stiff of losing her. That was the top and bottom of it. Seeing Barbara once a month was heaven . . . and hell.

You are not allowed physical contact when visitors come. It's strictly them on one side of the table, you on the other – with hawk-eyed screws delighting in detecting so much as a brushing of fingertips. What I really wanted to do was to leap over the dividing barrier, hold Barbara close and get down to some passionate lovemaking. There were times I was so desperate I wouldn't have thought, or cared, about having an audience. It is not true that they put bromide in your tea to dull your sexual appetite. Well, if they do, I must have had an out-of-date ration, 'cos it never had no effect on me.

Since any hanky-panky was out of the question Barbara and me talked about our plans for when I got out. It was a poor substitute, but during our conversations I promised faithfully that all the shady stuff was behind me. I was changing my ways. In future Ronnie Knight would be as straight as a yard of spring pumpwater – and twice as pure. The days of me being a small time no-good were over for ever. I'd never again so much as park on a yellow line. I would pay my rates in advance and subscribe to the RSPCA. And may me hair fall out if I told a lie.

When I got out on that lovely, lovely day, Barbara was waiting for me with a big, beaming smile – and a taxi. I had served my full fifteen month stretch because of being framed at the open prison and I remember that I floated to freedom as an eagle soars to his eyrie. Barbara was so breathless that her boobs were bobbing up and down with the excitement of the occasion. She said she had a big surprise and couldn't wait to show me. I'd got a big surprise for her, too. After months in the slammer I was having even more difficulty waiting. I was more interested in sex than surprises. Being in a taxi with the driver's beady mince pies glued to the mirror made it a bit tricky to show Barb just how pleased I was to see her. What the hell, I thought, a few more hours aren't going to kill me. I was kidding myself. Or at least trying to. The reality was that every second was torture. The heady delight of her perfume was driving me nuts.

The cab stopped outside a tailor's shop in Green Lanes, Harringay. A place called Carson's, I think. The flat was over the top of the shop and when I saw it I could not believe how lovely it was. What I'd been used to was being with my family in the tiny terrace, then the block of flats. With June I'd been living in a poky place at the top of a staircase, with the so-called kitchen on the landing. I'd been there all the time I'd been into the High Society good life. I had gone from there, straight into the other place. Then I walked into this little bit of heaven on earth.

There was a passage. It must have been more than forty feet long, bigger than I'd ever seen. The lounge was massive enough to hold a town council meeting and I remember that there was a very smart bamboo bar in one corner. There were two lovely bedrooms, a smashing bathroom. The kitchen wouldn't have been out of place at the Savoy.

While I'd been twiddling my thumbs in the cooler Barb had done it all out and furnished it for me. She had kept it a big secret. I loved that girl and kept thinking to myself how lucky I was. I'd walked out of a little square cell with only one door and all white walls and I'd come out to this lovely present. I was surrounded by bright carpets and curtains and classy furniture and fittings. She really was lovely that way was my Barbara. I'd taken a magic carpet ride out of hell into a heaven. That first night out of the nick in a place of our very own I really showed Barbara how grateful I was. I think she appreciated it.

*

Barb was back working at Winston's, that trendy haunt of the rich and famous celebrity set. Most nights I took her down at around midnight before the cabaret started at 2 a.m. Sometimes I used to go off on my own, doing the rounds of the clubs. But near enough I'd always pick her up.

At first it was all exciting to be back on the scene. But the routine soon began to give me an attack of the yawns. In addition to which I was short of the readies, having no work. I didn't take easily to being a kept man, with Barbara being the breadwinner. Some nights I didn't feel like going out. Sitting alone indoors was hard. I had to try to keep awake all night so that I could leave in time to pick Barbara up after the show. She always expected me to be there.

When I'd been scrapyarding I'd made a good living, like I told you. I'd put a nice bit aside, about three grand, but at the way I dished it out that didn't last very long.

I'd got Barbara, the flat and a pleasant enough little life-style. What I needed was a job. The solution Barbara kept suggesting was that I should stick with her and become her 'personal manager'. That was definitely no occupation for Ronnie Knight. It smacked too much like being a hanger-on to me. I was going to make my own name and forge my own niche in the world. And not by clinging to Barbara's skirts, either.

All the time Barbara was becoming more in demand. She often got up at the crack of dawn to start filming, would go on to do interviews, photo sessions or telly chat shows. Then do her cabaret turn at nights. I worried she was overdoing it, but she loved every minute. Thrived on it she did. With the adrenalin pumping round she could go on for days, with only a few hours rest.

Of a daytime when I was on my own I'd go see my old mate Poochy and other pals from the old days. But they didn't get out much at nights because they were all married, working hard and with nice families.

I felt happier, more at home with the old East End crowd than with most of Barb's showbiz friends. Not seeing so much of them meant I was a bit lonely at times, but I soon developed friendships with a few of the acting fraternity. One star I really loved was dear Ronnie Fraser. He was doing a film with Barbara, Reg Varney, Bernie Breslaw and little David Kaye, and I got really close to him. Ronnie was a trouper, a fine theatrical artiste. He was also a real piss artist. In those days he drank like the end of the world was nigh and only those souls would be saved who had pickled livers.

The phone would ring. 'Hello, my darling,' he'd boom. 'Would you be so kind as to come and pick me up on account that I am ever so pissed and find it rather difficult to stand up unaided, so to speak.

So I'd grab a cab and find him in one of his usual haunts. 'Come on Ronnie,' I'd say. 'Let's be getting you home.'

'Hold your horses, old chap,' he'd reply. 'I'm just partaking of another little drink.'

While I had been doing me porridge my son Gary was born. With a father's natural instincts I wanted to see him. So I drove round to the flat. I saw my little Lorraine playing outside. She was five and a pretty little thing. There was a pram nearby. As I looked at my daughter I remembered how I had used to take her out in the afternoons, how I'd been with her all the time when I was indoors. But soon as she saw me she got the pram and ran away screaming her head off.

I was stunned.

I got out of my Jag and started to leg it after her. Lorraine was yelling blue murder. All the neighbours started coming out, poking their noses in. I can't have this, I thought. So I got back in me motor, turned it round and went back home.

I never saw Gary till he was about twelve. And I've never seen Lorraine since then.

That unhappy little episode upset me. But not half so much as when the Old Bill came a-calling at the crack of dawn one fine day in August 1961, enquiring about my whereabouts a few days earlier. The reason they were asking was that they had good reason to believe that Ronnie Knight had taken part in an £8,000 robbery with violence at Fulham power station. There are times in your life when you fail to see the humour in even the funniest situations. On this particular occasion I could not so much as raise a smile at this comical suggestion. Barbara wasn't exactly falling about with mirth, either. Knocking us out of bed before the sparrows was up was not her idea of a fun time.

I knew the Old Bill had it in for me. I could not deny that the Knight brothers had earned a certain notoriety. I knew Jimmy and Johnny had been in trouble with the law. But I never did any business with my brothers or anybody else. The Old Bill never gave up trying to disprove my protestations of innocence. Time after time (Barbara reckons it was about fifty occasions during our time together) the custodians of law and order raided our home.

This would be the way it went. They would get us up and turn the place upside down, saying they were looking for certain missing goods. When they found nothing they gave a grudging explanation, saying as how they were required to act 'upon certain information received' and would be remiss in their duty if they left any stone unturned. The certain information they had on this particular occasion was that I had turned brutal armed robber to bash a few grand out of some poor sods going about their daily business. I ask you.

Like little terriers, were these couple of detectives on the case. Out for quick promotion by nailing one of the Knights, it seemed to me. 'Course I told them it was a ridiculous, trumped-up charge and would they kindly do me a great favour and stop messing me around. Naturally they believed me so much they went and charged me. This time they excelled themselves in their ingenuity, accusing me of being involved in robbery with violence. And just in case that failed to stick, they hung another one on me: that if I didn't actually take part in the robbery I received part of the stolen loot. £5. That's how much they said I'd handled. Five friggin' quid.

These sort of trying situations tend to hang over you. No matter how much you know it's all a put-up job, part of life's rich pattern, it does tend to get you down. I mean, a fiver. That really was scraping the barrel. Nevertheless I was up before the magistrates and charged. Thank God I got bail.

It wasn't until just after the following Christmas that the case came up at the Old Bailey. There was no dispute that I was fully acquainted with the firm involved in the robbery. When I say acquainted I mean it in the strictly social context. We had no business or professional dealings together whatsoever. We just knew each other from way back. Alfie Hutchinson, said to be the boss man, had earlier been sentenced to a ten. Peter Davis, out of Fulham, was sent away for a seven stretch, Terry Shaw, from Stamford Hill five and Fred 'Yocker' Robinson out of Willesden was treated to eighteen months for receiving.

They had done me on the basis of two condemning pieces of

evidence. One (hold your breath) was that they had found my phone number in Alfie's phone book. Two, when they raided my place they found a fiver identified as being one of the notes stolen in the hold up. The phone number ploy was laughed out of court, but the fiver was considered a far more serious piece of evidence.

It's a sobering thought that but for Betty Cronk I could so easily have yet again been delivered into the hands of the prison screws. Thank God for dear old Betty Cronk. She told the jury what a constant source of pleasure it was to have me as a neighbour. Amongst other friendly deeds I often used to help her out by taking her little poodle for walkies, for which kindness she was extremely grateful. Betty had been at my place the day that Alfie Hutchinson came a-calling for a chit-chat and to repay me £25 he had borrowed from me a week or two earlier. Fortunately Betty not only saw Alfie hand over the five fivers, she also noticed me stuff the cash into a vase, which was where the Old Bill found it. The other notes were 'clean'.

On January 18, 1962, I was acquitted as charged.

That case got a lot of publicity because at the time Barbara was really hitting the big time by playing a Cockney tart in golden boy Lionel Bart's latest hit musical *Fings Ain't Wot They Used T' Be*. The flashbulbs were poppin' as I came out of court and Barbara gave me a big hug. She told all and sundry: 'Ronnie is the most wonderful man I have ever met . . . I never doubted his innocence for a second.'

I was extremely put out about the way the Old Bill had tried to set me up on that charge. Very upset indeed. But what the hell. Life had to go on. And I had to deploy my talents to the serious business of making a few honest quid. I could not let bearing grudges hold me back. What I had to do was to look to the future. What, I kept wondering, should be my line?

Mickey Regan was a well known face in the West End and all points East. He was a well respected and connected gent. A bookmaker with a flourishing empire and a few other business interests on the side. Me and Mickey used to chew the fat down at the deliciously named Meat Trader Club in the Smithfield meat market. He was a fascinating character was Mickey, who'd made his mark in the world and knew what he was about. We always got on well, me and Mickey, and I fancied that I could do something with a backer like Mick behind me. I thought about it a lot. But I never got round to mentioning the possibility to Mick. Well, I found it hard to suddenly come out with the suggestion, uninvited so to speak.

Trust Barb and her good old push. While I was fumbling around trying to think of some way to broach the subject she just upped and out with it: ''Ere Mickey. Why don't you and my Ron do something together, a nice business? What do you say?'

Funny thing, says Mickey. But he had been thinking about taking over a club. Bit run down, but definitely with good potential. What do you think about that, Ron, he's asking me? What I thought – ears pricking up like a pointer's zoning in on a brace of plump partridge – was that was exactly my style. Ronnie Knight, West End club-owner. Sounded perfect. After a suitable pause to show I was giving the proposition due and careful deliberation I told him I'll have a bit of that, Mickey my old son. You can take it from me that I am most definitely interested.

The move was decidedly a move in the right direction. It gave my curriculum vitae a distinctly up-market flavour. No doubt about it. Absolutely none at all.

*

As wedding days go, it turned out to be a bit of a damp squib.

Me and my Barb finally tied the nuptial knot one wet, windy, and far from wonderful, chill morn on March 3, 1964. Barb hated it. Passionately. Gawd did she ever!

It was a 9 a.m. Register Office affair in good old Tottenham. It pissed down buckets. Non-stop, cold, driving deluge stuff. I found myself plunging into marriage number two because after June got the divorce Rosie started to drop a few hints about how any decent feller would be busting a gut to make an honest woman of her little girl. From her previous attempts to buy me off I had reached the realistic conclusion that Rosie didn't really fancy me as a son-in-law, but having her daughter living in sin was the worst of two evils.

Barbara always made a joke of how we came to name the day, by telling everybody that it was she who proposed to me. Her story was that I kept going on to her about leaving the other boys alone, telling her what to wear and how to wear it – and accusing her of behaving like an old fishwife. In addition, she would laugh, I constantly referred to her as 'my old woman' and generally regarded her as colonized territory.

So one day she told me: 'If you want to go on nagging me all the time like you owned me, why don't you marry me, then?'

Whereupon, in typical East End style, I retorted: 'Of course I'm going to marry you. I wouldn't have stayed with you all this time unless I intended to make you my missus.'

That was Barbara's recollection of our marital arrangements. That's the way she told it. That at heart I was just an old-fashioned East End chauvinist who took everything (and her in particular) for granted. Plus she put firmly on record: 'I broke all the rules when I popped the question to Ronnie. But I wanted him and that's all I cared about.'

I hang my head in shame to admit that events leading up to the day of reckoning are all a bit vague in my memory. I recall she got a bit uppity on account that I didn't go down on bended knee. And when some eagle-eyed nosy-parker noticed that she wasn't flashing any stones on her engagement finger Barb joked away about '. . . 'course Ronnie wanted me to have a lovely ring, but I'm not one for diamonds. All I need is that little band of gold'.

That's what she told the world. But deep down in the lower basement of my memory file I have flashes that she often used to let me have both barrels on the theme of me being unromantic and completely thoughtless. I sometimes have to chuckle when I think of Barb saying she wasn't one for diamonds. The girl loved jewellery. She fussed over her shiny trinkets like a mother hen incubating a clutch of eggs.

Funny how the old brainbox plays tricks with you sometimes. Do you know, there are days when the precise details of our Big Day all but elude me. I know it was our third attempt. On the first occasion Barb called it off at the last minute because the Press had got wind and she wanted a quiet affair. Then things were delayed when she landed a juicy role in a 'Carry On' film and she could not leave the studios.

When we finally got round to it Barbara got all dressed up for the occasion. She was peeved because she had lost half a stone for her movie part and in consequence her outfit fitted where it touched. She expressed the opinion that she looked a bleedin' old scarecrow. However, in my eyes she was pretty as a picture. A really beautiful bride. It was a pity that she got so drenched she ended up looking a bit like a drowned rat.

We took a taxi. Just me and Barb, my brother Johnny and a little Yiddisher boy called 'Bootie', who was a lovely looking lad, which could possibly account for how he got his nickname. You know, like as in 'beauty'.

It was a pretty miserable affair, which was a pity because I really wanted everything to be nice for Barb, 'specially after all she had done for me.

Barbara has always made a big song and dance about the fact that after the ceremony we nipped into the nearest boozer by way of a modest reception. The reason we had such a modest celebration was strictly a consequence of her career. Just before we had left home she had received an emergency phone call from the studio putting her 'on standby'. That literally meant that she was supposed to stand (I suppose sitting would have been acceptable) by the blower, ready to drop everything and tear round to jump in front of the cameras.

It never ceased to amaze me how all your acting types are slaves to orders. I suppose it comes from directors and producers telling them what to do and how to do it for most of their lives.

They say a bride never forgets her wedding day. Barbara never forgot this one. For years afterwards she kept on reminding me about what she called 'The Bloody Disaster'. Every time we had a cross word she would hark back to it. 'I got married when it was piddling down and you took me down the boozer afterwards,' she used to wail. She also complained because we hadn't dashed away on a honeymoon to some exotic island in the sun. But unless events mock me the real reason was that Barbara was too busy working again.

We did have a honeymoon, even if we did have to wait for a couple of months. Barbara had calmed down a bit by then, with the memory of a certain day dimming in her mind. She had just finished a long, hard stretch of shows and suggested we went away somewhere really special, somewhere we could spend all our time together. What a joke that little arrangement turned out to be. We did get away, but our planned romantic honeymoon was better than a plot for one of the 'Carry On' films.

Barbara and me were at some television studios, filling in time waiting for her to go on by chatting about where we should go for our break. Dear old Kenneth Horne, with that polished dome and booming voice, listens to us debating the odds and then comes up with a suggestion. He says he's just got back from somewhere called Madeira and goes on about what a wonderful, unspoilt little paradise it is. Frankly I'd never heard of the place. The only Madeira I knew had currants in and you ate it. Ken gave me the necessary geography lesson. It was some quaint little volcanic island in the Atlantic off the coast of West Africa. A Portuguese colony, sparsely inhabited and famous for its orchids and natural beauty. One of Sir Winston Churchill's favourite places, apparently. Well, it couldn't be all bad then, could it?

Being a city boy I cannot say I was exactly spellbound by Ken's enthusiastic commentary. Personally I had fancied somewhere with a bit more life and action. I would have been perfectly happy to settle for Brighton or Southend. But all considered and with a certain rainy day still vivid in my mind I decided to watch Barb's lips and nod in agreement at everything she said. This Madeira sounded to me more like a desert island. The sort of place pirates used to get marooned on . . . and go slowly barmy from boredom. But there was my Barb oohing and aahing, eyes wide in wonderment and obviously going a bundle on the idea. After the previous assault on my ears I counselled myself that discretion was the order of the day.

It sounds lovely. I cannot wait to get there. A veritable little paradise. I kept repeating my approval with as much enthusiasm as I could muster. Barb was thrilled to bits.

Now it might seem a bit odd. But at that stage in my life I had never been on what you might call a proper holiday. More than that. I had never been abroad. Nor travelled on a plane or boat. I was none too keen to sample the joys of sea and air transport, for reasons largely related to a highly sensitive stomach. But for my Barbara no sacrifice was too great.

Barbara bubbled with happiness, going round telling all our chums that we was off to this romantic tropical island. On a proper, really romantic honeymoon. Just the two of us and wasn't it wonderful and wasn't Ronnie just marvellous for springing the surprise on her. She told Kenny Williams, who was starring in just about everything on radio, telly and in the theatre in those days.

'Well blow me down . . . would you Adam and Eve it,' he drawled in that rich fruity voice of his. 'I fancies a bit of that myself. So why don't we all go together?'

It seemed a bit of a funny how's your father to me, taking your pals on your honeymoon, but Barb was very close to Kenny. They were like brother and sister. And she seemed to love the idea of having him around. So, naturally, I said I could think of nothing finer and that my only regret was that I didn't think of the idea first.

When we got to the airport Kenny had another surprise lined up. His old mum Lou was there waiting for us. And his sister Pat. Now we were going on honeymoon as a romantic little fivesome. My excitement knew no bounds.

Getting to Madeira was not the piece of cake I had thought it would be. In the first place the idea of flying made me come out in a cold sweat. But I told myself that it would all be over in a couple hours.

Then it would all be plain sailing. If only I had known what wretchedness lay in store I'd have committed suicide.

To get there we first had to fly to Lisbon in mainland Portugal. It was a nightmare. By the time we landed I felt like a dead rat from all the buffeting and turbulence. I was so grateful when we were back on good old terra firma. We took a taxi to the port and I was quite looking forward to a peaceful rest as we completed the journey by boat. I'd expected something like the luxury cruisers you see in all the movies, with swish dining rooms, the officers done up in their tropical whites and the beautiful women flitting around in gowns. Perhaps there was even a casino, where I could while a way a few hours. When I saw the rickety old tub we were booked onto I nearly died from the shock of it. The vessel was a little cattle boat, with goats and chickens wandering round the deck and sacks of grain scattered all over the place. I had seen smarter looking slums in the East End. To add to our joy it was dead of night when we boarded. The animals was squawking and clucking. There were no proper cabins, just a sort of covered area on the deck where you could sit.

We put to sea and my gawd it was terrible. The waves were smashing the boat about all over the place, the wind was howling. The weather was like the middle of a hurricane. And in about thirty seconds flat I was hanging my thumping head over the side. Sick as a dog. Although we was rolling and pitching and up-and-downing it didn't seem to bother the others. Specially not Kenny. I found out he had been in the navy and loved every minute of it. The more the bloody wreck dipped and rolled the more Kenny whooped for joy. I thought he was bonkers. You know what happened next? Just as I started to entertain the notion that I might just survive after all, Kenny starts complaining that he's hungry and could just tuck into a bloody big plate of stew or something.

'And what would you fancy to settle the old tummy, Ronald?' he asks me.

'I wanna die, Ken.' I told him.

He clucked, shook his head and kept telling me: 'It's all in the mind, Ronnie. All in the mind.'

Much as I loved Kenny I could cheerfully have strangled him for the way he was tormenting me. All in the mind! More like all over the deck. I hadn't never felt that bad in all my life. I went to the back end of the boat and stuck my head over the side. Me stomach was tied up in knots. I wanted to be sick again but there was nothing left. Barbara got worried about me and tried to help. But when you are dying you just want to be left alone. It's the only dignified way to go. If somebody had tossed me nonchalantly over the side to drown, my last thought would have been to thank them for the kindness.

I reckon I must have passed out.

When I came to there was Kenny glaring down his nose: 'Pull yourself together Ronnie. It's all in your bleeding mind.'

We finally tied up in the little port of Funchal. All I wanted to do was to step onto something that did not keeping going up and down, rest my thumping little head and let the passing-away process take its natural course. They wouldn't let me. They kept saying we had to get to the hotel. I lay on the bed, spark out with all me clothes on and went to sleep . . . or at least I nearly did.

It was Kenny again. He came storming in. 'Rooms? Call these rooms? They are broom cupboards,' he snorted. 'Come Ronald. We shall have strong words with the management of this establishment.'

I begged him to leave me alone. Just let me lie down a while till I feel better, I pleaded. But Kenny had got his dander up. He wasn't even listening. Down the stairs he dragged me, marching across to the reception desk wwith the regal air of the King of Siam. With the bewildered manager and assorted staff gathered before him Kenneth began his performance.

In that imperious voice of his he addressed his audience: 'My name is Kenneth Williams. I am a very big star of the theatre in England and my friends' – he swept his arms in our direction – 'are also very famous and important persons, who are unaccustomed to being incarcerated in rabbit hutches.'

'If you do not find us proper rooms befitting our station then I shall ensure that this indignity does not escape the attention of the entire British Press who just happen to be very close and loyal friends of ours. We are much loved and revered.'

Cor, Kenny did drone on. And the looks of distaste he dished out would have made fresh milk curdle. My considered opinion was that he had overdone it and that we would be tipped out on our arses. Not that I could give a damn, the condition I was in. All I needed to make my happiness complete was a quiet corner where I could lie down. If it was littered with broken glass I didn't care. Through my dizzy haze I heard the manager start to grovel a suitable apology. In a twinkling I'm lying in a lovely soft bed in a big, airy room. It was blissful.

After a good kip I felt bright as a button on a guardsman's Sunday tunic. The only health problem I had after that harrowing experience was worrying about my sides splitting. Kenny was at his hilarious best

– and when Lance Percival joined us for the second week I'm certain I had a few hairline fractures of the ribs.

One night we decided to have a look at the hotel cabaret. After the usual opening dancing girl routines they wheel in a great big cage centre stage. The lights go up and there's this stripper chained inside, losing little bits and pieces of her flimsy outfit as she struggles to escape the clutches of her wicked captors. Well, you can imagine Ken's reaction. He really camped it up. Ooohing and aahhing. 'Poor little thing will catch her death, bless her,' he gushed.

Sitting behind us is a group of people and one of the big-mouths starts getting smarty-arsed and taking the rise out of Ken. I reckon he'd had a few because he started to get really out of order. In the end I walks over, grabs the clown by the arm and politely but firmly suggests he accompanies me to a quiet corner of the establishment.

'That gentleman you are catcalling,' I tells him. 'That's little Kenny Williams. He don't mean no harm to nobody. He's a lovely man and he's just having a laugh.'

'I don't give a monkey's cuss who he is,' the geezer spits back in me face. 'Names don't impress me.'

With that I gave him the gentlest of playful squeezes. 'Well, my name is Ronnie Knight,' I whispers. 'And if I hear so much as a little peep out of you I'll knock you from the top of this hotel to the fuckin' bottom and back again. How do you fancy that for a break in the usual routine of a night out?'

His silence spoke volumes.

After that he sat quiet and attentive as a mouse in a nest of vipers. We had a lovely, trouble-free night.

Next morning we were by the pool getting a bit of the old currant bun. Kenny was there as usual, dressed in his best shoes, shirt and suit. The reason being that not only did he not sunbathe, he was passionate about not letting even the lightest of rays touch his delicate little body.

But that trifling idiosyncrasy was nothing compared to Kenny's major nightmare. He was an insomniac. Couldn't keep his eyes shut for more than a few minutes at a time. Worst of all he was unable to ease his misery by taking sleeping pills. He had some fascinating medical condition that made his throat constrict so he couldn't swallow anything like that. So what could he do? When he told me I thought he was having me on. Since he could not get tablets down his throat the doctors had found the only solution. They prescribed special suppositories he could push up his bum.

'It's true, Ronnie. Absolutely true,' he gushed. 'Just one little capsule strategically placed and I sleep like a babe.'

Any doubts I had about the validity of his tale were dispelled when he showed me the capsules that did the trick. Rather on the large side, I thought. It made my eyes water just to think about it.

So after two fun-filled weeks we bid farewell to sunny Madeira. Being a city boy I cannot say that the orchids, fish and pretty birds did a lot for me. But it had been an interesting time and I'd had enough laughs to last a lifetime.

And my Barb did enjoy herself.

5

The joint Mick Regan had his eye on was the Artistes and Repertoire Club at 142 Charing Cross Road. Right in the heart of the West End. The story was that the geezer who owned it was up to his neck in trouble, with a pile of debts to add to his considerable list of woes. Mick said that on a busy night you could be guaranteed more action down at the local morgue. Lovely sense of humour, had Mick.

Mick takes me down to give the place the once over. What do you think? he asks. All right, I said. I could see it had potential. I reckoned I could pull in the punters, especially with my mates and Barb's showbiz connections. So I said to Mickey we'd give it a go. We took over the place. This was it for me. Ronnie Knight had found his little niche in life. Fate had led me by the hand to my calling.

It was a new world and I took to it as enthusiastically as a little duckling to water. It was my sort of scene, the kind of place I'd always felt at my best. The happy difference was that this time I was on the clever side of the bar. When I realized the sort of money that could be made it brought a lump of gratitude to my throat.

After we had carried out some tasteful renovations and given the club a new look, the customers started pouring in. I fronted it up and wallowed in the role. I was mixing with friends, important faces and the showbiz lot. And I could afford to dress up in the very best. I was a very happy man. My new calling had the old scrapyard lark licked into a top hat, that's for double sure. In the bad old days I'd had to earn a crust by slogging me boots off all day, up to my armpits in muck and engine oil. There had been the Old Bill banging on your gate every five minutes wanting to know where every button and washer came from. This life up West was another planet, light years from the balloons and bloody goldfish.

My meteoric transition proved the absolute truth of one of your good old adages: how easily you get accustomed to a dramatic change in your circumstances when they take an upward trend, that is. Only a little while ago, when I was doing my penance behind bars, I would have given anything just to have a quiet crap in a bit of peace and quiet. Now I was a Face around town, a respected club-owner, the money rolling in and with a choice of de-bloody-luxe bathrooms. The change in financial fortunes was nothing short of miraculous. And what with both me and Barb out socializing most times it didn't cost us much indoors.

When we were out almost everything was on the house either at my club or where Barb was working. Everybody wanted to look after us. It's a funny fact about life. When you have got nothing, you have to struggle and fight for every little step up the ladder. When people think you've made it they break a leg trying to force more on you. Success breeds success, no doubt about it. I've always thought that to be one of the unfairest ironies of life. But you cannot deny the truth of it.

In no time at all my A and R is the top club in town. The place is packed out opening 'til closing. It's like a little gold mine, churning out the nuggets regular as clockwork and twice as fast. My goblet of happiness was running over.

In the bar you could not believe how things was booming. We had hit the big time with a bang. Our biggest problem was worrying where we were going to put all the punters. We were just round the corner from Tin Pan Alley. Pretty soon all the rock and pop stars started to come in of an afternoon. Bill Wyman and Keith Richard from the Stones had been pretty regular customers before we moved in, but when the place began to get jam-packed they found quieter drinking holes. Budding pop stars like Freddie Mercury and the Queen lot used to drop by during rehearsal breaks from the recording studios. Good as gold they were. Never any trouble. None of your wild-men stuff. I'd heard all the rumours and gossip about them, all about how they was supposed to be ac/dc and that, but they never caused no bother. No sweat at all. They were always dressed in white, tight-fitting clothes, with long, long hair. I used to marvel how they managed to get in and out their trousers. But it was no business of mine. They were good lads. A pleasure to take their money. Even the biggest superstars seem nice and ordinary when they are just sitting around, taking the waters and minding their own business.

We hit on the brilliant idea of having live music during the day, and it was just about the only place in town doing it. What a right note we played with that one.

In the beginning we were hiring groups. But pretty soon all these famous stars were turning up with their instruments for jam sessions. It was bloody terrific, with everything from rock guitars to violins. At times it was almost like a big-band session. Everybody got to hear about it. We were the hottest property on the map. The showbiz celebrities found it was a place they could come to without being mobbed or bothered by screeching fans. They knew they could have a good time and nobody was going to get excited about what they did.

Naturally enough some of Barb's 'Carry On' crew used the club. Especially Kenny Williams. He was a born entertainer, that man. A comic genius. He could make looking out of the window the funniest thing you'd seen that month. When I was with Kenny I needed earplugs to stop myself listening to him and bursting into fits of giggles like a silly kid.

In no way could you say that Kenneth Williams was a ladies' man. On the other hand in all the years I knew him I never witnessed anything to the contrary.

One night Kenny's holding court as usual when this good-looking young woman ups and wanders over to him. I thought she was going to ask Kenny for his autograph. I was about to hand over me pen when this sweet thing stands in front of Ken and suddenly outs with: 'Everybody says you are an old Queen. Well, are you a homosexual?'

On my life I wanted the floor to open up so I could dive in and stay covered until closing time. I didn't know whether to kick up a fuss, tip her out of it, take no notice or what. All I knew was that I could feel the blood rushing to my face. Kenny gave her one of those long, searching looks of his. Then he said, serious as the village preacher: 'Now listen to me, my little cheruby. If you want to see my arse, you don't have to go to all this trouble. You've only got to ask.'

Whereupon, without further ado, he dropped his trousers, turned round and treated her to the sight of his wriggling little bottom. He turned, did himself up with splendid dignity and carried on as though nothing had happened. That really turned the tables on the cheeky young woman, who I had by now noticed had had her fill. She watched Kenny's performance with increasing embarrassment and when he had finished she obviously felt a real idiot.

When I first got to know Danny La Rue I thought quietly to myself that it was a bit funny that a bloke became super-rich and famous by dressing up in women's undies. It was the sort of trick some people did and got sentenced for their trouble. But Danny is a genius at the knack of keeping his drag act humorous and light-hearted, never ever tawdry. Even when he had his best suit on and a nine o'clock shadow I could not help thinking of him as he is on stage, where you cannot deny he looks pretty as a picture. Many's the time I stood up to offer him my chair!

In those hilarious early 60's days the real wag, the club clown, was Ronnie Fraser who, I've said was one star I really loved. He was working hard, had lots of stage, film and telly work, but he refused to let it interfere with his drinking habits. One night he was pulling the leg of a new barmaid. She looked all hot and flustered so I went over to see what the old devil was up to. 'He keeps insisting he wants me to make him a Ronnie Fraser special,' she whispers. 'I don't know what it is.'

With a wicked grin on his rotund face Ronnie interrupted. 'In that case young Miss, I will enlighten you. To prepare a Ronnie Fraser special you take two measures each of gin, vodka, whisky and whatever takes your fancy, pour it in a glass and hand it to me.'

She broke into a giggly laugh. The poor girl thought he was joking.

Unknown to his millions of fans Ronnie has a special talent. He is a brilliant mimic. Sometimes he almost landed himself in real trouble. It's no secret that a lot of very heavy villains used to use the A and R. The likes of the Kray Twins, the Richardson mob, 'Mad' Frankie Fraser and one or two other lovely people. Although they never would have admitted it, I knew they liked rubbing shoulders with the stars. Well, a lot of these characters had quite distinctive voices. Some of the big, tough heavies, possessed weak little pip-squeak voices. It is putting it mildly to say they were somewhat sensitive about their comical vocal cords.

Ronnie, being such a brilliant impressionist, could take them off to a T. After he'd had a few (which he usually achieved in record time) he would start the fun and games. Gawd, he did make me squirm. I could see when he was about to start his devilish antics. Many a time I'd try to steer him off. There were some very serious people there who would not take kindly to having the piss taken out of them. But there was no stopping the old sod once he got going. He would draw in a deep breath, turn to me and blast: 'I say, I cannot readily recollect the name of that chap what keeps the boozer up in 'ampstead.' And it would come out in exactly the tones of one of the toughie brigade. My little heart used to flutter, fearing that it was all going to lead to a bit of

69

grief. But they either pretended not to hear or took it in uncommonly good spirits.

The only time Ronnie really dropped us in hot water was when we was out at some charity do one night. One of the gimmicks was to raffle off a racehorse. The bidding got up to the thousands mark . . . and there's Ronnie going like a good 'un, upping the bidding by a pony a time. Tried to warn him, I did. But he was in full flood. He was away and there was no stopping him.

Next morning he was contriteness itself. 'Ronnie, my darling. I seem to have acquired a real-life racehorse. I don't have nowhere to put it, but even more embarrassing I cannot raise the money I bid. I am somewhat skint.'

In the end I managed to square it. But it was not easy, I can tell you.

Ronnie was a good mate of Ian Hendry, who I believe would have been a very big star but for his drinking letting him down. When he was making *The Hill* with Sean Connery, Ian used to try to get his work done in the mornings so he could get up to the club most afternoons. Ian never caused any trouble. But the booze got him in the end.

One star who used to get on my wick was Harry H. Corbett, who played the son in the 'Steptoe' television comedy. Usually he minded his own and kept to himself. But sometimes when he went over the top with his 'I'm a big star' ways he was a real pain in the groin.

Corbett was one of those whose card we had marked down. We called them The Tossers. They were well known, sometimes quite famous people who couldn't hold their booze and got stroppy with it. We kept a close eye on them and if they got out of hand we quietly sorted them out. Our top priority was to keep good order.

Running a club's a bit like being a Sunday School teacher. You shouldn't have favourites. But I couldn't help loving Dorothy Squires. What a ballsy lady she was. For most of the time I knew her she was with Roger Moore, long before he got the James Bond part and really hit the big time. He was playing 'The Saint' then or something. Anyway Dottie was nutty about him. Worshipped the size tens he walked in, she did.

You always knew the minute Dottie walked into the club. She had this terrific, larger-than-life personality and shone like a beacon on a moonless night. Although she would be playing at somewhere grand like the Palladium she'd be only too happy to get up and do a turn for the asking. She was also a dab hand at helping me keep the peace. If

70

anybody got out of hand she'd glare at them and roar: 'Oi, you lot. Fuckin' well turn it in.' They'd say all right Dot and shut up. Yes indeed, a real lady she was.

I prided myself on keeping everything low key at the club. As time went by and I gained additional experience to add to my natural talents, I considered myself to be a diplomatic mediator. If there was any trouble you could handle it in two ways. Either you boshed 'em and threw them out, or you tried reasoning. On account that the first solution caused grief and could lose you customers, I always favoured the gentle approach. My initial line of attack was always: ' 'Scuse me, but would you mind going because your presence is no longer welcome in this establishment.' Usually they would see the sense in it, especially if my partner Mick strolled over. Mick was six feet four tall. And big with it. With the light behind him he looked a most formidable figure.

Sometimes, 'cos I'm only around five-nine, the troublemakers would give me a bit of lip. If there was a stranger in making a fuss I'd tell him to pipe down. He'd say: 'Who the fucking hell are you?' or some other such pleasantry. It was at times like that I felt a switch of tactics was called for. I'd say: 'It just so happens that I happen to be the governor. Who the bloody hell do you think I am? You got a choice. Either you get your arse out of here or I'll take personal pleasure in kicking it out.' It didn't happen very often, I am very glad to report, but I found a show of firmness when called for usually did the trick.

If there was any nastiness in my establishment it was invariably caused by strangers. Then I'd lay the blame on whichever member brought them in and warn them that in future they had better make sure their guests toed the line. Nine times out of ten the trouble-makers would come back and apologize, saying how the drink was to blame and they were sorry for taking liberties.

On the rare occasions somebody got roughed up a bit we used the utmost discretion. We would call an understanding cab-driver, who would whisk the victim to the nearest casualty department and ensure they were properly attended to. Everything was all nice and quiet. We didn't want to involve the police. They had enough on their hands, without bothering them with silly little incidents.

We did have our fair share of the Old Bill amongst our clientele. In those days one of the most regular faces on the London club scene was that of Commander Ken Drury, who was the absolute supremo of the Scotland Yard guardians of law and public morality. For some reason I could never quite figure out we were not on his regular round of top London clubs. He visited them regularly with a ready smile, a 'how you doing boys?' and a friendly bit of chit-chat. The main complaint about Mr Drury seemed to be that he was never what you might call in the front line when it came to standing his corner. To his credit, though, he was so concerned about the growing vice and porn going on down the road that he used to keep a very close eye on them. Never off duty, that copper.

What I was astonished to be told was that Mr Drury was taking rake-offs from various little enterprises, including three grand a week from Jimmy Humphries, the gentleman behind most of the seamy and steamy sex parlours. This odd couple could often be found of a certain time of the week down at the Hogarth Club in Soho, where it was heavily rumoured transactions of a fiscal kind regularly took place. It was that sort of deal that was to be Mr Drury's downfall. When he appeared in court and got sent down for five years not a lot people wept tears of sorrow.

The disgraced copper was lucky because he was sent to Ford open prison, saving him from a lot of pain and discomfort he would have suffered in other jails. Mr Drury served twenty months before being released on parole. It must have been the longest time in his life. I had found being a con absolute murder, so what a torment it must have been for the former top-brass policeman. The experience took its toll. He died a few years later. I can only say that in all the time I knew of him he never so much as hinted that lining his pockets might in any way improve our relations with the law.

Many other members of the Old Bill came in for a quiet snifter and a nose around, presumably putting in a bit of your extra-mural overtime to justify their villain-spotting expense chits. Now and again they would give us a little scare with a raid on membership or out-of-hours drinking. But it was just a bit of show. Just to let us know they were there, to keep us on our toes. They didn't seriously want to close us down, did they? I mean, half the criminal element in London used to frequent the club, so the Old Bill always knew where to find them if they wanted a word. If they'd have put us out of business they would have had to go scouring all round London unearthing the rascals. The status quo was good for us all. What you might call a mutually beneficial arrangement.

What never dawned on me in those carefree days was that by

mixing freely with the criminal element I was digging myself a hole from which a whole crop of trouble was about to grow. I was going to be branded as a villain. Not just an average no-good crook. More in the master-class.

6

Two sets of words came out of the East End. Whichever combination you use, they have become part of British criminal folklore.

The Twins.

Ronnie, Reggie.

The Krays.

Whichever way, they add up to . . . . Double Trouble.

Ronnie and Reggie Kray are currently serving life sentences for a cocktail of crimes including murder. Ronnie is incarcerated in top security Broadmoor and Reggie in Lewes Prison, Sussex.

During the Sixties the brothers carved out a reputation as East End gangsters. The Press described them as mobsters, who ruled their territory through fear and extortion, operating protection rackets and most of the organized crime. That's what was said about them when they were sent down in 1969 for thirty years.

There is absolutely no doubt that The Twins were very, very tough customers indeed. To be fair I must concede that me being a close mate of theirs might have caused some suspicious folk to question my pedigree. Was I guilty of wrongdoings by association?

The truth is that I first got to know Ronnie and Reggie when we were all spotty-faced teenagers, hanging around the streets looking for something to do and somewhere to go, just like thousands of other kids in the East End. It was at the good old Tottenham Royal where we first got chatting. They was a couple of smart looking lads, kept themselves to themselves and seemed nice, respectable guys. They never came over as nasty or cocky. They didn't throw their weight around and despite what some people might think they were not surrounded by a gang of ruffians. They had just a couple of other mates, that's all.

We had a few drinks, Ronny and Reggie, Poochy and me. 'Where you from, then? Anything exciting happening, then? Fancy another drink?' That's how it was. Your normal sort of small talk from young blokes out of a Saturday night, hell bent on having a 'good time'. We'd all be around sixteen, or seventeen when we first became mates. We got involved in one or two minor skirmishes, but nothing very serious. Not what you would classify as serious trouble.

We used to meet up at the dances most weekends and we became pally enough for me to invite them to my wedding. As I recall they were model guests and good as gold.

Now if there was one thing you could say about the Kray Twins it was this: they were as strong and healthy a pair of lads as you would find in a day's march. They were readily accepted into Her Majesty's armed forces, drafted to the Royal Fusiliers and – their one little bit of luck – were stationed near Tower Bridge. So they were still in town.

Somehow Ronnie and Reggie just did not fit into the system. Military discipline, spit and polish and marching up and down was just not their cup of tea. So next thing you know they are on the trot, up on their toes and out of uniform. They had a nasty name for what they did. Absent without leave, or was it desertion? I cannot recall. But I remember they were sent up country to Shepton Mallet, to some place from where it was more difficult to scarper. When they came out, things was back to normal. Inevitably The Twins were older, wiser and somewhat tougher than what they were when they went in.

While they had been doing their bit I had not only become a father, I had done very nicely out of the scaffolding business, fitted myself up with a trendy wardrobe and got myself one or two of life's little status symbols. The prize amongst which was an old-fashioned, traditional, black London taxi-cab complete with luggage carrier space and one of those great big bulbous hooters that used to 'hoink-hoink' by giving it a lusty squeeze. It was the first motor I ever had and set me back about four hundred quid. Did I love that motor or did I? I drove it round with my nose stuck in the air, proud as a pig with two curly tails. Although she was about thirty years old, she was in nice condition. A lovely runner. There were lots of similar Morris models still in active service, so my runabout was often mistaken as your genuine article.

It was a smart enough vehicle to travel in when you were going somewhere nice, to a restaurant or down to the country pub. You could go anywhere in it. Wouldn't even have been out of place parked at the Dorchester. There was no little green bags to blow into them days, but the old motor's appearance saved me from other forms of attention that often came the way of young blokes driving around in the early hours. At a fleeting glance they could mistake me for a genuine cabby taking a fare home, though some idiots in the back often thought it was the height of amusement to put their hands through the sliding window and hoot the bleedin' horn!

Ronnie and Reggie took to my motor a treat. They loved it. I used to pick them up at weekends so we could travel in style to the Royal, and I ferried them to their various venues for their amateur boxing bouts.

That's one thing they had been good at in the Army. They took after their big brother Charlie, who was a very highly rated pugilist and could easily have become a top professional. At one time they were offered the chance to go over to Canada to join some big boxing stable by an important trainer who spotted their potential. But they could not drag themselves away from their East End roots.

The Twins was more than useful in the ring. Which is more than could be said about me because, quite frankly, getting bashed about the head and face, with one in the kidneys for good measure, was not my idea of a fun experience. But the Kray brothers loved getting stuck in. I used to go with them sometimes down to train at the Fitzroy Gym, which again did not strike me as the best way to spend an evening.

One night the three lads jumps in my cab and we roars off to Leyton Baths where they are all on the same bill, one of the rare occasions they all fought together. It wasn't too good a night for them. Charlie was up first. He was a damn good fighter and there was a bit of hissin' and booin' when he lost on a narrow points decision. Reggie won his bout easy enough. It was up to Ronnie to save the family's honour by making it two out of three. Young Ron was going great guns till the last round when his opponent fought back dirty and gave him a serious head butt, which completely threw Ronnie out of his stride. He lost.

They was gloomy and despondent afterwards. I was trying to console them as we walked through the car-park back to the motor, when Ronnie suddenly sees the bloke who had given him one with his head.

'That's the one,' says Ronnie. 'I want a quiet word with him.'

He walks over to the guy. There appears to be a sharp exchange of words between the two. 'You nutted me in there,' says Ronnie all indignant.

Then bosh! Ronnie lets out a snaking right punch. That was it. The bloke collapsed like a sack of potatoes.

I never did see either of them in any other punch-ups outside the ring, though I was reliably informed that they knew what street fighting was all about.

They were not nasty people unless someone had a go at them and took liberties. The fact is that their reputation as distinctly hard men meant that most of the gangs feared them and kept out of their way. Only fools and headbangers behaved otherwise. One or two little teams, like The Angel Boys, Finchley Road mob and other ambitious types stepped out of line and later wished they had not bothered.

I do know some things about Ronnie and Reggie Kray that they never broadcast. For one, they did a helluva lot of work for charity, the church and other worthy causes. I have personally known them to donate loads of cash to down-and-outs and others in need of a helping hand. I knew churches you could drop by where the congregation would be singing the praises of the Twins for favours done and no questions asked. There was one church in Bethnal Green Road that they was always helping, with cash for renovation work and aid for the poor. At one time almost anybody in the East End who needed serious favours used to go calling on the Twins.

I am not whitewashing them. Just telling the truth. When I first began to understand just how much they contributed to charity I thought they was terrific boys.

They worshipped their old lady, Violet, and she wasn't half proud of them, I can tell you.

It was the same with all the muggings and brutal beating up of ordinary, decent folk in the streets. If people were knocked about in their patch the Twins took it very seriously indeed. Personally, in fact. They would take it upon themselves to find out who was responsible for the misdemeanour and administer short, sharp shocks on the culprits, who invariably vowed to mend their ways. A Kray's purge on the small-time hoods worked wonders on cutting down the assault and petty crime figures in the area.

Maybe it was a perverse form of rough justice, but I will tell you this: the East End was a safer place for ordinary folk in those days. Little old ladies could step out of a evening for a nice glass of stout down at the local without fear of having their heads bashed in. That's more than you can say about now. Now it is not safe for a prizefighter to be out after dark. Muggers thought three, maybe four times, before committing misdeeds because they knew there was more than an even chance that the Twins would find out and give them a dose of their own medicine.

Same thing with women. Ronnie and Reggie always showed ladies the greatest respect and good manners. They treated the wives and girlfriends of their close associates with the utmost civility. If you was in their company and there was ladies present, swearing was not allowed. The Twins did not hold with it. Anybody who broke the golden rule was out on their ear.

They was also very emotional people, were Ronnie and Reggie. If anybody suffered a bereavement, or somebody close was seriously ill, they used to get extremely upset.

As often happens with relationships, mine with the Krays sort of petered out. For no particular reason. They went their way and I went mine. We got together later on when I was with Barbara running the A and R and they were in a similar line of business, opening their own aptly named Double-R club in Bow. That was about the time they were starting to get really well known and earning a reputation as gangland villains.

The boys loved mixing with showbusiness personalities and were never happier than meeting up with old East End mates who had made good. People like Ronnie Knight. 'Course me and Barbara were a perfect set for them. They was always inviting us to their parties and treating us as celebrities to open the new clubs and restaurants. When they opened their up-market club The Kentucky, they made an offer to us that was hard to refuse. They insisted we were present for the opening night. That turned out to be somewhat embarrassing, seeing as how Barbara was doing an important show and just could not make it.

'In that case,' says the Twins in unison, 'there's only one thing for it. We will postpone the opening till Ron and Barbara can make it.'

And that is exactly what they did.

They came along to Barb's big night at the Odeon cinema in the Mile End Road for the premiere of *Sparrows Can't Sing*. They had shot a lot of the film down on the docks and Ronnie and Reggie had worked as 'minders' to the stars, like Jimmy Booth and famous director Joan Littlewood. It was a fantastic night, with little Barb being pictured in between Ronnie and Reggie and thousands of people waving, shouting and cheering their heads off. Suddenly Barbara started on one of those infectious little giggles of hers.

'It just occurred to me, Ron,' she whispers, 'that there's so many people here because Ronnie and Reggie went round knocking them up saying they would take it very kindly if you would turn up on the night.'

In other words an invitation that people felt they just could not refuse!

We met a lot. We talked over the old times. But we never became as close as we were in those early and exciting Tottenham Royal days. You never can put the clock back, can you? Somehow it just doesn't work.

Whatever the Kray Twins got up to after those days, I really don't know. But it is fascinating to see how today they are becoming sort of cult figures, with all their books and a movie being made about their lives. They are reputed to be raking in millions of pounds. I do not know about that but I do believe it when their agent says a lot of the profits will go to charitable and needy causes, 'cos I know beyond doubt that's what they did before.

They've had quite a lot to say about me in their books, talking about our relationship all those years ago. I can only tell how things happened, the side of the Krays that I knew. We were kids together. We had some good times. Some good laughs. We were good friends.

*

We didn't operate a class barrier at the club. Nor did we seek references. Membership was open to all those who could afford it, minded their manners and kept good order, the latter being a matter beyond negotiation. So we had barristers from some of the innermost temples, businessmen and the aforementioned members of the constabulary all mixing happy as you like with the showbusiness people. And scattered amongst them from time to time, just like chaff and wheat, was bound to be some of those colourful characters who kept the Old Bill in business.

The thing about bank robbers, bandits and the like is that they don't go around with their trade or calling rubber-stamped on their foreheads. Inevitably, then, a lot of what you might call tearaways and more sinister denizens of the underworld were pretty frequent faces at the A and R. They seemed to have a lot of spare time on their hands. But I took the charitable view that being at the club kept them out of mischief.

No doubt about it, the A and R was very much the 'In' place for all sorts from all walks of life. The Twins, of course, used to drop by now and again, together with the Richardsons, Frankie Fraser and an assortment of other notorious individuals. They were all the sort of people you either loved or hated. should it happen to be the latter it was a smart idea to keep your opinion to yourself and keep smiling.

Some of them were hard men, no doubt about it. Others had done a lot of bird and just wanted to have a good life, since they were never absolutely sure where tomorrow might land them. After a few drinks they might start to talk a bit tough, but if you kept them quietly out of the way they hardly ever went over the top. The secret was merely to contain their natural high spirits.

On the other hand you could never afford to get too complacent with some of the ex-cons. Care and caution was the key phrase. Take a specimen like weedy Jimmy Essex. He wasn't much to look at. A bit like a balding garden gnome with no teeth and a pathetic mush. You had to feel sorry for him sometimes: but never enough to forget that he had done a couple of murders. He was an out-and-out no-gooder as would ever be your misfortune to bump into on a dark night. Like I said, he was never any trouble. But me and Mick made it a golden rule never to turn our back on him should a spot of bother unexpectedly flare. The rumour was that he only stabbed people in the back. You were all right so long as you kept him face-to-face. It was a golden little tip worth remembering, a spot of inside inform-ation that could save on your tailor's bills.

I learned early on from my elders and betters that no matter how well you are doing at one particular business it never hurts to poke a few more irons in the fire to sort of spread your investments. One of my little sidelines was with Freddie Foreman. I had first got to know Freddie through my close mate and partner Mickey Regan. Freddie was avidly described in the popular Press variously as a 'strongarm lieutenant and hitman' in the Krays' firm. We had fifty or sixty pool tables situated in pubs all around and it was a very nice business. All we had to do was make the weekly rounds collecting the takings, and a few hundred sovs landed in the back pocket without fail. This extremely lucrative number was all very above board. The arrange-ment suited us both admirably. Whatever Freddie chose to do in other enterprises was none of my affair. I did not know and had no desire to pry.

During that golden era, one of the facts of life that took the glitter off the cake for some owners was the question of insurance. That was how the little service was billed by those offering the premiums. Insurance. Somehow it sounded much more sound and reliable than protection. There is little doubt that it was a booming business. Just where you had a Woolworths you would invariably find your Marks and Spencers. So it was with the night club and drink scene.

Wherever you unearthed establishments of that sort you would find enterprising persons keen to cash in on the profit margins.

But I can honestly say that never once during my fourteen years in the West End club business was the sordid subject of protection money or other such nastiness mentioned.

Jimmy Humphries, the porn merchant who was keeping certain lawmen in a grand style to which they rapidly became accustomed, was an old villain. But with his profitable outlets in Old Compton Street, Fish Street, Brewer Street and Walkers' Court – a load of strip clubs – he had become a main man. As Jimmy got on, legging it up the social ladder like a circus acrobat, he began to cherish respectability above all else. He would dress himself up so that in a certain light at a certain hour of the night he looked like a real gentleman, a bit of a toff. In the end the porn king became a very wealthy geezer indeed. He bought Hastings Football Club, a greyhound track and a big farm. You can't get more respectable than that.

Ruby Sparks was another old underworld character that fascinated me. Ruby wasn't his real name. But that's what everybody called him. So one day, out of natural curiosity, I asked him why he was blessed with a girl's monicker. It turned out that when he was a kid he was playing round Hatton Garden one morning when he sees an open door. He walks in cheeky as you like and is interested to find hundreds of lovely red glass marbles all over a table. Unable to believe his good fortune Ruby gets down on the floor and starts having a little game, knocking the shiny red balls all over the place. Suddenly, this man comes in and nearly has a fit. The red stones that Ruby thought came out of bubblegum machines were your real life precious jewels worth a king's fortune. So that's how Ruby got his name.

Stories like that always used to tickle my out-of-town visitors – our 'country members' I called them. They were people who came down to the Smoke on a bit of business from places like Glasgow and Birmingham and other outlandish regions. Generally speaking they were all top boys from their home territory. Being of a suspicious nature I figured that they were not all involved in matters strictly all legit and above board. They were also not the sort you messed around with. That being said I often never knew nothing about the out-of-towners until they was all nicely settled in the club minding their own business and having a drink. Whatever their backgrounds I can only speak as I found. And I found them to be as well behaved as a choirboys outing. They caused no offence and took no liberties.

The Glasgow mob held a special place in my affections, of the financial variety. Blimey could those blokes drink. I had never seen nothing like what they could put away. Not that I was complaining. It was all good for business. Jesus, the takings were fantastic when that lot hit town. I could see the percentages soaring.

Now, while this boom was keeping the bank manager happy the club was getting a bit of a reputation as a hangout for villains. The name Ronnie Knight was also being bandied about a fair bit. What was happening was that the names A and R and RJK were getting frequent airings in nicks and courts.

This is how it came about. Some rogue on a bank job would tell the Old Bill that he couldn't have done it 'cos he was up at the Artistes and Repertoire at the time discussing the latest Cabinet changes with a dozen of his mates. And if they did not believe him, then they suggested checking the facts with Mr Ronald Knight, the joint-proprietor, who just happened to be chairing the debate to ensure that all points of view got a fair and proper airing. So, before you know it, I would have a couple of gentlemen to see me on a certain line of enquiry. Sometimes I could remember what was suggested. Other times I could not. But the overall effect was that I got involved in events that were absolutely none of my business.

When supergrass Bertie Small was dishing out the poison on twenty or thirty people many of them would use the club as an alibi. Worse still, some characters who were involved in notorious trials, like the Wembley Bank Job, where a fortune was nicked, had been regulars.

A good counsel for the prosecution spouting his head off in court could make the A and R sound like a club for crooks. That sort of thing was happening all the time. We kept getting recommended to police divisions all over London. Inevitably this meant a surge in the number of officers paying us a visit, which was not entirely good for trade and was extremely time-consuming. It might well be that wanted men would also mention that they had been to places like Churchills and other such up-market joints. But for some reason it was old A and R that seemed to stick and got a bad reputation. Looking back I think that it was during them days that I began to get somewhat tarred with black myself. Because some of the bad boys used the club and because I knew them certain people put two and two together and came up with some silly conclusions.

At first I used to think it was very funny when I heard rumours about Ronnie Knight being a Mr Big in the underworld. I wrote it all off as tittle-tattle: just one of the prices I had to pay for my success in clubland. I never dreamed that anybody would take it all seriously. Many's the time I had a laugh about it with Candy, my favourite barmaid, a dynamic coffee-coloured lady who was just about the best in the business. I had known her on the Soho scene for years – and when she came a-calling asking me and Mick for a job we could not believe our luck. She was brilliant at her trade. I never tired of just watching that girl dispensing the drinks like she was on well- oiled casters and never losing a cheery smile on her beaming little face.

Candy's most amazing skill was being able to take in massive orders all in one go – without ever getting it wrong. A party could come in twenty handed and yell out a score of different drinks. She would have the first on the bar before they had finished ordering. After that, all they had to do was nod 'same again, Candy' and she would do it all again. Candy's incredible memory was invaluable when the club was packed. Sometimes the place got so busy that a break-out party from Broadmoor could have been having a knees-up for all I knew.

I bumped into people, got introduced to them without no idea of who they were or what line of interest they pursued. One suspicious-looking gent I remember keeping an eye on because he looked every inch a no-good turned out to be a 'respectable' lawyer. He was wearing the hunted look on account that he was doing a naughty with a bit of fluff and was worried sick that he'd bump into somebody that would tell his missus and really drop him in it.

What I'm trying to point out is you could never tell by appearances.

At other times I'd get to meet characters who reminded me of my kindly, jolly uncle Jack. Then somebody would quietly fill me in on their colourful backgrounds, involving all sorts of mayhem and misdeeds, and I would have to sit down with an aspirin to overcome the shock.

A case in point was a very interesting character called Eric Mason. What a nice friendly sort to have frequenting my place, I thought after meeting him for the first time. One night there developed what could have turned into an ugly incident. These two or three miscreants were stepping out of line and I had found it necessary to deliver my peacemaker's ultimatum. This time I could see it wasn't having the desired effect, 'cos I detected a hint of bloodlust as they lunged towards me. Suddenly they snap to attention like a Grenadier at the Queen's birthday. In the soft lights I detected a delicate hint of green around their gills. When I saw their hands trembling I thought I must have grown horns and a tail. I looked them straight in the eyes.

But the little rascals were staring over my shoulder. I turned round. Standing right behind me was none other than Mr Eric Mason. He didn't have to say nothing. But he treated them to a certain look that suggested pushing their luck was not a prudent manoeuvre. I do believe that I detected an interesting smile playing on Mr Mason's craggy face. After that little encounter they earned scout points for good behaviour.

What I learned later was that Eric Mason was a very hard man indeed. A bank robber and villain extraordinary who had been involved in some murderous gangland battles. One claim to fame was that he was the last prisoner in Britain to be lashed with the cat-o'-nine-tails. I've since seen the scars. But that was nothing more than a pimple on the nose to this tough hombre. One night he had been found more dead than alive after a battle with the Richardson mob. He had so many broken bones that he rattled when they lifted him into the ambulance. But what really got the surgeons fascinated was the way the axe had sliced through his hand, pinning it to his skull. Every time I look at Eric now I picture him with the chopper sticking out the top of his head.

No matter how hard I worked at trying to spot the difference I never did manage to solve the mystery of how to tell a villain from an errant Baptist minister. Of course, I knew the regular, small-time little scallywags, mostly from the East End. Their social failings were an open book. But I continued to take the view that their out-of-club-hours activities was entirely a matter for them and their consciences. Had I gone round poking nose into their intimate affairs and asking leading questions I faced a serious chance of being told to mind my own and to get on with my knitting.

Mind you, I could sometimes tell when some of the suspect members of my clientele had enjoyed a little tickle. It was that unfailing nose of mine. I'd probably seen 'em at the bar a week earlier, slowly sipping at a beer and obviously counting the pennies. When they'd been up to no good they would be standing there with a bunch of pals, dispensing joy and mirth and buying drinks all round. On the quiet I'd think to myself: 'Hello, who has been giving them some money . . . what have they been up to?' Then you would see in the paper that some job's been pulled. Mind you, I could never really be sure.

While I was pondering the permutation of possibilities my concentration was invariably distracted by the old till a-ringing up. When they had money they were all good spenders. No doubt about it. I questioned matters no further.

Looking back today, I still don't see what I could have done about me getting labelled as One of Them. They came in. I had a nod and a chat. That was it. I didn't want any attention. I didn't have no clout. I didn't court a shady reputation. All I wanted was to run a successful club and make a good, honest living. What kept me going was the memory of slogging me guts out on the scrapyard and pounding the cobbled streets with my little fishy friends. And what kept me on the more or less straight and narrow was those nightmares about ever again going back behind bars.

I finally realized how serious my situation was getting during some well publicized court case. This grass was telling a jury how the job in question had been planned in the A and R. The inference being that it was right under my highly developed nose. One of the villains was supposed to have given it the seal of approval by standing up and pronouncing: 'I think it's a good thing. The job's on. We'll pull it next week.' All this plot-hatching was alleged to have been going on while I was at the other end of the bar. It was said in court, but it was entirely news to me.

I don't deny that sort of thing never happened. I do not deny that I realized that certain people of ill repute would talk shop on my premises. Maybe I might have had my own suspicions. But I took the view that it was none of my business. No more than it was if a captain of industry used my place to plot a takeover bid. But when it comes out in print it looks like the club is the headquarters of the criminal fraternity. And that Ronnie Knight knows all about it. That was not true.

But it was not all gloom and doom. Far from it. Apart from the financial rewards that came my way, I got a lot of fun and laughter out of some of my customers. We shared a laugh and a joke. Some of them was right little rascals, but somehow I could not help liking them. Even if it cost me.

There was this cheeky young devil who had a grin like a contented Cheshire cat, who was always asking for a few quid to see him over. One day he says to me: 'I must owe you a tidy bit now Ronnie. How much is it, then?' I'm thinking to myself that I should have trusted my instincts that he was a nice boy and ought not to have harboured nasty thoughts that he might not pay me back. Since I had not kept meticulous notes on his loans, I did a bit of mental calculation and figured that he owed around £250, probably a bit more, but out of the kindness of my heart I would let him off. So I said two-fifty. His grin broadens even more and quick as lightning he comes back with:

'Well, I'm a bit down on the luck, Ron. Any chance of making it £500?' I always was a sucker for lines like that. He got it. Which now I come to think about it, reminds me that I never did get it back.

Here's a secret that I've always kept close to my chest. Ronnie Knight used to be a sort of 'Agony Uncle' to cons doing long stretches. My voluntary social work was to help out villains who had fallen foul of the law and were paying their due penance at one of her Her Majesty's guest houses. Having done a spell of bird myself I knew how important it was to have someone on the outside you could trust and in who you could confide your problems.

Since it often happened that their close mates was similarly indisposed on account that they had pulled jobs – and got nicked – together, they needed a trusty confidant on the outside, someone who could come and go as they pleased. So if prisoners, many of them old club customers, wanted a spot of advice or help they'd call in Uncle Ronnie Knight. I know some of them were real social outcasts and thorough rascals. Amongst them were those who had committed really nasty crimes. But I felt I could not give 'em the cold shoulder when they were at their lowest ebb. They needed somebody to lend a sympathetic ear.

Over the years, throughout the Sixties and Seventies, I suppose I visited hundreds of prisoners, many of the Category 'A' collection doing long stretches. I'd get a letter imploring: Dear Ron, DO come and visit me . . .' So I'd take a few hours off and motor down to Wandsworth, the Scrubs or wherever the unfortunate souls happened to be serving their time. Just walking through them prison gates never failed to give me the heeby-jeebies. It brought the grief flowing back like ten thousand volts stuck up the leg of a wet suit. I remembered all the misery and degradation of life behind bars. Once or twice I panicked and felt I just could not step inside. Then I thought of the poor bastards in there waiting for a bit of company, a chat and a helping hand and I managed to see it through.

Nearly always the aggravation being suffered by the inmates could be summed up in one word. Women. These tough guys would sit facing me, trying to put on a cheery, carefree disposition. But in seconds it'd all come tumbling out. They'd had a 'Dear John . . .' Their woman had gone walkabout and they were devastated. Their last bit of security and hope had gone. The news that their missus had done a moonlight flit – usually with an old pal which made it worse – did terrible things to men on long stretches. I'll never forget what I witnessed when I was inside. You could tell the ones that had had the letters a mile off. One minute they would be all right, smiling and making the best of things. Next you would see the poor buggers shuffling round, faces like uncooked pastry and all red-eyed.

The first thing you think about when you get sent down is the wife and kids. All the wrongs you've done them. How you have caused them pain and misery by your wrong-doings. You are riddled with guilt. You worry about what the old woman's doing with herself while you're inside. It gets to your guts. You get consumed with suspicion and jealousy. You hope and pray she's going to stay true and faithful. But when you are doing a ten, even a two, you know in your heart that the chances are pretty slim. She's going to jump into bed with some bastard sooner or later. That's for certain. And there's fuck all you can do about it.

When the 'Dear John . . .' drops your world finally collapses. I'd been lucky. I'd had Barbara and a good few other friends to see me through my darkest hours. So I never complained about going on my missions of mercy to administer to those less fortunate than what I'd been.

When you are behind bars, you cannot talk in strict confidence to another con. Tell a heartbreak story and you are soon the laughing stock of the nick. But there is more to it than just the busted pride. The worst thing is that you don't often know just what the real truth is. You've just picked up a bit of chit-chat. Maybe some charmer is stirring it. It's so private. You don't want another bloody soul to know about your personal affairs. So you need a mate on the outside that you can turn to. Someone you can trust.

My going to see them didn't look suspicious. Practically every villain knew me, so it just looked as if I was paying a nice little call to talk over a bit of unfinished business. That minimized the risk of cell-block gossip, which makes your average women's institute meeting look like a nunnery during high mass. They didn't want anybody to know that their missus had buggered off with somebody else. They did not want it put about. It wasn't just macho pride, either. If your family broke up it could affect your chances of parole. You were much more likely to get out early if the beaks thought you was flying back to the nest and a good stable background. They always seemed to consider that a little woman back home was a steadying influence. That's the way they saw it and that's what often influenced their decisions when time off for good behaviour day came round.

Woman trouble was a real ball cruncher. The offended parties talked to me openly and freely. They knew that their innermost secrets were secure with Ronnie Knight. I have never had a reputation as a talking man. What they all thirsted after was knowing: is it true? They had heard it was Fred Screwdust or somebody. Would I find out, let them know! Quick! In the strictest confidence.

The heartache bit came when they managed to bring themselves to almost beg: 'Ron, if you possibly can and that, would you try and stop her or get her back for me?'

Some real tear-jerking stories unfurled. One man I had known for years called me down on the pretence that he wanted someone to take care of his greyhounds. Really he had heard some interesting gossip about his trouble and strife. Since I was out and about he wondered, all casual like, if would I mind having a little nose around? No trouble at all, I assured him. I was sure it was all a nasty smear, but I would make a few enquiries. The poor sod. He didn't know the half of it. Not only had his missus buggered off. She'd scooted with one of his old mates; the runaways had sold every damn thing. The house, the car, the bloody lot . . . the greyhounds. She had even nicked his nest-egg stash of ten grand he had painstakingly soldered into an old telly, ready for when he got out.

Going back and telling him the horrible facts was one of the hardest things I had to do. He'd done two of a ten-year stint. He was destroyed. I felt very sorry for that poor fella. It upset me to see him sitting there, fighting back the tears and knowing deep in his heart that there was sweet Fanny Adams he could do about events. As I got up to leave, after relating the painfulness, all I could think to say was: 'When you get out come up and see me.' I know it wasn't much to offer in consolation. But what can you tell a man who has lost everything? Including his stash! That poor bastard looked like he had been condemned to the electric chair.

Other cons were a bit more volatile when it came to their notice that the she-cat was up to the hanky-panky business. More than one prisoner enquired if I would be so good as to 'sort the fuckers out', referring to both erring wife and current boyfriend. I'd point out that clobbering folk was not the role upon which I was engaged. Not my line of country. Nevertheless I would undertake to make a few discreet moves on their behalf. Once word got round that I was anxious to have a word with the cuckoo, it invariably resulted in the culprit getting on his toes. He would go missing. Obviously if I did bump into them I would administer a whack, while delivering a running commentary on their suspect parentage, positioning of their anatomy and short-term health prospects. Nearly always they would gush out their sad regrets and claim they were sorry. But the lust of the loins being such a powerful force, it was usually but a twinkling before they betrayed their best intentions and returned to the welcoming arms of the prison widow.

If I whacked the guilty bloke it was out of a strong emotional feeling. I could still see those heartbroken Johnnies shuffling along the landings with their little dog-eared letters stuffed in their top pockets. So I whacked the boyfriends because, Jesus Christ, it could have happened to me. I would have expected one of my mates on the outside to do the same. Maybe I got too emotionally involved.

The runaway wives had it tough too. They were given the glacier treatment and sent to Coventry by all and sundry. Some disapproving folk reinforced their distaste with the way they had behaved by throwing in a sharp kick up the arse. If one of the wayward wives walked into our club with a new bloke swinging on her arm we wouldn't serve them. Call it a touch of maliciousness and you would be absolutely right. We also put the word round to other clubs with a strong request to blacklist them. When the opportunity arose I always told the women what I thought of them. Not a long lecture. Just a few, well-chosen phrases.

But there was another little service I gave, which involved somewhat more than merely not revealing intimate secrets of the matrimonial kind. More like absolute, complete and utter trust. And that, as we all know, is a commodity that can sometimes be in worrying short supply. This was the dilemma certain wrongdoers found themselves in when the Judge interfered with their social arrangements for the next few years. They often had one or two personal and private possessions of such delicate nature that they needed somewhere safe and secure to place them. Somewhere away from prying eyes and official probing where their little odds and ends would be safe, carefully minded by someone trustworthy beyond question.

The little knick-knacks came in different shapes and sizes. Framed pictures, bits of pottery, various objects d'art and little things like that. One similarity that all had in common was that they were extremely well packed and sealed. I made it my duty to ensure that they was placed in complete safety until such time as their rightful owner turned up to claim them. What was contained within them I will never know. But the story about what happened to a certain televison set belonging to one luckless soul almost caused an epidemic of coronaries among the prison population.

7

All was wonderful on the West End club front. My business affairs could not have been better had they been blessed twice a week by the Pope and the Archbishop. I'd acquired another club just round the corner, the Tin Pan Alley, and had added a few sidelines to me longbow. Workwise speaking you could not have found a happier individual on a day's safari through paradise.

On the matrimonial front, however, Barb and me were heading for the rocks. There's always something in life, ain't there? Busty, blonde Barbara. The sexy, saucy starlet. That's how the papers always portrayed her. Those striking boobs got more coverage than the weather forecast.

She had really hit the big time. The 'Carry On' movies had become a national institution. So had Barbara and the other stars like Sid James, Charles Hawtrey, Peter Butterworth, Jack Douglas and all the other funny men. Barb had blossomed into becoming a big star and how she loved every live-long second of it. She was never more at home than on the film set or the stage. Hanging around so many actors, it never ceased to amaze me how they all adored being in the limelight. It was their oxygen. Funny way to be.

If there is one sphere of life where success really breeds success then it's got to be the entertainment lark. There is no business like showbusiness if you are the flavour of the month. Tough luck on the thousands of poor hopefuls who sit around on their backsides day after day waiting for the chance to play a horse's arse in a flea-bitten panto.

The more work Barb got, the more came piling in. She was getting offers from all over the country, signing up for touring shows taking her away from home for six or eight weeks at a time. They had a really smash hit with Joan Littlewood's *Oh, What a Lovely War*. Rave reviews and everybody kissin' everybody all over the place in traditional theatre style. Everybody and everything was marvellous.

Wonderful. Only it wasn't very lovely for me, 'cos Barb went off on tour for a year in America. Anybody who believes the fairy story about absence making the heart grow fonder needs a by-pass operation.

We moved to Stanmore, into a lovely big, five-bedroomed house with everything you could ever want. The pad was in a snooty little cul-de-sac called Aylmer Drive, with a big garden and orchard. I bet that place would fetch more than half a million quid now. When we first took up residence I was over the moon. I'd always fancied myself as a bit of a chef and used to love helping out in the kitchen, preparing the veg and getting things ready for a nice lunch or dinner.

But as Barbara got more in demand it began to be like a ghost house, with just me rattling around in it for weeks on end. When she came back she hired a chauffeur-cum-handyman and later a male housekeeper, so it got to lose even the suggestion of homeliness.

I got really fed up with all this going away lark. I'd say to Barb that she didn't need to do it any more. I was making more money than I knew what to do with. It was coming out of me ears. Every night I'd come home with a big pile of notes, I'd turn it out on the table and Barb could take anything she liked. Hundreds of crispy cash.

A lot of stirrers later tried to make a three-act play out of the fact that Barbara paid the mortgage when we lived out in Stanmore. Those lovely people hinted that I was living off of Barbara's back. But that was a lot of last week's garbage. The truth is that Barb paid some of the big bills out of her account because it was better for tax purposes. The accountants sorted all that lot out. Me, I provided the readies. Piles of it. That bought all Barb's expensive jewels, furs and finery. Money was the last thing we needed to fight about. We never did. She could have anything she wanted. We both could. But it didn't make us any the happier.

What really got me talking to the flowers on the wallpaper was being on my own all the time, while Barb was swanning off with some show or other. I'd tell her straight that I'd had enough of being on my own all the time. It was no way to run a marriage. I expected a few home comforts at the end of a night's toil. Not just a friendly lick from the dogs and a takeaway supper. Lying in bed alone getting the sweats was no way for a healthy, red-blooded bloke to be carrying on. Many a solitary night I'd spend there dwelling on the cruel irony of it all. I was married to Britain's cutest sex-pot, with half the male population envying me. And I was getting less loving than your average monk. In a way it was worse than being inside. At least there you knew your chances were pretty slim. My current situation was bloody crazy.

I lived the ration-shortage life with Barbara for years before I even began to think about nibblin' in pastures new. In those days I knew how much she loved the entertainment world, how she got a real kick out of doing her stuff. So I had never suggested she should give it all up. Just be a bit more selective so we could spend some time together. Just like your Mr and Mrs Average. That's all I wanted.

Anyway, no matter how much I asked it made no difference. Every little job that came up she would grab like she was in line for an Oscar. I learned that about actors. They are so bloody insecure they'd volunteer as a postman if people got up early enough to watch them perform. Barbara's reaction to my protests was always the same: 'But it's a challenge, Ron,' she would gush. 'It's just the break I want for my career.' Some Shakespeare came up once, something completely out of her line and paying charity-box money. But she couldn't resist doing it even though it meant her being away for weeks on end.

The thing was, I loved the girl. I really did. But I had to live with the fact that with Barb it was work and career first and second, with good old Ronnie down the field a poor third. No wonder I was short of me oats!

But flesh and blood can only stick so much for so long. I would get so brassed off I'd blow a fuse and warn her it was her friggin' precious career or her marriage. So make up your friggin' mind, gel!

'All right. All right,' she would promise. 'I won't do it no more. I'll get my agent just to do the TV and shows close to home. How's that suit you, eh?'

Then it would be all lovey-dovey, a normal sort of marriage and everybody happy. Oh yeah! For a couple of weeks. Then Barb would dash in excitedly one day, bubbling with enthusiasm about landing a brilliant new part. 'It's really marvellous,' she'd keep saying, just what she had dreamed about. So it was back up north for a few more weeks. Time for another lovely spell in the monk's mode. Charming, I used to think. Fucking charming.

That's how the years passed. That's how it went on. When it got really bad and I felt I'd had enough Barb would always harp back to the old chestnut about me becoming her manager. It would be a perfect set-up, she kept on saying. We could spend all our time together, travelling the world. Yeah, I could just see the scene. The sexy star and her lapdog old man trailing behind, listening to the whispering campaign.

In the end our marriage ended up like millions that had gone the same way. You try to make the best of it by seeking little diversions. Inevitably you seek a little light relief by putting your pecker around here and there. It's only natural, after all.

Many a time when I was on my own I thought about what had happened to our lives. I was making a handsome living. I loved the nightclub scene. We had a beautiful home, furnished with loving care and a bleedin' fortune. We could live the High Life much as we pleased. Big showbiz parties, the social whirl. Wining and dining. Sometimes in those fancy restaurants that cost an arm and a leg, I'd remember the old days when I'd scoured the menus looking not at the food, but at the prices. I had ordered not what I fancied, but what I could afford. Now there I was. Big Wheel. Big Earner. Big Spender. Life a Big Sham.

When you are unhappy you tend to indulge yourself. With some it's the demon drink. Others balloon up through stuffing themselves with food. My big weakness was spend, spend, spending. I bought wardrobes of stylish clothes and had a hot passion for powerful cars. Jags, Daimlers and Mercs were my particular fancy, with the Mercs a firm favourite. My habit was to change them every year, about the time they got to needing a really good polish.

Jesus, I was a really big show-off. I'd go to one of the West End showrooms and admire the latest model on display. That's right, the one slap bang in the middle of the front window.

Without so much as enquiring about the cost of the commodity I'd get the manager and inform him: 'I like it. I'll take it.' Watching their faces was always a pleasure. They'd start huffing and puffing, telling me sorry sir but you can't have that particular one as it's for display purposes only. Then they'd plug into the tune about waiting lists.

'If I cannot have that one there,' I'd point dramatically towards the object of my affections, 'then I shall friggin' well take my custom to more obliging accommodation'.

It never failed.

But it was all your diversion. Pulling that sort of stunt didn't give me all that much of a buzz. The bottom line was that our marriage had had it. It just wasn't right. How could it work with Barb away all the time? We couldn't have friends round. Holidays were out of the question. We didn't do anything together any more. Can you believe it, but there was only ONE day out of every year when we could be sure we would be together. That time was on December 25th. Christmas day would be our big re-union. But we would barely have time to exchange presents and have a kiss under the mistletoe before my little wifey would be scooting off for the Boxing Day pantomime or something.

That was it. Happy memory. Happy families. Happy Christmas. For the rest of the holiday it was a case of Ronnie Knight Solo. All alone. Everywhere I went there were couples, close together and having a lovely time. I'd sit there on my jacksy feeling like a spare pecker on a honeymoon. My friends would gather round, oohhing and aahhing about poor old Ron having no company. I began to feel like a social outcast . . . uncomfortable and out of place, half the time.

When you are on your own you realize just how much the social world is geared up exclusively for couples. Odd men out don't fit in unless somebody's trying to do a nice bit of match-making. And in my case, at that particular time, I was not in the matching stakes.

Most of the nights I'd go out with me mates. Poochy and the old crowd. I was also spending more and more time at the club. It became a home from home. I was happier there than going back to a cold, empty pad. No matter how plush and expensive it was kitted out. A home with no love ain't worth a candle in a storm.

I have never been what you might call a pushy type of bloke. Like I've explained, I lacked a bit of confidence and leaned towards the shy side. That is not to say that I considered myself an ugly duckling. I knew that Ronald J. Knight could look the goods and hold his own. I was a bit of a womanizer, but no more than most who got the opportunity. But Arabian-Knight stories I've seen about me being a Great Don Ron, a rampaging superstud, are a joke.

It all goes back to me Booty Knight days, when all the little girls gave me some stick. That plus the fact that being a Knight was a bit like being a leper. Any girl who went out with one of us boys got the earache from their mothers, on account that we were bad little berks and no good would come of it. All that early rejection knocked my confidence for life. Perhaps that's why I'd become a dresser in my early teens. Another compensatory factor to make up for my failings.

Sure I liked the ladies, but I'm damned if I could make the first move. Even now I find it takes a lot of courage for me to start talking to someone first. My style always was to let the girl make the running, for them to come and chat me up from the off. Once they got friendly I was all right. Within a twinkling I'd be in second gear turning on the irresistible Knight charm. But I needed a show of encouragement before I could pluck up the necessary gumption to move in.

When I first got involved with Barbara I had been smitten. So bowled over that I had thrown caution to the wind. She was a very forward lady and taught me a thing or two. She changed my life. With Barb it had been the really big sex thing – and I could not believe the things she wanted to do.

For all those years we had been together there was no one else in my life. That's for absolute sure. I had all the chances in the world, mixing with the young showgirls. Some of them thought I could make them stars and were eager to offer a little down payment, grateful-wise. But like I said I was not available. (Even if I had been it would have had to be suicidal to start putting it around with leggy dancers and actresses. It would have been like broadcasting my indiscretions on the BBC world network.)

I had it offered to me on a plate with all the trimmings, served hot, cold or anyway I fancied it. But I wasn't dining out. Even when Barbara was away all the time and I got pretty desperate, I somehow found the moral strength to stay true, even if I did have to bite my tongue now and then. Some of the propositions aimed at me by forward young ladies were so direct they'd have made a sailor blush.

I stayed completely faithful to Barbara for seven, almost eight years. I loved the lady. I had respect for her. I didn't want to hurt her, even if my libido did begin to think I'd taken the vow. But being human, it was bound to happen.

One night I was in the club feeling particularly lonely and sorry for myself. I was thinking: what's Barb doing leaving me on my own for seven or eight months at a time? This lady came over. We got chatting and that was it. The floodgates was opened. Ronnie Knight was available.

I had a few affairs. They were all with nice girls. If some lady seemed to fancy me it was there. I always made it clear that there was nothing serious. Usually it was a one night stand. I was not in the love league, just having a little fling here and there. We both had a good time and that was it. There was one golden rule. I never got involved with women who were married. I had respect for their husbands. I could never forget the Dear John guys in jail.

I ensured that everything was nice and discreet. Nobody got hurt. There was no real commitment. Just a warm, friendly time. My little flings meant I wasn't always on my own.

A certain car dealer, name of 'Clocky', so named because of rumours of his penchant for reversing the mileage on motor vehicles to indicate they had barely left the showroom, was another acquaintance who owed me. 'Clocky' happened to be on hand one time when I found myself somewhat in difficulties because my lovely new Merc, in for a service, was not ready in time for me to take a certain, discreet little weekend trip down to the South Coast. Quick as a flash 'Clocky' comes up with the solution. He has available a wonderful Rolls Royce Silver Cloud, in pristine condition, that he will be delighted to place at my disposal for the weekend. He further suggests that not only will it solve my problem, but will go some way to squaring the financial arrangements between us. So a few hours later I'm purring down the A2 with six or seven litres of engineering magic in front of me and a heady whiff of your Chanel wafting over from the passenger seat. The white Roller had a habit of cutting out from time to time, the clutch needed jamming down to the boards and I made a mental note to mention to 'Clocky' that there had been just enough petrol in the tank to reach the nearest pumps. But all was lovely as I sat there contentedly heading for a weekend of love and laughter . . .

Lovely, until I suddenly realizes the steering is pulling over to the offside. I stop extremely carefully because it is pouring buckets outside. The cause of my trouble is a puncture. The names I called 'Clocky' when I discovers there is no spare are not fit to print. So I have no alternative but to jack up the car, take off the wheel and hitch a lift to the nearest town, where it took three or four taxi rides to find a garage with a tyre to fit the Roller's tractor-sized wheels. It's two hours later when I get back . . . to find my companion being kept company by a couple of highway patrol policemen.

I greets them like long, lost friends and sets to work replacing the wheel. Since by this time I was covered in mud and grease and my suit was ruined I had given up worrying about the downpour. Having replaced the wheel, I was about to wish the officers a fond good night when I caught them bent double inspecting the other tyres.

'Do you know they are all virtually bald, sir?' asked the more talkative of the two custodians of the law.

A vision of 'Clocky' hanging upside down from atop a high rise block suddenly flashed before my eyes. Then other happy little thoughts entered my head. One began with I. For Insurance. I turned on the charm full blast, urging my companion to get the eyelids a-fluttering and willing her to add a bit of Eastern Promise to her looks of helplessness. It worked. The officers did not ask for any documentation.

'Sorry, sir. But I am afraid we cannot allow you to drive the vehicle in this condition. It is illegal.'

The way I felt at that moment, hanging would have been too civilized for 'Clocky'.

All my skills as a persuasive talker went into arranging the little compromise that ended with me driving gingerly to the garage for a set of completely new tyres that set me back the price of an average small car. The kindly officers followed me every inch of the way, to ensure that nothing untoward befell me. And I had to admire their diligence. They were determined I would not be heading for similar trouble. When I had got four spanking new tyres on the old Roller and was already dreaming of a bathful of bubbles they pointed out that, ahem, it was illegal to proceed without carrying a spare!

My relationship with 'Clocky' was never the same after that.

8

My David was a lovely boy. Some people said he looked like me. We were very close, me and my little kid brother. He was just short of twenty-one, with a lovely wife, a baby and a nice little home. He was such a happy-go-lucky lad, poised on the brink of life with a flourishing scaffolding business. The future looked rosy for him.

The day my David lay dying in my arms, a knife wound through his heart, was the most terrible thing that ever happened. I will never get over the guilt I feel. It was me who was responsible for his death.

Time is one thing you cannot buy or change. When something's over and done there's nothing you can ever do about it. I know that. Because if I could ever have brought David back with my own life he'd be here today.

David died after I stuck me oar in when I found he had been badly knocked about in a pub brawl. Somebody had taken liberties with my little brother and I was having none of it. It had all started when David went into some pub down the Angel. David was never any trouble to anybody. So he is just with a couple of mates having a drink when a certain fella went up to him and said: 'Your brother Johnny took a liberty with me the other day.'

So my David turns round all smiling and that and says: 'Well, don't you go bellyaching to me, mate. You know Johnny. If he done you some wrong, then you sort it out with him. What are you pulling me for?'

I know that's how it went because when I made enquiries at a later date I had it from a couple of witnesses with no mileage to make out of it. Anyway this fella tried to belt David. My brother's mate, barmy Billy Hickson, who was about six years older than my David, saw it coming and got one in first. Then it all started. Four other fellas come along and start on my David. They really did the business on him, punchin' and kicking the hell out of him.

I was up at the club when someone came in and told me what had happened. I went to see my Dave. They had done him no good at all. He was a bloody mess. They'd hit him with ashtrays and bottles. The kid was in a terrible state and his little wife was all in pieces on account that Davey looked terrible. I could have cried for the girl. She was beside herself with worry and concern.

Life on the streets and in the clubs had taught me that when trouble comes and gives you a poke on the nose there is absolutely no point in trying to be nice and forgiving. Try to avoid a confrontation and they will either think that you are a prize berk, or that you ain't got the balls to do anything about it. While you are pissing about weighing up the whys and wherefores they will get their lot in first.

Although I'd never weighed much above eleven stone I'd always kept myself in nice condition. Rumours went round that I'd had commando training, Karate and heavy stuff like that. It was a load of codswallop, but I didn't discourage the gossip. I always figured that if a certain reputation was beneficial to your well-being, why discourage it? The only official training I had was down at the boys' club one night when I was a young tearaway. I saw a couple of lads in the ring having a bit of a knockabout and I thought to myself I fancied a bit of that. In my mind's eye I could quite fancy myself as being pretty useful with the fisticuffs. Yeah, I mused, I don't mind dishing it out, flashing round the ring like a champ and keeping 'em at arm's length.

So the trainer gloved me up, put me in the ring with this weedy looking kid and I rushed in, bristling with confidence, to give him a quick pasting and thereby save him from unnecessary punishment. This reedy fella hit me three times. Least, I think it was three. The head, chest and kidneys. That was it. I was out of the ring in a flash. I told them, I didn't fancy getting my head knocked off for nothing.

Later I learned how to look after myself out of the ring. On the streets you can forget your Queensberry Rules and niceties of gentlemanly conduct. Rule Number One: hit first. Showing weakness was for mugs. You might as well lie down and beg 'em to kick your teeth in if you was going to back off in a street clash. It was no place for faint-hearts. You either fought or you ran like hell.

As I stood there looking at the sorry state of my little brother I knew that one day he had got to face up to the bastards who had given him a pasting. And I would make sure that when he did, he would have his brother Ronnie standing by his side.

At first I tried to forget about any revenge or reprisal for what had happened to my David. But it bugged me. I couldn't get out of my mind the memory of his poor, battered little face and hearing his wife sobbing her heart out. It started to get me down so much I couldn't think of anything else. I became obsessed with squaring it up. So I started making a few enquiries. I went round to see a few people. They all swore blind that they didn't know it was my little brother they had done. They swore it so much I began to think that maybe after all it was just one of them things. A few hot-headed remarks. A pub punch-up. Matters getting out of hand. It happens.

Then I realized that one of them called Johnny Isaacs, the one what started it all in the first place, knew damn well that it was my David they were doing. That bastard had known all right and he hadn't said a dicky. I told the others who had set about my David. 'You stuck up for Isaacs and give it to my brother, so don't try conning me.' They apologized. They said all they had seen was Isaacs getting it from Billy Hickson and that they had gone to help out. 'We didn't know that Isaacs had been taking liberties with your David,' they assured me.

They said: 'Ron, would we have touched your little brother? Hand on heart.'

I believed them.

So I went and found this Isaacs, stand-in for a dog turd, and I gave him a good whackin'. Then I went back and had a slanging match with my David. I mouthed him it was all his fault. What had he been doing out on the town round the pubs when he should bleedin' well keep out of trouble and think of his little wife and kid back at home where he should have been anyway. He didn't say nothing back. He was a quiet boy, my David.

Sweet Jesus Christ. If only I could have let it lie at that. But I couldn't. It kept eating at me, nagging away at my guts. I kept thinking to myself. They done my David, knocked him black and blue. And all the time Johnny Isaacs had known that it was my little brother they were kicking the hell out of. It obsessed me. So I talked it over with my Johnny and we decided we better do something.

So we go to see these people, taking David and the mad Hickson. We went to the Latin Quarter Club in Soho.

I will never forget the date. It was May 7, 1970. When we got to the club I told anybody who would listen that I wanted to make sure that nothing like this ever happened again. I wanted that they should say sorry to my David, promise him that it was all a big mistake. Then everything would be squared. Then I could forget it. It would be forgotten.

100

Things didn't turn out like that.

Isaacs is not there.

Billy Staton, who runs the place, is first up. He comes along and holds out his hand like to say 'Hello Ronnie'.

As he came towards me this Hickson headcase went berserk. He began screaming and shouting and went for this Staton.

I got hold of Hickson and banged him against the wall so hard he gasped like a punctured tyre. 'You little prat. What you doing?' I shouted.

It was too late.

They was all up. Fists and feet were flying.

War broke out.

Somebody tried to give me a whack. I stepped aside and got one in first. That was it. The brawl had started and there was no stopping it now.

One of them was an evil-looking git name of Alfredo Zomparelli. 'Italian Tony' they called him, which I thought was fitting for a barman. In the middle of the ruckus I saw 'Parelli dive towards the kitchen. He came out brandishing a tool, a wicked-looking carving knife. The polished fifteen-inch blade glinted in the light.

When all this had started David hadn't been on the scene. He'd gone to the toilets downstairs. He must have heard the commotion going on upstairs and starts running up to us.

This nutter 'Parelli stands at the top of the stairs waving the tool around like crazy.

David tries to dodge past him to get to us. 'Parelli leaped at him as though he was a scalded cat.

David got it twice in the chest. The second went right though his heart.

He went down like a sack. I could see he was hurt bad. I ran to him. I bent down and turned his face towards me. Once 'Parelli realized what grief he had done he was shooting out at top speed.

It was a terrible sight. Something I will never forget. The blood was pouring out of David's chest, spurting in great hot, wet flushes. His eyes were staring straight at me. He couldn't talk to me.

I prayed. Oh, my God. Did I ever?

I kept repeating 'Are you all right David? Are you all right?'

All the time I kept seeing our old mum's worried face. Just like she was there watching everything with sad, watery eyes.

I was down on the floor cradling David's head in my arms when the police came in.

'For God's sake get an ambulance,' I cried.

But by then I knew that my David was mortally injured. He was lying so still. He couldn't say anything.

All the way to Charing Cross Hospital, I prayed.

'Keep him alive, please, please, anything. But keep him alive. You can have all the money in the world . . .'

I was hysterical with grief and guilt.

I kept thinking of David's wife Barbara and little Lisa.

My David couldn't say a word.

The nurse stopped me from going into the operating theatre. I said he was my little brother but she said she didn't care who I was I had to stay outside.

For half an hour I sat and prayed while the doctors worked on David.

Then they told me my David was dead.

I had to get out of the hospital. The cops tried to stop me. But I forced my way past. I suppose they saw my agony, because they didn't try to detain or follow me.

I walked. I ran. I was blind. Insensible. All I could see was the poor, white dying face of my brother David.

I blamed myself. I'd tried to sort people out for hurting David. I'd made them pay and say sorry. Why couldn't I have left it at that? Why had I had to take David round so they could grovel?

Why? Because of Ronnie Knight's pride. I'd dragged David along to show off, to let him see the respect I had.

It had cost him his life. God help me.

All the time I kept asking myself: why hadn't they done me instead? It should have been me that died. It was my fault. I'd been around. Seen a bit of life. But my David was just starting. He'd got his own little business.

The effect David's death had on my family was terrible.

Every time his name came up it was like stabbing a knife into my mum's heart.

When we laid David to rest on a spring morning a part of me was buried with him.

*

After the funeral all I could think of was revenge. Every living moment was focused on getting the one that had done it. I became obsessed by finding 'Parelli and making him pay for all the pain and misery he had inflicted on my family. I hated him. I went out looking for him. But he had always gone on his toes. It seemed that the rat had crawled into some dark, stinking hole where he belonged.

What I discovered later was that the Italian had been smart enough to dump his bloodstained clothes in a locker at London's Leicester Square station. Then he got into a car, crossed the Channel aboard a ferry and fled back to where he came from, probably some rat-infested Italian slum, where I reckoned he must have felt at home. But three weeks later the turd flew into London's Heathrow Airport, looking all contrite, and turned himself into the police. He had had plenty of time to think about getting his story straight.

In November, just a few months after he had killed my David, 'Parelli stood in the dock at the Old Bailey and denied that he was guilty of cold-blooded murder. He pleaded guilty to manslaughter, claiming it was self defence. And the court let him get away with it. It turned my stomach.

Zomparelli's story was that he had been sitting at a table in the Latin Quarter when I walked in with John, David and the lunatic Hickson. He claimed that violence suddenly erupted with chairs, bottles and glasses shattered all over the place. 'Parelli's case was that although he was minding his own business two men had jumped him and started to attack him. He said he rushed to get a knife, a double-edged kitchen blade, just to defend himself. Then, he sobbed to the court, he didn't know anything until my David collapsed. He made it sound like my brother had thrown himself on the weapon. He deserved an Oscar. His performance paid off beautifully.

He got a miserable four years.

Four years for my brother's life!

The cops had rubbed salt into our grievous emotional wounds by charging me, my Johnny and the mad Hickson with fighting and making an affray, which we denied.

Hickson was convicted and got a twelve months' suspended sentence.

With me and Johnny the jury was out nearly all day, but they could not agree on a verdict. Judge Sir Carl Aarvold ordered a retrial.

Next day, November 25, Johnny and me were acquitted after the prosecution offered no further testimony against us. They said that witnesses had either refused to give evidence or had gone abroad.

We walked out of the court thinking that a great injustice had been done and with Judge Aarvold telling us: 'Be careful in future . . .'

*

My raw hatred for Alfredo 'Italian Tony' Zomparelli swelled and festered like a throbbing carbuncle. When he was let out after serving only thirty-odd months that loathing became an uncontrollable monster that destroyed all my logic and reasoning.

I wanted my revenge. 'Parelli was mine. I knew he was out on the streets. I went hunting for him like a lion after a warthog.

Immediately I got the word where he was hanging out I would hightail it over, no matter what. I would drop everything, anything and move. But he had always slunk away by the time I got there.

He must have developed a sixth sense. He could smell me coming a mile off. But I never gave up the search. I hoped and prayed to God that I would find him so I could kill him. I was going to make him pay for what he had done. I was going to rub him out. It would please me. He was scum. I would be doing the world a favour. I would have done for him sure enough. No doubt. No matter what it cost me. God knows how I hated prisons but I would have danced back inside for the rest of my natural. Every day I would have awoken with a song in my heart.

If I could have done Zomparelli myself no price on earth would have been too high to pay. That would have satisfied me. Then I could have looked up to my David and said: 'I done it for you, David.' I would have been proud. I'd have been glad even.

I used to think that love or maybe even jealousy was the most powerful emotion in the world. Now I knew that compared to hatred they were nursery rhyme stuff.

*

After he had been released 'Italian Tony' had started running a bucket-shop travel agency in Frith Street, Soho. This enabled him to pursue his passion for hanging round sleazy porn joints and exercising his pea-brain as a pinball wizard. It was poetic justice that when he bought it he was engrossed in the stupid game.

He got his just desserts one lovely night: on September 4, 1974, a few months after getting out.

He was playing a pinball machine in a Soho amusement arcade called the Golden Goose when justice was done in a Chicago-style slaying. The rat got a .38 in the chest and three in the back. And no one could deny that it was as nice a professional job as you could wish for. I cracked a bottle of champagne to celebrate. My only regret was that someone had beaten me to it.

The Golden Goose was in Old Compton Street, just across the

road from my club. Right on my doorstep as you might say.

Naturally enough the murder made the papers in a big way, with wide speculation about why he had been blown away in an expert contract killing. Underworld whispers were that 'Parelli had been taken out because he was trying to muscle in on the amusement arcade rackets, which was a highly prized and profitable enterprise, jealously guarded by those in control.

Another theory was that 'Parelli was the London Connection in a Mafia-controlled international car racket, involving stolen Ferraris and Maseratis. That made me laugh. He could not reliably have been entrusted with a supermarket trolley.

It was also whispered that he was a courier in a drug and prostitution racket operating between Rome and London.

The Old Bill even flew in a Italian detective inspector, an expert in the weird and wonderful techniques employed by the Mafia. At least that was the story on the grapevine, and richly harvested by the Press.

Of all the possibilities on offer the one the Old Bill seemed to favour above all others was that 'Parelli was the victim of a revenge killing, perpetrated by person or persons located not a million miles from the scene of the crime. All things considered I felt it would be only a matter of time before the lawmen nipped sharply round the corner and came a-knocking on my door. I had never exactly made it a state secret that I wanted 'Parelli dead. I had spent weeks trying to uncover the turd so I could do the honours myself. He was my Number One enemy.

So after they had permed the possibilities and duly deliberated, they concluded that there was a certain amount of circumstantial evidence in the air. There were no prizes for guessing who was their prime suspect. The Old Bill had cottoned on and wanted to sew up the case in double quick time. Who else could it be? They beat a path round to my door and started making suggestions of a leading kind. Like, they knew I had done it, so why didn't I just come clean so as to save the poor old taxpayer the cost of an unnecessary investigation?

After a few further polite preliminaries the Old Bill enquired if I would be good enough to accompany them down to the station. They kept me down the nick for three hours. That was 180 minutes for them to find a thousand different ways of trying to get me to confess.

I admitted that I had wanted 'Parelli croaked. I had never made any bones about that. I recited my innermost feelings on the subject, holding nothing back. Somebody else had got to him first. They had done me a big favour. I was grateful that they had saved me the chance of soiling my hands. I was extremely sorry, but I knew nothing more about it. I could help their enquiries no further.

Indeed, the first I had heard about 'Parelli's demise was when I got home in the early hours and found Barbara crying her heart out with shock. She said Sid James had phoned and broken the news. I told that to the police. I could see they were not totally convinced. Fortunately at the time of 'Parelli's murder I was in the club. Dozens of witnesses had seen me. They swore my alibi because it was the honest truth. So they let me go.

They did not do so with what you could call good heart.

At the inquest in March, 1975, it was said that 40 people had been in the Golden Goose when 'Parelli was blasted away. He was having a game on the appropriately named 'Wild Life' table when a gunshot rang out and 'Parelli slumped to the ground.

The assassin was said to have stood there very calmly and to have fired three more rounds at the Italian. They penetrated his back and chest. Death was virtually instantaneous. Police told the coroner that more than one thousand people had been interviewed . . . so I was not alone. The verdict was that 'Parelli had been murdered by person or persons unknown.

*

Nigh on half a dozen years flashed by before the Old Bill again got round to picking me up for questioning on the subject of the late, lamented 'Parelli's departure from this world. The lads made what the Press revelled in describing as a 'dramatic dawn swoop' on sleepy Aylmer Drive on the morning of Wednesday, January 4, 1980.

Barbara, bless her, failed to see any merit in the way the officers went about their lawful business with happy smiles on their faces, despite the ungodly hour of the crisp morning. I do believe they seemed to be enjoying their work as they went through the well-orchestrated routine and offered me a ride down to the police station.

This time I was knocked out of my stride on account that they charged me with the murder. I noticed a hint of relish in their attitude as they confidently predicted that they had me by the short and curlies. Nicking Ronnie Knight, they beamed, made all the late nights and early mornings absolutely worthwhile.

Indeed, the Old Bill was so cock-a-hoop that my well-founded confidence began to waver.

I knew I was innocent. Equally I was long enough in the tooth to realise that if you really try you can sometimes pin things on people.

106

And the passing of sixty moons was time enough to burn the midnight candles on the subject. You cannot accuse the Old Bill of having no sense of humour. They love a bit of fun. They didn't let it out all at once. Just dribs and drabs about their cast-iron case.

The message they were playfully trying to convey was that Ronnie Knight would be ill-advised to go ordering any new shirts on account that they would probably be out of fashion by the time he got round to wearing them. But for the life of me I could not raise a laugh at their attempts to introduce a modicum of humour into the situation.

What I began to deduce was that some villain had fingered me as the culprit with such conviction that the policemen felt confident enough to build a case around it, after all these years.

I was absolutely right. I soon discovered that a supergrass was squealing that I'd given him a shooter and paid him a grand to gun down 'Parelli.

Gawd love me, I was being set up. Framed. Large as life.

The gentleman volunteering the information was a sinister, snivelling gangland killer called George 'Maxie' Bradshaw.

When his name was first mentioned I truthfully replied that I had never heard of the little pile of dog's business. I didn't know the mug from Adam. That brought a wreath of great big smiles onto their faces.

It was a picture to see them all so happy. Aha, they rejoiced. They had got me again. There was indisputable evidence that not only did I know the man of the moment, he had been a regular visitor to the A and R. And they could prove it beyond any shadow of a doubt. So get out of that on a wet Sunday!

I racked my brains, rummaging through the old memory file but for the life of me I could not figure out who this mysterious Bradshaw could be. I hadn't never clapped eyes on him before.

One thing about being stuck in a cell is that shortage of time is not your biggest enemy. It tends to drag when you are not enjoying yourself. So I had no excuse for not concentrating on the subject in hand: Trying to work out who Bradshaw could be filled my every thought. Eventually I remembered this creep who used to come up to my club with Alfie Gerard, an old mate of mine. He was a right weirdo, this Maxie character. He had dark, long curly hair, a funny, little drooping moustache and a beard.

I recollected that the first time he offended my line of vision he reminded me of that old television cowboy, the ''Cisco Kid'. And that's what I nick-named him. The bleedin' ''Cisco Kid'. He must have been blind as a bat because he wore those thick, jam-jar glasses . . . and contact lenses on underneath. He looked like your typical escapee from the happy farm. Mad as a March hare on the funny powder.

Once I tagged who this Bradshaw was, it all came flooding back like a slow-motion action replay on World of Sport. Bradshaw was the pain in the colon what was always trying to get into our company at the A an R. He'd come over and greet me like he was my long-lost soulmate and plonk himself in the middle of our little group. Every time he got within spitting distance he gave me a prickly sensation down my spine. My dislike was so intense that I'd cold-shoulder him out by turning my back on him and giving him a push now and then, so that he was in absolutely no doubt about my feelings. He didn't like me for that.

I recalled that I had asked around who this little creep was. I found out he was a real rascal. He used to go round holding up banks, shooting people's legs off and things like that. He was the sort of man you couldn't wait to invite to your next cocktail party.

So this paragon of all things bright and wonderful was the law's star witness. This punk is telling the cops how I'd got him to blow away 'Parelli. I wouldn't have hired Bradshaw to swat flies.

The law thought they had got me dead to rights because I'd denied knowing Bradshaw. They were not at all unhappy about my relapse, because they concluded that I had pretended not to be familiar with him because I had something to hide. They would say that they had shown me a picture of this swarthy little geezer I'd named after the Mexican cowboy, who I knew from coming up the club.

What they omitted to mention was that the photo they showed me was of a geezer with no specs, no tache, no beard, no nothing. The coppers said that this snapshot was of Bradshaw, the man I had hired to do the business. This bloke with hair shorter than a college boy's, all fresh faced and without those distinctive jam-jar specs.

'Maxie Bradshaw,' I said. 'He was the '''Cisco Kid''. This bloke looks more like Stan Laurel.'

The coppers' faces told me they didn't see the funny side of my levity.

Back in the cells something was really bugging me.

What I could not figure out was why this Bradshaw creep would go and blast the Italian off the face of the earth just to set me up. Sure, I knew he didn't take to me on account that I had frozen him out up at

108

the club. I had not hidden from him the fact that his face turned my stomach. But it was a somewhat drastic measure to do a murder just to put one over on me. Even for a dickhead like Maxie Bradshaw. No. It just didn't figure.

So I asked one or two people in the know what they had on Bradshaw. What I found out was that dear old Maxie had the oldest motive in the world for giving Eyetie Tony a dose of lead poisoning. It had nothing to do with me. It had everything to do with a woman. As usual. This was how the intriguing story read. While 'Parelli had been doing his spot of bed-and-breakfast for knifing my David, his lady love was obviously not exactly pining for him. She had been shacked up with Bradshaw. She must have been because the Italian used to bash women about. He had a bird at the end of Old Compton Street, near my club. He was always pretending she was a football. When he wasn't doing that he used to go round demanding money off people. Those two little examples showed the nicer side of his character.

But when he had slithered out of the stir, this lovely little lady decides she made a terrible mistake making it with mad Maxie. She shifts her obliging ass back to the Eyetie.

This leaves Bradshaw out in the lurch and with a dose of the consuming jealousy gnawing away at his guts. It all seemed so simple to me as I sat there in my lonely cell working it all out. Maxie had got the needle at being cast aside. Being a creature of great intellect and subtlety he decides the only honourable solution is to go out and blast the Eyetie's head off.

What puzzled me most was this: did Bradshaw have the wit to try and kill two birds with one stone by implicating me? Or did person or persons, who shall be forever nameless, give him a hand with his line of thinking? God forgive me if my suspicions are ill-founded. But you have got to admit the sweet set-up had an unpleasant aroma around it. I have never known the truth behind my speculations. What was beyond any doubt was that I was charged with murder.

Bradshaw oathed that I'd put out a contract on the Italian's life. He let it be known that he was merely obliging me like the good old pro he was. No matter how much I suggested to the coppers that my jealousy theory had some merit they were unmoved. As far as they were concerned I was guilty as a fox caught in a chicken run with feathers up his arse.

So they did me. Then they pulled in Alfie Gerard's son Nicky and charged him, too. Bradshaw said Nicky was the one who pulled the trigger, while he stood guard . . . and I pulled the puppet strings and paid the bills. The police were brimming so full of confidence that they were bubbling over like a vat of chipfat. They wanted my scalp. They wanted me sent down and were determined to do it. That's all they cared about.

There are times in your life when you can only conclude that even God gets bored. Instead of doing good things all the time he fancies a bit of devilment. Like getting people fitted up for things they hadn't done. It was ironic. I had to admit. I'd been out scouring the streets like a bloodhound after my brother's killer. Only to be denied the pleasure of putting him away. Now here I was back inside, looking through the wrong side of prison bars accused of doing what fate had robbed me of achieving.

Despite my innocence I was getting increasingly worried that I was going to be away for a very long time. No matter how sure you might be, no matter how tough your character, those sort of worries get to you in the end.

*

It was like a flashback. Brixton again, where they held me on remand. After sampling the joys of Wandsworth a few years earlier Brixton wasn't that bad. I could have things brought in, the little niceties that make the monk's life slightly more tolerable. Like decent meals, fresh clothes, reading material and other odds and ends.

Funny. Me and Barb hadn't really been hitting it off for years. Now I was in trouble, up to my sweet little neck, Barbara turned up trumps. She was an angel, visiting all the time, cooking for me and making sure the inner man was well catered for – even if sex was off my menu. I thought it was funny that after all our problems, of us never having time to be together, here she was acting the perfect little wife. The meals she had sent in came on the biggest plates ever made, straight up to me on No.4 landing, last cell before the recess.

As I was troughing up one night, grateful for the small mercies in life, I felt sorry for the couple of boys in the next cell. They had no friends, no visitors, no nice bit of grub. So from then on I ended up sharing most of my meals with them. I don't know whether they were grateful or not. It was just doing a kindness and I didn't look for anything back.

Being in my line of business I knew quite a lot of the clientele in Her Majesty's establishment. But it seemed to be crammed out with supergrasses dying to squeal their heads off for the promise of a bit of time off, a cell with a view or possibly just a kind word.

110

As the days stretched into weeks, then into months, what really depressed me was talking to geezers also on remand. Some of the poor sods had been there for eighteen months or more. It struck me as a great injustice being nailed up for months on what was really nothing more than suspicion. I started having nightmares about it. I got worried that it would drag on and on. When I'd done my fifteen months' receiving time I'd gone straight in from a fairly tough background. Now I'd had a good few years of your old Dolce Vita. The best of everything. From the most expensive clothes, flash cars, fancy restaurants and other little goodies befitting my playboy lifestyle. It tended to soften the underbelly somewhat, making the traumatic return to basic life in the nick extremely hard to enjoy. Now I was back in the degrading old routine. I found it harder to take.

Wake up at 6 a.m. Wait for breakfast. Then it is your dinner. They open the cell up again and you walk around. Exercising they called it. You don't have to work in Brixton. If you wanted to do a job it was down to you. You got paid a few bob a week and you could go down to the canteen. I wasn't short of the readies, so I could have what I liked. I didn't smoke, but I used to carry a stack of cigarettes. And I built up a store of tinned stuff, so much that my cell looked like a busy little supermarket. Ronnie Knight went back in business. Well, you had to do something or else your little grey cells started to die for lack of what to think about.

The screws started accusing me of trading for a living. I told them it was all for me and my friends. Plus I liked to help out the prisoners who had got nothing. I always felt sorry for them that didn't get any visitors. Any diversion helped to keep my mind off what I had coming in the way of a stitched-up trial.

When I had first been charged I hadn't been able to get out on bail because they would not let any of my family stand the £200,000 they wanted. Some mumbo-jumbo about if they put it up I would be on me toes and abscond. My Jimmy, the eldest, could have done it straight away for me. But no. They wouldn't stand for that. So it was down to Barb. She rallied round like the good old trouper she was, working day and night trying to persuade people to put up the necessary. God knows how, but somehow she managed to do it.

I'd been out on bail until the committal trial in the middle of 1980. In their blessed wisdom the beaks decided I wasn't safe to be left wandering the streets. They broke the bail and threw me back to the screws.

Now I'd been in Brixton five months. Almost half a year of my life

9

I am looking at the Old Bailey judge and I am thinking: 'You cannot be swallowing this, your lordship. You just cannot believe these fairy stories.'

My carefully considered opinion was that the prosecution was stretching its case way, way beyond the limits of credibility. They were painting me as some shady underworld club-owner who had masterminded the ruthless contract killing. They contended that there was no room for reasonable doubt. That was the scenario. That's how they had got me down. All cut, dried and ready for roasting. And there was this lovely, hired assassin George 'Maxie Bradshaw' piping up that of course I was the villain behind it all.

Six months earlier in that never-to-be-forgotten year of 1980 – January 17th to be precise – Bradshaw had been sentenced to life imprisonment for the murder of one Alfredo Zomparelli. He had pleaded guilty though he had maintained throughout that he had not actually done the foul deed, but merely stood by as Nicky Gerard pulled the trigger. At his own trial Bradshaw, a strapping six-footer aged twenty seven, had been described as 'the biggest supergrass of all time'. Fascinating was the only word to describe the story he came out with at his hearing. Absolutely spellbinding stuff.

Scotland Yard Chief Supt Robert 'Tug' Wilson told Mr Justice Comyn that this Bradshaw git – the one and only ''Cisco Kid' – had shown great courage for squealing on 105 criminals he said had taken part in a variety of murders, bank robberies, wage snatches etc., etc., etc., To all of which Bradshaw himself had been a party. So if you cannot take the word of a murdering thug, who can you believe?

The reason Bradshaw had developed a social conscience, it was said in all sincerity, was that 'because of his lawless record he realized only something very positive could prove that he wished to return to a decent way of life'. In other words after being locked away for the rest of his natural for just about every crime in the book he had now seen the error of this ways and felt it his duty as a reforming citizen to shop all his fellow gangsters.

He stood there in court cool as a chilled cucumber while the ever-grateful Supt. Wilson heaped on the praise about how he had shown 'a great deal of courage' in turning squealer and in consequence now faced 'extreme danger' from those very villains he had fingered. Now fancy that!

So keen was he to show his repentance that day the light dawned that Bradshaw also admitted a few other indiscretions . . . involving arson, armed robbery and a catalogue of grievous bodily harms. The reforming Bradshaw had also asked for 107 other offences to be taken into consideration. This little lot added to his form by including fraud, theft, conspiracy to rob and the frequent use of firearms, his favourite weapon apparently being a sawn-off shotgun: though it seemed any old shooter would suffice in a crisis.

Just a few days before the murder of 'Parelli, Bradshaw had got in a bit of practice by shooting some geezer in a scrapyard. He told the Old Bill that he done it to 'teach him a lesson'.

You had to hand it to the little rascal. Once he started to let the cats out of the bag he held nothing back. Once he decided to blab on his baddie buddies and climb into bed with the Old Bill there had been no stopping him. It all came pouring out in seventy-four statements he made peppering out the names of the hundred-odd gangsters with who he had done a spot of business. And guess who he included on the bumper shopping list he handed over to the law enforcers? You've got it . . . RJK himself.

There he was, this murdering, brutal, full-time robber and gunman, bleating that I had led him astray by putting him up to wasting 'Parelli on a thousand pounds contract.

Now you might think that with a character reference like that Bradshaw's evidence would not exactly endear him to your members of the jury. Especially as at his trial Judge Comyn had told Bradshaw: 'Yours is a terrible and terrifying story. A story of years of wicked crime.' You might think it. But you would be wrong.

My immediate prospects looked a gloomy shade of black. The prosecution had pulled out all the stops. They were determined to get me inside, even if it meant whitewashing a rat like Bradshaw to do it. I wasn't a gambling man, but after the first few days of the trial I would not have taken odds on me walking out of this sweet little set-up a free man. Here before my very eyes was not one, but two splendid specimens of all that's decent in humanity being somewhat economical with the truth about their dealings with me. They were like a macabre double-act, feeding one another lines to swear my life away.

The second character – the prosecution's eleventh-hour star witness – was one Gerald Knight (no relation, thank God). He goes on oath like a decent boy scout to tell the jury how he had heard me plotting the murder of Italian Tony in my club.

I first made the acquaintance of this cream of British manhood a lot of years back. He used to come up drinking champagne every five minutes making out like he was the goods and a citizen of some clout and importance. What he really was was a con merchant of the highest order. And he being a sucker for an honest face, I fell for it, didn't I? Like a boozy sailor for a bit of skirt at ten o'clock on a Saturday night.

He got me involved in a deal in the property business. One day he bent my ear, carted me off to some premises and showed me round, all the while extolling the virtues of being in the booming market. Gerald Knight assured me that property was where the smart money was carefully being placed. 'Course I swallowed the patter like an innocent babe. I couldn't wait to put the money up. That old devil avarice was at it again.

When I finally got round to realizing that all was not strictly above board it was too late. This dirty Knight had upped on his toes and skipped, leaving me with a dud cheque for seven grand and a promise on my lips that the next time I saw him he was in for a special whacking.

Being ripped off by some common trickster was not the sort of information I wanted broadcast on the BBC world service. So I kept it close to my chest, concealing also the added fact that he had also stuffed me over a little line we were doing in watches. That sideline, I recall, had involved marketing a few Cartier and Rolex jobs (that I had been assured were absolutely your genuine article) at knock-down prices. It was a rewarding little enterprise, ticking over nicely and bringing in a good few sovs. Being a busy little begger I'd left the tiresome matter of keeping the books to Gerald Knight. I really should have known better. I had only myself to blame. Knight came back to Mother England after serving some porridge over in Belgium for the same game he had done me on. When he gets to London he learns that there's a cell waiting for him in Brixton. He also discovers, to his apparent dismay, that Ronnie Knight is currently in residence at the said establishment. Highly suspicious of what lay in store for him when I got my hands around his greasy little neck it seems he started frothing at the mouth and begged the Old Bill to do him a kindness and accommodate him in alternative surroundings. In return for which favour he dreamed up a nice little cock and bull story orchestrated and choreographed by willing experts on the very subject to further put my neck in the noose. Now there he was standing in the dock swearing my life away. And throwing his hands up in horror at the very suggestion that he had done any business whatsoever with the accused Ronald Knight.

This is how it all came about that Knight knew I was behind the killing, he confided to the twelve men and women good and true.

He came up to town from Brighton for the day with his old dad and had said: 'Come on dad, we're going to have a drink at the A and R club in London. I want to meet this Ronnie Knight, I fancy a talk with him.' He told how he comes into the club and said: 'Hello Ronnie Knight. How are you? We have the same name of Knight. You are Ronnie and I am Gerald. This is my dad and we are very pleased to meet you.'

While we was exchanging such everyday pleasantries, said this Gerald Knight, another guy walks into the bar. According to Gerald Knight I glares at this newly arrived character and in a definite huff I yells out: 'Where the fuckin' hell have you been? You know I want you to do this murder for me.'

'I'm sorry Ron,' says this man (according to Gerald Knight). 'Shall I sit down?'

Whereupon, Gerald Knight is telling His Worship and the assembled courtroom, I turns to him and politely intones: 'Would you gentlemen kindly excuse us, only we've got a little bit of murdering to discuss.'

There it was, straight up. He was coming out with it like he was in the confessional.

Despite the gravity of my situation I could not help pondering the lack of imagination of the part of the back-stage scriptwriters. How could they have ever let him go in with a story like that? I am not normally one to criticize, but it struck me that the plot was a trifle unimaginative. If they were going to use him to fit me up they should have told him to say something with a touch more credibility. Something like he had overheard a whispered conversation in a dark corner. Or that I'd dropped out hints about the dirty deed after I'd downed a few drinks. But a story like that! Jesus!

During those chilling November days in 1980 as the trial lumbered on, my future was looking decidedly bleak, I knew how the poor sods must have felt standing on the sloping deck of the *Titanic*. It was all unreal. But it was happening. Nothing you could do about it.

'Maxie' had continued the show with a creditable performance about how I had set it all up and lured him into the murder. He said I had produced a spanking, brand new .38 revolver and had put up a grand to have 'Parelli blown into the next world. In the most graphic detail explaining the background to our death-deal Bradshaw had recalled how Nick Gerard had one day asked him if he had ever considered killing someone for money. Quick as a flash he replied that he had often considered the possibility and the answer was 'Yes'.

Later I am supposed to have invited Bradshaw to do 'Parelli.

The lying git went on about how me and Gerard had taken him to a coffee bar to quietly finger the Italian. We were supposed to have hightailed it back to my club where I handed over a package containing the .38. It was spellbinding stuff to listen to. Bradshaw was giving it his all. It was like watching a cobra dancing to a charmer's flute. Bradshaw was at his finest when he described the memorable day of the killing. Warming to his role, he related how he and Gerard had got dressed up in dark raincoats and glasses. Gerard, he informed us, had even gone to the trouble of sticking on a false moustache. Painstakingly, the puffing toad threw in a line about taking the Tube to Soho before entering the Golden Goose.

At first, he said, they could not see 'Parelli in the arcade. So they hung about a bit. Five minutes later they copped the Eyetie playing a pinball machine. I'll never forget Bradshaw's next line: 'I instantly recognized Zomparelli from our previous encounter in person.' He came out with it like he had been rehearsing all night.

Then, he said, Gerard told him to 'go ahead'. He walked into the arcade and stood by with a .22 just as the Minder. Nicky Gerard was supposed to have walked up to 'Parelli, raised the gun and 'shot him at arm's length plus a couple of inches'. Then the two assassins walked into the street and melted into the crowd. So help me God.

End of story. And the end of Ronnie Knight, if the prosecution had their way. Mr Kenneth Richardson, QC laid it on heavy. He said it was a 'cold blooded professional murder'.

He told how police had been unable to charge me until recent times because I had a cast-iron alibi. Their big breakthrough had come when the guilt-ridden Bradshaw started to spill his guts. I do believe I heard a few gasps from the jury when it was mentioned in passing that Bradshaw had confessed to more than a hundred different crimes.

My Mr Ivor Richard did not let the moment pass. When he cross-examined the self-confessed supergrass he got Bradshaw to confess that between 1974 and 1977 he pursued a career as an armed robber, applying himself to the task with all the fervour of a beaver at nesting time. During that distinguished period he admitted to shooting and wounding 'between eighteen and twenty men'. Furthermore he had figured in some thirty or thirty-five robberies (the precise number eluded him) and his share of the £200,000 stolen had been around £75,000.

Such was the character reference of the witness for the prosecution. They was asking the jury to accept the word of a killer, arsonist, bank robber, hit man, thief, liar and cheat. A man of substance.

Still, in life you can never be sure. The truth does not always prevail. My future was on a knife edge, with Bradshaw one side and Gerald Knight the other.

For some irritating reason Knight's treachery angered me more than what Bradshaw was doing. He had done me for seven thousand quid, conned me stupid and was now trying to put me out of circulation for a long, long time.

During one of the breaks in the proceedings Barbara comes over and whispers: 'Ronnie, I think I've still got the cheque that Gerald Knight gave us . . . I never throw things like that away.'

I say yeah, Barb, do me a favour. Don't lets start hanging our hopes on dreams. I mean nobody saves cheques for seven years. It's impossible.

We had put it in the bank four of five times. And it had come bouncing back to us like it was practising for Wimbledon. In fact I could almost swear to remembering screwing up the cheque in disgust and tossing it into the waste where it belonged. When I shuffled back to my lonely cell that night I was feeling lower than Harrods basement. I don't mind admitting that I was at the end of my tether.

Next day Barb comes bouncing in with a great big grin on her face. She cannot have won the pools, I thought. What's up? She's only gone and found the bloody cheque! The one the con artist Knight had signed seven long years ago. It had taken Barb all night sifting through boxes of old documents before she turned it up. It was like a shot in the arm. I do believe it meant I was in with a real chance of proving what a lying person Knight really was.

When my brief quietly and unobtrusively produced the cheque in the hushed courtroom you could cut the tension with a cricket bat. It wiped the smile off Knight's lying face when the cheque was stuck under his nose. Watching him squirm with the shock of it all filled my heart with so much joy I almost fainted.

First he tried to deny it. Yes, he had to admit it looked like his signature, he said. But he remembered that he had lost a cheque in some man's garage, somebody he did not even know and whose name he could not immediately recall, but who he seemed to remember had died soon afterwards. He also believed that this past-tense gent used to do signatures, so it must have been him what done it.

I couldn't help myself blurtin' out in the court, 'so turn it over then!'

When he did his face dropped a mile and just missed his boots. There on the back was his name and address, the address the alleged deceased could not possibly have known. And Knight had signed it again.

He went white. Then grey and then a nice pastel shade of green.

'I don't wanna talk no more,' he stammered. He was gone. He could not get out of that one.

His whole credibility was destroyed by that cheque. It showed him up for the cheat and liar he was . . . proving beyond doubt that not only had he done business with me, but that he had also crooked me and had good reason to want me safely tucked away.

The judge was not amused. He gave Gerald Knight a stern glare. 'Get him out,' he barked.

After what had just happened I was hoping that Mr Justice Wien would do the decent thing and stop the trial. Be fair, I thought. Their little game is well and truly up. But His Lordship was having no early end to the drama. He was determined to see it through to the bitter end. He must have been enjoying the show.

Maybe I was biased, but from where I was sitting it was beginning to look more like a farce. In fact it crossed my mind in a moment of unexpected flippancy that a 'Carry on Courting' would make a rib-tickling comedy. It was the wrong place and the wrong time for such levity, I know. But if you can't have a laugh now and then life ain't worth living. It was the same during the war. Doodlebug and V-bombs raining down like confetti and people still had time for a smile and kind word.

I could not understand why the wise old judge would not call it a day.

119

As the proceedings dragged on I reflected on the current circumstances and immediate prospects of R. J. Knight Esq.

I'd come into court thinking I hadn't really got a chance. Honest. Only my natural optimism kept me going. I had sat through hours and hours of prosecution evidence thinking Jesus Christ, how much more can they verbal me up. I'd listened to Bradshaw and Knight tip-toeing through the truth with hobnailed boots on. I'd thought to myself how can anyone believe this little comic soap opera. Then when it seemed the whole prosecution case had been torn apart and exposed when Barb found the cheque, the judge had still decided to keep going. After that anything could happen.

It was terrible knowing that the end of the trial is coming closer and closer. You keep thinking to yourself, God love me, have I got to spend the rest of my life in prison? Life. Ten or twelve years behind bars. That was what it would mean, no doubt about it. Had I got to spend all that time in there for something I never done? It drags on and on and on and in the end you don't know where the hell you are. It gets to be like watching a movie. Unreal, like it's happening to someone else.

Then suddenly it all snaps back into sharp focus.

The judge is up there looking like Jesus C, doing his summing-up routine. The prosecution winding-up claptrap is still ringing in my ears. They spoke with such passion and conviction that if I hadn't known I was innocent I would have been tossing a coin.

Then the jury gets up and goes out . . .

Your heart pounds so loud you start looking round for what's making the noise.

You could germinate a cactus seed in your mouth.

The jury is back in five minutes.

I think 'Cor blimey, that was quicker than expected'.

But it's only a technicality. They want to see statements that I had made. I cannot be sure because at the time my nerves was stretched tight as a fiddle bow, but I think the judge said no, they could not. His ruling struck me as a bit mean on account the rest of my life could be hinged on a few phrases contained in those statements.

So back behind the scenes trot the dozen people who are going to decide my future.

Beyond any shadow of a doubt time was suspended. Every minute took an hour to tick by.

I sat downstairs. In the prisoners' reception room.

Sweating.

One of the screws he come up to me and says: 'Cheer up Ronnie, old son. You are out of it.'

I don't know whether to believe him or to put his merry quip down to his mischievous sense of sadism.

Then the word drops. The jury is coming back. They've been out two hours.

How to God I climbed those Himalayan stairs and got back in the dock I'll never know. My legs had turned to jelly. The old ticker was on full revs and the brain was swimming in chocolate sauce. At moments like that you clutch at straws. As I squinted at the jurors I thought I detected a certain knowing look in the eyes of one of the women. That look seemed to say that it was going to be all right. Did she even give me a nervous little smile? Or had I imagined it? Hope springs eternal.

Then the foreman stood up. Everything switched into slow motion. It was all happening in clockwork. I was transfixed, because deep down in the base of my skull I kept thinking that I was going to go down for life . . . Life.

'Not guilty!'

That's what he said.

'Not guilty!'

I had almost missed it.

I heard Nicky Gerard going on with: 'Thank you, gentlemen. Merry Christmas. You have most certainly made mine.'

I looked over at Barbara. Tears were streaming down her face. Some paper had carried a big story about how she had said she wouldn't want to live without me if I was sent down.

I heard her cry: 'My God. Oh, my God. My Ronnie . . .'

I felt a bit of a spare dick at first because I couldn't think of anything to say. If I'd given it a bit of thought I could have come out with something really prophetic. Like that US astronaut who went walkabout on the moon and gave us the classic line: 'A small step for me . . . a giant step for Mankind.'

The best I could do was to face the jury with a silly look of gratitude on me mush and whisper the immortal line: 'Thank you. Thank you all. Justice has been done.'

The God's honest is that I had expected to go down. I couldn't get over being acquitted. Now I was free.

It was the best feeling in the world. I didn't know whether to laugh or burst out crying.

Outside in the streets . . . cor blimey. There was hundreds of people cheering and shouting. I looked at everybody and waved to them. My little ticker sang like a skylark.

I looked at my Barbara and I thought to myself what a trouper she had been. Not only had she worked miracles to raise that quarter-million pound bail. Not only had she visited me practically every day during that nightmare six months on remand. More than that, she had stood by me through the drama of the court hearing. And if she hadn't turned-up that seven-year-old cheque I would probably have got life for something I never done.

Barbara had been a perfect angel. How could I break it to her that I didn't love her any more?

10

My murder trial was beginning to seem trivial by comparison to the tricky situation in which I found myself.

Barbara and me had come out of the heavy courtroom drama like a fairy tale Prince and Princess. For once I was getting what the showbiz fraternity called 'a good Press'. Barbara standing by her man in his hour of need had touched the hearts of the great British public. It seemed all very romantic and lovey-dovey; true love triumphing over all.

Only I hadn't told Barbara that there was a new woman in my life, a certain lady whose acquaintance I had made a considerable time earlier, long before I was lifted over the shooting business. She was a woman I realized I could not live without. All those wretched months I'd been in jail, with Barbara visiting almost every day, I'd been smuggling out secret messages to my new love and getting equally hush-hush letters in reply. While Barb was fighting my cause like a champion I had been terrified she would find out what was going on behind her back. The worry of being rumbled had been as scary as my concern about what the jury would decide.

Many a time in my nightmares I heard the jury convict me . . . of two-timing Barbara. And when I looked up in disgrace to the judge the face scowling beneath the judicial wig was Barbara's. It brought me out in hot and colds, I can tell you.

None of us are perfect. To err is human, they say. So, if I have a weakness in life it is this: I cannot bring myself to hurt women. I just cannot just look them in the eye, say, 'Well, it's been nice knowing you. Ta-ra'. Some flint-hearted Lotharios might be able to behave so callously, without care or concern for the hurt it might inflict. But not Ronnie Knight.

It had been the self-same situation when I first met Barbara. Although I was mad about the girl and desperately wanted to move in with her I found it virtually impossible to break the sad news to her indoors. A thousand times I had rehearsed a little speech, to break it as nicely as I could to June that the flames of my love for her had flickered and died. But every time I took a deep breath and looked her straight in the eye to tell her the truth, I got cold feet. Instead of saying 'I am sorry June, but I can deceive you no longer,' I would side-step the issue by enquiring about the health of her dear mother. Call me a down and out coward. But that's the way it was. June had remained oblivious to my philanderings until the very last. Although I had been virtually living with Barbara I'd stayed with my missus right up until the time I got lifted for the receiving affair. It wasn't until I was safely behind bars and I refused to see June any more that she finally got the message which saved me the difficult task of actually having to face up to her.

My tangled love life had gone full circle. Now the dilemma was that I was living with Barbara and was in love with a beautiful girl called Sue Haylock. I could not help but reflect how funny life turned out sometimes. Here I was, a suave forty-odd, head over heels for Sue, a willowy and gorgeous girl in her late-twenties, which struck me as about the right sort of age gap.

Lots of rumours have done the rounds about Ronnie 'Don Ron' Knight's alleged sexual exploits. What some malicious people used to put around was that Ronnie Knight could not keep his pecker in his pants. If I'd got up to half the fun and games attributed to me I'd have been in a wheelchair by now with a hearing aid and a glazed look in my old eyes. But those tales of my amorous adventures were based on nothing more than salacious gossip and spicy chit-chat. I long ago realized that some people have nothing better to do with their uneventful days than to dream up mischief. I have already come clean about my modest share of extra-maritals. Unfaithful I was from time to time. A stud in the super-league class I most certainly was not.

During our long separations I'd heard lots of stories about my Barbara. About how she was supposedly having passionate affairs with most of her leading men, including that beefy Hollywood superstar Victor Mature.

I loved Sid James. Adored the bloke. He was one of life's special characters. The craggy-faced actor was probably the superstar of the 'Carry On' crew, and I always enjoyed being with him . . . despite the story that went round for years that Sid was nuts about Barbara.

It was rumoured in the press that Sid kept telling her that he could not live without her, and that he had begged her to give me the old heave-ho and join him in domestic bliss. I learned later that this was an arrangement completely unknown to Sid's lovely missus Valerie. It was also news to me, on account that it was an event Barbara never felt warranted bringing up at our little breakfast table conferences. It was inevitable that I'd get to hear about Sid getting too amorous in their love scenes and that he was trying to sweet talk her into bed. But I never listened to the yakkity-yak tales about them having a raging affair. I knew that they spent months of their lives together when they were filming or were away touring with a play. I recollect that there was one particularly ugly scene when Sid was supposed to have gone purple with rage with big Bernie Bresslaw – just 'cos Bernie, who was gentle as a lamb, made a completely innocent and matey pass at Barbara.

It is true that most times I went backstage to pick Barbara up I'd find her not in her own dressing-room, but in with Sid next door. Wherever they went she was always in Sid's company. But I don't reckon there was anything going on between the two of them. I would bet on it.

I was never jealous of him or the way he made up to Barb. And if she ever mentioned it to me it must have been when I was lost in some deep creative thought or another, because I certainly do not recall her ever broaching the subject of Sid in terms sexual. She would tell me she and Sid were doing a play together, had difficulty with a particular scene, or even maybe had a tiff. But nothing more risqué than that. You are not likely to forget if your old woman starts dropping out that one of your mates is making her the big offer and wants her to do a bunk with him.

Either way, it made no difference to me, did it. You know what the stars are! They are always kissing and cuddling one another. It's what they call the artistic temperament. Whenever you are with the theatricals it's kiss-kiss, lovely-darling, kiss-kiss. Cuddle-cuddle. Strewth. They are at it all the time. It's the same even when they are working together day after day. The still go on hugging and crying like they haven't seen one another in a blue moon. They embrace one another after the interval! It's just their little ways. It doesn't mean there's anything going on there.

That's how it was with Barb and Sid. Our relationship was OK.

One day Barbara comes up to me and asked it I'd got any spare cash. She said she needed some readies for old crinkle face. Sidney, it transpired, was in somewhat urgent need of £100. It was a modest sum. Naturally I was happy to oblige and counted out the money on the spot. But being blessed with a naturally curious nature I could not help enquiring why Sid needed cash. After all he was not short of a quid or two and his credit was good.

What it was, you see, was that Sid was a gambling man. His old woman, being well aware of Sidney's life-long reputation as a gentleman of the turf, had arrived at a way of preventing him from falling into too much temptation. Valerie had done a deal with the production company, ensuring that all fees were made to her. That way she controlled the purse strings so that Sid had no chance of blowing away all his hard-earned money on a gee-gee of his fancy. Sid told me his wife used to like to give him so much a week to indulge his passion for trying to pick a few winners. Having spent any amount of my golden youth in the close company of well-heeled bookmakers I knew that Sid was a long-term loser, like most of your amateur punters. Nevertheless Sid loved his little flutter. He used to borrow off of me near enough weekly to finance his little hobby. Just as regularly he paid me back when he got his allowance. I won't have a wrong word said about Sid James. When he died it really upset me.

Yeah, things had happened to both Barb and me in the past. We had both had our little ups and downs. The path of true love had not run smoothly. But despite it all we had stuck together all those years.

With Sue it was different. From modest beginnings our affair had blossomed into the real thing.

I'll never forget the first day I first clapped eyes on my Sue. It was up at the club, one magical lunchtime. She was in a party I knew, which included a publican, his wife and Sue's companion, a big-wheel car dealer called Tony. The first thing I noticed about Sue was that she had this infectious sense of humour. She had everybody laughing, tears streaming down their faces.

They were all dressers, which being a member of the fraternity, impressed me no end. She stood out like a prize pheasant in a crow's nest. She was wearing a little bonnet, with a veil over the front. A very striking lady, I thought quietly to myself as I gave her the once-over. Lovely face. Nothing wrong with the rest of her, either, from where I was sitting.

This publican nodded affably in my direction and sent over a drink. A little later I returned the compliment and before you know it we're all together having a nice chat. Somebody introduced me to Sue.

'This is Ronnie Knight, he owns the club. He's Barbara Windsor's old man' Being tagged as 'Mr Windsor' had happened so many hundreds of times that it didn't bother me no more. I just grinned and shook their hands, offering a friendly 'Hello and nice to see you all'.

I had to admit it to myself I was interested in getting to know more about this lovely little lady upon whom I was feasting my eyes.

At that first meeting me and Sue went through the tried and tested social niceties like pleased to meet you, you look nice and what can I get you to drink? After a little time the party all bade their fond farewells. They upped and walked out. Including Sue.

For several days later in my vivid imagination I kept seeing that impish little face, hearing the bubbling laughter and thinking that this Sue was one helluva lovely girl. Every time I walked into the club I found myself hoping and praying that I would be treated to that dazzling smile of hers. Then one day there she was. Sitting at the other end of the bar, opposite of my end where I always was. So I gave her a smile a mile wide, added a wicked wink and sent her over a drink, a Campari as I recall.

I thought to myself: 'I have definitely got to get to know this girl a damn sight better, 'cos she's making them people laugh all the time.' Since I was short of a few giggles at that particular period in my life, I fancied sauntering over to join the merriment. I needed the tonic. But since I hadn't been invited I could not bring myself to barge in. I never have been a pushy sort. I kept looking at Sue. I sensed that she was giving me the jolly old once-over as well. But every time I tried to catch her eye she'd quickly turn the other way and start blushing like crazy. I liked that. In a day and age like we was living in I liked a girl who could still manage a blush.

My interest was definitely alerted. Ah, ah, I thought. She's getting me at it. Here we go. I waited a while. Then throwing discretion to the faint-hearts I bowled over and chatted: 'Hello, darlin'. I've seen you somewhere before ain't I?'

I could have bitten my tongue off. But being the sort of lady I had figured she was, she did not compliment me on the original line. She just gave me one of them special smiles. I thought 'She's really lovely . . . what a character! One of the guys.'

My interest being thus aroused I decided to make a few enquiries. One of her company filled me in a bit about her background, with the warning: 'Sue's a real laugh . . . so don't be surprised if she leaps on the bar and does a dance.'

Meanwhile, from across the crowded room Sue was definitely giving me the eye. And that look told me she was not playing hard to get. I moved in. We started to chat. That was it. I asked her about her fella Tony, the Rolls Royce salesman. She had left him, she explained. They had been very close. But this Tony apparently had a drink problem of somewhat serious proportions. A lovely fella, but a lush. The booze had got the better of him. Sue had walked out. She was very sad about it. Tony had treated her well and she had tried to look after him. But you know what it's like with the alcoholics. There's no helping them when they get to a certain stage.

I asked if she was sure that what she was doing was the right thing. She nodded. I could tell that she had not made the decision lightly. Later, when I met this Tony bloke properly, we got on really well. He was so fond of Sue that he told me she had to leave him or he would drag her down. He even said to me: 'Take care of Sue. Look after her. Please.' Now wasn't that a nice thing for a fella to say?

As Sue had explained things to me at our first real chat she looked so sad and forlorn that my heart went out to her. Deep down I realized that even then I was falling in love in a big way. If the London Philharmonic had suddenly popped up in the background I would not have been in the least surprised.

Later on know-it-alls put around the news that I set Sue up in a little love-nest so we could have a comfortable little affair just round the corner from where I lived with Barb. Another not-true. Sue had her own money and after leaving Tony bought her own very smart apartment in Mulberry Court, Mulberry House.

I soon learned that she was a very independent lady. She was also very shrewd and businesslike and could look after herself. So that was it. It was the old hearts and flowers routine again. However, as usual it was not your usual straightforward little arrangement. Our affair had a few complications. The fact that I was married to Barbara being one of the more major drawbacks.

After a few weeks of conducting ourselves discreetly, I realized that I was head over heels about Sue. I have no wish to sound corny or slushy. But to my astonishment I was forced to the conclusion that for the first time I was really in love. I mean really. During all those years of loneliness when Barbara was away all the time and I was having my little bits on the side I dreamed that one day someone special would come into my life. Now it had happened with Sue. I wanted her. She wanted me. It was the business. No doubt about it. The thought of ever losing Sue, of being without her, filled my veins with ice-water.

Barbara and me in 1962: 'I fancied her so much my front teeth ached.' (*Syndication International*)

Left: Barbara and me at Blazers Club in 1979: 'I was a Face around town, a respected club-owner'. (*S&G Press Agency*)

Below: Leaving the Old Bailey after being cleared of the murder of Alfredo Zomparelli, 1980: 'The God's honest is that I had expected to go down . . . Now I was free. It was the best feeling in the world.' (*Hulton-Deutsch Collection*)

'Outside in the streets . . . cor blimey! There were hundreds of people cheering and shouting . . . my little ticker sang like a skylark.' (*Syndication International*)

Opposite: Barbara comes back after one of her many tours, 1981: 'She was getting offers from all over . . . anybody who believes the fairy story about absence making the heart grow fonder needs a by-pass operation.'

At the villa in Spain, relaxing with friends, 1989: '. . . this place was probably the nearest I was going to get to my idea of heaven.'

Top: (*left to right*) John the Bread (a local bar owner), Eric Mason, me, Manchester George.

Above: (*left to right*) Ronnie Popley (landlord of the Greengate Pub, Bethnal Green Road) and friends.

Top: (*left to right*) Ian and Gillian Atkinson, me and Anne Fletcher.
Above: (*left to right*) Sue, me, Gillian Atkinson and Eric Mason.

Me and Sue: 'I love that girl sure enough . . . we share the same dreams.' (*Syndication International*)

On the other hand there was Barbara. How the hell could I hurt her? It wasn't in me to break her heart. Barbara still had strong feelings for me. I was sure of that. She cared about me in the best way she knew how. But the passion of Barb's life was – and always had been – her career. That consumed and dominated her. It was top of her priorities. That's the sort of dedication it takes to make a star.

Sue put me first. I liked it better that way round.

I would probably have been worried had I not known that Sue was a settled lady with her own means. She had respect. She was her own woman. If she had been broke I'd probably have suspected that she was looking for a sugar daddy. That would seriously have dented my pride. As it was I had been the one to capture her. I had done most of the chasing, not the other way round. So I was confident that Sue was not after me money.

From day one Sue sorted out my intentions as regards to her – and my relationship with Barbara. The first time I asked her out she did not beat around the bush. She looked me straight in the eyes and asked: 'What are you doing messing about with me? You're a married man.'

Under the circumstances I had to admit that it was not a unreasonable enquiry. So I told her all me troubles. It all came pouring out, how I hardly ever saw Barb, how I was really very lonely and desperately needed someone to love . . . and be really loved back. But I levelled with Sue about not being able to hurt Barbara. Sue had been through her own heartache and hard times with Tony. Yes, she said. She understood how I felt and how things were. She took me on those terms. There was no deception, nothing sneaky or underhand.

From that day to this, despite all life's little trials and tribulations, my relationship with Sue has been as perfect as a summer's day. It had to be well anchored in love and trust to survive the inevitable gale-force hurricane that was blowing up on the horizon.

Sue soon became my life. She began to see just how much Barbara was away and to realize that I had not just been laying it on. I think that she began to understand how things were and why I had been so fed up with the loneliness. She could see why I could not take it any more. Sue looked after me. She took me out. I could talk things over with her. Everything from business to personal problems that bothered me. She became more than just a lover. She became a good mate. And she has always taken the view that had Barbara been around more I would probably have been as good and faithful as a lap-dog.

With Sue by my side I felt confident and secure. I kept thinking of those twenty years when at anniversary and birthday parties and New Year I'd be the only single person in the room of happy couples. For the first time I began to understand what a good married life could be like. That might seem a little strange, as me and Sue were having an illicit affair. But once we had got things together I was content and didn't so much as pass a second glance at another woman.

I had made my choice that Sue was for me. The way we had to conduct our lives was not what you might call ideal. There were times when I honestly did not know if I was coming or going – or had already been there. When you are deceiving you cannot help but spin a tangled web that inevitably trips you up now and again. But for all the complications involved I was very happy.

Sue was a great cook and adored fixing cosy dinners at her flat. She was a stay-at-home lady, enjoying nice nights by the fireside. To be fair to Barbara, she had been pretty nifty in the kitchen, too, but she was hardly ever there. That's why we had to have housekeepers and other staff, which with my working-class background did not suit me at all.

Another thing I liked about being with Sue was that she was very close to her family. Many a weekend, when Barb was off touring, me and Sue would jump in the motor and potter up to see her mum and dad in Cambridgeshire. Her parents are lovely people. I was soon very close to them and enjoyed our visits. Out in the country we'd stop off and buy fresh farm veggies and Sue and her mum would prepare lovely meals.

Going back to Barbara, when she occasionally returned to our home, it became more strained and difficult. We were beginning to act and feel like strangers, like ships passing in the night. Every now and again there would be a nudge-nudge, wink-wink story in a newspaper, or some joker would drop out that Barbara was supposed to be having an affair with some actor or another. But if I mentioned it casually in passing Barb's answer always was: 'Never believe what you read in the newspapers, Ronnie. If they don't know the facts they make it up.'

At that particular period in our fast-fading marriage I accepted that we had got to be realistic about our situation. With Barbara away all the time I leaned towards the probability that she did not spend all her spare time crocheting. She was a healthy, red-blooded girl was Barb. I suspected that she was having a little bit on the side here and there. Well, what do you think? I did not begrudge her a thing. She never denied it. She never actually come out with it. I never confronted her. The question of fidelity became a taboo subject. A case of what the eye didn't see the heart didn't grieve about.

Once, years earlier, Barb had asked me if I was jealous of all the famous and handsome actors she worked with. At the time I suspected she was testing me out, maybe just to see how I would react. I had learned that women do that sort of thing sometimes. Like when they ask you how they look. You say lovely and they snap back that 'you're only saying that'. They can make your head ache sometimes. I'd told her that the only thing that made me jealous was her work. It was her job that was always dragging her away from me.

But that had been long ago. In those days I still believed and hoped that she would settle down one day and that we'd be together for always. Now I was torn in two. Like an alcoholic at a wine-tasting. I could not get Sue out of my head. I lived for the times we were together. I dreaded the thought that anything could go wrong to spoil our happiness.

The point had arrived where being with Barbara had become almost painful. But she had been my wife for almost twenty years. We had been through hell and high water together. There had been some warm, loving times. Call me a coward. I just could not write it all off. I did not have it in me to say: 'Well, Barb, that's it. It's been nice knowing you, only I have someone else and I'm moving on.'

I realized that I did not even have to go that far. It was not necessary to rub salt in by saying I'd fallen in love with someone else. It would have been easy to make up some plausible excuse. I could simply have said I was fed up with her being away all the time, which was true. I could have thrown myself about. Yelled that I couldn't stand it no longer. Jumped up and down. Stormed out saying that was the end of that little lot. But do you think I could do it? No more than walk naked down the Mall in the rush hour whistling 'God save the Queen'. I didn't have it in me. I suppose I *was* a coward.

What I kept hoping and praying was that one day Barb would come home, give me a pitying little look and say: 'I'm ever so sorry, Ron. But it's all over. I've found somebody new.'

That would have been the easy way out. I waited for her to say it. She never did. So I kept stalling. Sue was not too impressed by my lack of decision. On the one hand I was telling Sue that she was the only girl in the world and that I would die rather that be without her. I was whining that my marriage was a sham. All washed up, with both me and Barbara miserable as sin staying together. On the other hand I was doing sweet Fanny Adams about the situation.

The inevitable day dawned when Sue sat me down, twitched her nose and sniffed: 'You just haven't got the spunk to tell Barbara, have you?'

Sue was absolutely right. One hundred and ten per cent spot on. No, I haven't, I had to admit. I saw no point in beating about the bush. I had to be honest. What a bloody state to be in.

Sometimes I worried that I would be hurting Barb if I gave her the elbow after all them years. In more rational moments it often occurred to me that she would welcome the glad tidings that I was leaving the next day. Perhaps it would come as a welcome release. Was she hoping, just like I was, it would be me who would pluck up the necessary courage to come out with it? Maybe that was the case. Perhaps she wanted me off her back. Then I'd think, Jesus, what she went through at my trial. She got all those people to stand my bail and visited me through thick and thin and all that. No, I decided, I most definitely could not take even the most minimal of risks of causing Barb any grief or pain.

The man Barb's with now, the chef she runs the restaurant with, well I'm pretty sure she met him while we was still together. She never so much as mentioned it, which I would have welcomed. It would have saved us all a lot of trouble if she had told me the truth. Whether or not Barbara was playing away from home at the time I will never really know, but she still stuck a private eye on my tail, proving the point I have made many times: where women are concerned you never can tell.

When I first begun to suspect that I was being followed about my daily business I put it down to my guilty little conscience playing me up. All things considered it had every right to do. I had this funny, sixth-sense feeling that my every movement was being shadowed. In an attempt to unmask my pursuer I took to suddenly swirling round in the street, glancing in shop windows and hiding in doorways. My tactics did not trap the mystery man, but I did get some funny looks from passers-by, who obviously wrote me off as a fruitcake.

When I first mentioned my suspicions to Sue, she laughed fit to burst. 'Don't be silly,' she chortled. 'Why on earth should anyone want to follow you? You're imagining it all,' my Sue told me.

Like hell I was.

After a few days of the now-you-see-me games I finally copped him out. He followed me from the club. When I got into my motor he jumped into a Jag behind and stuck to me like we was welded together. I took a twisting route through all the back streets. He hung on. I stopped. He stopped. My animal instinct told me that he wasn't one of your Old Bill.

I'd have staked my life on that. At first that happy thought came as a mighty relief, since I did not relish being the subject of a police investigation – even though I hadn't done anything to warrant being kept under scrutiny. In situations like that you worry about becoming paranoid. But I told myself there had to be rhyme and reason for it all. I looked in the mirror and said: 'If that gumshoe hasn't got Ronald Knight under surveillance then my name is definitely Fred Astaire.' So I drove around a bit more till I was certain I had lost him. Then I turned the big Honda's nose round and headed towards Edgware and Sue's welcoming two-bedroomed sanctuary.

I was delighted to find Sue's mum Marj was there with sister Sally's lovely little baby. It was a warm and friendly family scene. I felt part of it, all nice and happy. But the bliss was about to be disrupted by the unexpected appearance of Mrs Ronnie Knight, a.k.a. bubbly actress Barbara Windsor.

It transpired that I had seriously underestimated the tenacity of the private eye. The smartypants had obviously managed to keep tabs on me all the way, sneakily letting me think I had thrown him. Then he had put in a malicious little phone call to Barbara. She hightailed it over to the scene of the crime faster than Jack Flash.

Sue was leaving to take her mum and little niece to Kings Cross to catch the train back to Cambridge. We opened the front door and who should be standing there but Barb. I remember she was wearing a pair of trousers, with a scarf round her face, like she was trying to disguise herself. So I knew something was up. She stood there with a strange, intense look on her face. She didn't say anything at first. It seemed down to me to make the first move.

'Hello,' I said. 'It's all right. We are just going up to the train.'

Considering the heart-pounding emotional stress I was under it was the best I could manage in the way of a nonchalant and non-committal greeting. I tried to make the pleasantry sound nice and casual, like I'd been expecting her at any minute and was pleased to see her. From Barb's reaction I gathered that all was not tickety-boo. She began to scream obscenities at me that made earlier memorable outbursts seem like friendly banter. I soon deduced that she had learned a good few more cuss words since her last performance. Had she ever!

As you know I've always been embarrassed by people looking at me. So with dozens of neighbours, casual pedestrians, motorists and shopkeepers enjoying the show it made my acute shame considerably worse. I wanted to curl up and die. What did Barb want to go and do something like this for? I kept asking myself. She knew it would upset me.

Sue had just pushed her mum into her little black Mini when Barbara turned on her. Barbara might be only a tiny tot, but she was lashing out and scratching like a wounded banshee. The names she called my Sue! Well, I wouldn't repeat them in front of ladies. Her language would have given the Board of Censors a blue fit. She re-wrote the Old English Book of Obscenities.

She slagged Sue. Then she had a go at me. 'I'll bloody kill you,' she screamed.

The audience of enthralled bystanders was growing by the minute. I didn't know where to put myself.

Barbara tried to grab Sue's hair, seemingly intent on doing her best to swing on the strands. Fortunately Sue neatly side-stepped Barb's lunge. I saw Barbara looking at Sue's little niece and I could see she was thinking that maybe it was Sue's baby. No prizes what she might have added to that line of reasoning. Like who was daddy, then?

Fair do's to Sue. She tried hard not to get involved in a slanging match, while Barb was going at her like a she-cat. I felt really sorry for Sue's mum Marj, 'cos she was a refined lady, not used to witnessing the air turn blue. Barbara's outburst was a verbal assault on Marj's sensitivities. What a commotion.

The whole tatty business had gone far enough. 'Turn it in!' I ordered in my sternest. Barb carried on yelling and screaming. So I told Sue to get in the motor with her mum and the kid. They drove off with Barbara screaming something not nice about barmaid tarts. She had apparently remembered seeing Sue sometime earlier up at the club. Since Sue had been on the scene for some time, Barbara suspected that the affair had been common knowledge. Women are very sensitive about these things.

The cab driver that had brought Barbara over had been gawping at the entertainment. As I paid him off Barb simmered down to just over boiling point. She jumped into my car, turned to me and said: 'That's it. Finished.'

A great feeling of peace flooded over me. Like when you've just made love. I had been all excited and tense, me nerves tight as a fiddler's bow. Now I felt lovely and calm. All those years of pressure seemed to be floating away on a dreamy cloud. I didn't need Barb to tell me we were through, 'cos I knew.

But I swear I hadn't wanted to get caught this way. It was a bit undignified. All those people had been looking. It was humiliating.

I could not deny it, though. It was all my fault. No doubt about that. I'd had a hundred chances to tell Barbara in a decent and civilized way. And I had chickened out every time.

As we drove along Barbara gradually calmed down. She turned to me all red-eyed and puffy-faced and blurted: 'I can't believe what you have done to me. How could you treat me like this?'

I took the huff at that.

I said to her: 'You can't believe it! That's lovely that is. You're always away six bleedin' months of the year, especially at Christmas. What do you want me to do?'

She tried to interrupt, but now it was all out in the open I wanted to get it off my chest. It was all those frustrated years of resentment coming out.

'You didn't give me a monkey's while you were gadding off all over the place, leaving me. I'm only a human being, you know.' I laid it on as heavy as I could, developing the theme of married couples staying together, me living like a monk and what did she expect.

By the time we arrived back at the house in Stanmore we were both drained. We had said all there was to say. We sat around for a while, neither of us knowing what to do, or how to do it. I'd expected Barbara would try to kick me out, but she didn't. She went quiet, almost withdrawn. I couldn't think of anything constructive or meaningful to throw in by way of easing the tension. So I said I wanted to go to Spain.

Barbara sniffed and replied: 'Why don't you pack your bags and go, then?'

I said yeah. So I packed my bags and went.

As I went out the door I said: 'Ta-ra.'

I couldn't wait to get back to my Sue.

She had taken a right old verbal mauling from Barb, cor love me if she hadn't. But she was in good spirits. I reckon that like me she was relieved all round that the lies and secrecy were over and done with. We were together now and didn't have to pretend. It was a lovely feeling.

Both of us decided we wanted to go out to the villa in Spain to sort ourselves out and decide what to do with the rest of our lives. We were excited at the prospect of jumping on a jet and being on our own. But we had some loose business ends to tie up first. We had to decide what to do about the clubs I now owned – and my stake in the famous Chinese restaurant in London called 'Mr Kai's', which was a favourite eating place of the rich and famous, including stars like Joan Collins and Twiggy.

Another club I'd bought after the Tin Pan Alley was a nightspot on the Finchley Road, called 'The Hillsdown', which had proved yet another nice little earner. Sue had more or less been running the place. We'd hit on a good gimmick at the Hillsdown of charging the same price, a quid, for any drink you wanted. That was Sue's brilliant suggestion and I told her I thought it was a smart bit of business thinking.

'Business nothing,' she beamed. 'I got the idea because I can't add up.' She had been completely in charge of the operation in a managerial position – not your common barmaid she was made out to be. Not, I hasten to add, that I had got anything against barmaids, common or otherwise. Barbara had spent her professional career playing a series of big-hearted, big-boobed, Cockney barmaid types, so I could never work out why she was so bitingly critical of girls of that particular calling.

One of the binds with late-night clubs was that the Old Bill had a way of barging in when they were least wanted – like bang in the middle of after hours drinking sessions. We had a foolproof method of announcing the arrival of the blue serge brigade: a warning light flickered behind the bar. By the time the hob-nails hit the carpet we were all just one big happy – and private – party enjoying a nightcap after all the toils of the evening. Nothing illegal about that.

Mick and me made arrangements to sell the A and R and the Tin Pan, so Sue and I could set off for our journey in Spain. I had no trouble disengaging from my share in the Chinky at a fair profit.

The solution of what to do with the Hillsdown came early one morning when Sue dropped by to check what stock we had in hand. It was a little task that did not take long on account there was nothing there. What was there were four Indians in the place acting like they owned it. They were walking round, measuring up and umm-humming about converting it into a takeaway or something. Sue was a bit taken aback because the joint had been stripped bare.

The certain gentleman I had been involved with partnerwise, who shall be nameless, had sold it from right under my nose. Even the cigarette machines, which did not belong to me, had vanished. I took the unexpected turn of events philosophically. We hadn't lost too much. And the way things had turned out it saved me the bother of having to find a buyer.

So that was it. The end of Ronnie Knight, West End club-owner. The end of a memorable era. Ronnie Knight was heading for Spain for a nice long rest. And with him was going the lady he loved.

There was only one more loose end to tie up.

The rather delicate (and top secret) matter of The Naughties.

11

French Lou was the one who led me astray. Lou was a colourful, bon viveur, gourmet and man about town. As befitted his station, my continental acquaintance was always immaculately turned out, favouring cashmere suits and crocodile shoes. He was a gentleman of varied commercial and business interests, with an ever-open eye for interesting new propositions. It was Lou who first introduced me to the financial delights of The Naughty Game.

The Naughties, as I was soon to find out, were those saucy little Soho strip clubs where your sexual perverts used to get their kicks. You would not believe the kinky goings-on that were going on. There was something to suit every taste. There was your straight strip clubs, the soft porn dirty acts and your hard-porn corn. Gawd love me, the things they got up to in some of them places. Talk about turning you off! Then there was the sleazy, backstreet 'massage parlours', much to the relief of some of what you might call your more desperate punters.

At that particular time in the social evolution of Britain's capital your old and well-tried decency laws were being swept aside on a wave of freedom and so-called liberal morality. In consequence the brothels boomed and banged away round the clock, providing intriguing menus for 'extras and specials' longer than the à la carte at the Savoy.

Considering the sky-high prices the wide-eyed punters were prepared to pay for a little bit of what they fancied, is it any wonder that all your entrepreneurs wanted a slice of the flesh market? The girls working the parlours made very presentable livings indeed. But they worked the most unsociable hours. At the end of a heavy shift their poor feet must have been killing them!

So 'Ze Leetle Norties' was the charming, Froggie way M. Lou used to collectively describe his thrusting sex empire.

What had always fascinated me on my very infrequent sorties

around the notorious red light areas was the wide range of clientele hanging around. You could always tell them, 'cos they mooched around aimlessly, looking at roofs and roads – anything but the saucy posters that really interested them. You had your sleazy little ferrety-faced tosspots, with whom I would not have entrusted the family cat. You had your innocents abroad, mostly horny young geezers up from the country looking for somewhere to put it – and risking catching something very nasty indeed in their indecent haste. And you had what was by far the most interesting bunch. Your upper-class, professional types who were either not getting the necessary in suburbia or were partial to a bit of whipping and rubbery – and whatever else went on behind closed doors.

No one could ever have accused me of being a prude. Perish the thought. But when it came to sexual perversion it gave me the creeping abdabs. The kindest view you can take on these matters is that it takes all sorts.

I had known French Lou for years and was well aware of his Soho outlets, enterprises that he did not readily drop out in everyday conversation. One of his most successful operations was flogging fine wine and spirits, a subject upon which he was a master. Lou supplied a lot of my requirements at the A and R, during which time we got to know and like one another.

One day the saucy Frog asks me if I'm interested in putting thirty grand into a new venture he's got lined up. That was another plus about Lou. You could never accuse him of confusing you with double-talk. He just came straight out with it.

In my boyish naivety I thought maybe he was opening one of those trendy wine bars, because, as I say, old Lou knew his plonks he did. Used to have some beautiful reds, whites and rosés. Lovely merchandise.

Lou explained that this interesting deal had come up, only he was somewhat over-extended finance-wise and needed the cooperation of a party he admired and could trust. Since we had a certain rapport and had always worked together to our mutual satisfaction he could think of none finer than yours truly to be by his side. So if I'd care to put forward the necessary funds to help get the ball rolling he could virtually guarantee a handsome return.

'You don't have to ask too many questions, just trust old Lou,' he parried my enquiries.

In the past I had put up a few sovs here and there with Lou, without wanting to know the ins and outs of every little detail. Never once had

I regretted trusting my instincts. But this was thirty grand we were talking. Big pommes de terre by any reckoning.

'Sodding well tell me what it's all about and maybe I will be interested,' I suggested as politely as I could, my natural sense of curiosity getting a grip of me.

'Well, confided Lou in that irresistible way he had, it was all a question of setting up . . . one of the dirties'.

Not, he hastened to add, hard porn or a brothel. Nothing so sordid. He would not dream of asking me to get involved with the heavy end of the meat market, as he knew the sensitivity of my feelings on the subject. What he had in mind was more in the way of a specialist little showplace. A sort of theatre in the round. The house would produce nothing more sensational than a few wholesome young ladies doing a nice little titillating dancing routine, showing a bit of the old how's your father, but most decidedly nothing that could in any way, shape or form be called sordid.

My curiosity was stimulated. Tell me more, I implored. Well, it seems some creative genius had conceived a novel idea to get the pervs all worked up. The name of the game was to screw the maximum return with the minimum outlay – with nothing too sleazy in the irresistible bait. My initial reaction was to tell Lou what he could do with his proposition. Ronnie Knight, respectable club-owner, a man about town, mixed up in the low-life naughty business? Wash your mouth out. It didn't bear thinking about.

It was at about this point that my continental comrade began to enlighten me on the sort of profit margins one could reasonably expect to reap on an undertaking similar to that under discussion. Call me greedy. Say I was a natural little chancer. Or that I just could not say no to a challenge. But biz was biz. I told Lou that he had found his man. We had a deal. Before finally shaking hands with Lou I did a modicum of personal research into the viability of the enterprise. The considered weight of opinion was that having a stake in the Soho Porn Racket was a few points more financially rewarding than shares in a goldmine. Those in at the start of the fleshpot boom were making fortunes, swanning round in Rolls Royces and holding shooting parties at their country estates, with a title or two among their honoured guests. I fancied a bit of the action. The drawback was that Nice People didn't get involved in the seamy, steamy business. Had it not carried a certain social stigma the porn business would have been floated on the stockmarket. So before clinching it with Lou I made my conditions perfectly clear: if he so much as mentioned my name in connection with anything unsavoury he'd soon be crying in his onion soup. I did not even want it known that I occasionally scanned Page Three. I did not want the fair and unsullied name of Ronnie Knight associated with the existence of any sleazy activities of any kind . . . never mind having a pecuniary interest in the sinful and sordid business.

'There's just you and me, Lou. And if word ever gets out then I won't have to put my thinking cap on about who blew the whistle, will I now?'

It was at this point that my little French friend began to huff and puff with uncharacteristic stammerings. Indeed, so considerable was his distress that I fancied he lapsed into parleying in the old Français. The cause of his difficulty turned out to be the fact that there was a third person involved, a mysterious partner who like me insisted on being of the strictly sleeping variety. True to his word, Lou steadfastly declined to identify my faceless business associate. And since I had already warned him of the grave perils involved in loose talk, I could hardly take him to task for his reticence.

At a later date, in a state of vino veritas, Lou was to carelessly drop out a mention of a certain individual in connection with our mutual enterprise. He referred, in passing to 'The Commander'. Barely had the phrase escaped his lips than he gnashed his teeth and stamped his foot one on the other in fury at his indiscretion. I let the moment pass. But I do fancy that a vision of blue and brass flashed before my eyes. I conjured up mental pictures of polished boots and peaked caps. 'Ello, 'Ello. What's going on 'ere? I thought. But no amount of pumping would get Lou to confirm my suspicions that our joint associate had very long arms and a pointed head. Wickedly, I realized that I had always found it very interesting that our theatrical establishment never fell foul of the eagle probings of the law, I wondered if there could possibly be any connection.

Since I was now something of an impresario (in a certain manner of speaking) I felt it was necessary to discover how my modest little showpiece functioned.

This is how it worked: around a central stage area was arranged in a circle about a dozen cubicles, just like private little phone boxes. The punter paid for one of the cubicles. In front of them was a tiny peepy-hole, through which they could spy the girls performing their exotics on the central stage. Now this is where the stroke of genius comes in. Suddenly a little shutter falls and cuts off the view, usually just as the girl at the centre of attraction was about to do something particularly risqué. The things they did with those rubber snakes made the mind boggle! Well, bless me, it seems the punters nearly broke their finger nails ramming in the extra quids to once again open up their peepy-hole.

And get this for a real financial masterstroke. At the end of the show, that lasted but a precious few minutes, the gasping, peeping twits were handed a Polaroid camera. They were invited to take snaps of the strippers 'in any pose'. The fivers flew like toilet paper in a Vindaloo house. There they would stand, camera in their hands, shaking like nudists at the North Pole. A little bell would ring, out would pop the girl. Looky-looky. Flash, bang and thank you very much for your contribution towards the management's outgoings.

Although I was confident that Lou would button his lips, I must confess that I was ill at ease at joining the ranks of the great strip-joint Johnnies. When the rewards of sin began to roll in (at around three grand a week) I do declare that it tended to ease the mental anguish. But I still was not proud that I had sold my principles for mere profit, handsome though it was. There were moments when I felt deeply moved, almost ashamed. I hated it. I lived in dread that respectable people would find out that I was in The Naughties up to my sweet little neck. It got so that if anybody started talking in general conversation about strip joints I used to break out in an itchy rash.

For most of the time I avoided Soho and the sleazy environs like it was a leper colony. When I did have to venture there I took circuitous, back-street routes in the hope that nobody would spot me. If anybody had seen me, especially my nearest and dearest in the Old Bill, they might have put two and two together and guessed that I was up to no good. So after a while I decided that dark glasses, a hat and turned-up collar would help disguise me. I toyed with the idea of going the whole hog, with a wig and false moustache, but the dread of getting spotted looking like a pervert was even more petrifying. It would have been just my luck to have got picked up for loitering with intent. The humiliation of appearing in court would have destroyed my reputation.

'When asked about his peculiar form of attire the defendant answered as to how he was merely trying to avoid being spotted on account that he was visiting a certain establishment of disreputable character, your worships.'

I could imagine it. Me standing there in court, head bowed like a perverted sheep-shearer. So I settled for the turned-up collar.

I used to go out every Friday night for the very good reason that Friday night was pay night. We added up the week's takings, deducted the necessaries, with me and Lou taking ours – not forgetting 'The Commander's' right and proper slice of the cake.

The dirty mac brigade might have disgusted me. But they were keeping me in a most luxurious life style. No doubt about it. What a motley lot they were. Once or twice I'd listen to 'em talking. Many were very la-di-dah. I know for a fact that a few well-known people, from lawyers to businessmen, used to frequent the Soho sin houses. There was even talk of top coppers and judges slinking in from time to time. One or two fish-and-chip newspapers carried stories along those lines. But I never saw any myself. What tickled me most was that they all wore macs. It was as though putting on the old waterproofs somehow made them invisible. I got the feeling that some of them would have come in with their wigs on and still thought they were protecting their identity if they had an old Burberry thrown over their shoulders.

Still, I gave up pondering the frailties of human nature a long time ago. If somebody either had to out of necessity, or chose to pay for a flash of the brush, then that was their tough titty. It is something that I, personally, have never quite been able to fathom. It struck me as a bit like going into a restaurant, paying to glance at the menu, then being kicked out.

Whatever else you might say about The Naughties you could not fault it as a sound business investment. I got to thinking that the depravity of man (as opposed to the ladies that is) was a pretty safe speculation. Forget your gilt edges. Invest in the guilty.

So it was that I also found myself involved in what was daintily called an 'escort agency'. Now, so far as I knew, that's exactly what it was. A few nice girls a bit down on their luck who didn't mind spending the night out with a few old buffers for fair reward and gain. Obviously I was not intimately involved with the day-to-day running of the agency. So I could not positively vouch that there was never a bit of hanky-panky on the side.

I now realize that I must have been really ashamed of that particular period of my career, because until I came to rack my brains I had completely obliterated it from my memory bank. But since honesty is in the offing and I propose to hold nothing back, I feel I must reveal even the most acutely embarrassing skeletons in the cupboard.

Now I think about it, my biggest critic was my old A and R partner

Mick Regan, who was quite a puritanical guy. He hated it. Absolutely. And he never let up telling me what he thought about me getting involved.

Escorting was a prosperous business. It must have fulfilled a social need because we could hardly keep up with demand. And if we were filling a gap in the market, where was the harm? I reckon that at one time we were also keeping about forty girls gainfully employed. There was money in it. No doubt.

What with one thing and another, during the Seventies and well into 1980 I had been pretty well set up. I had had me interests in the A and R, which was my base, the Tin Pan, the Hillsdown, the Chinese, the Naughties and other bits and pieces. I had also been known to dabble in the occasional one-off project. Was Ronnie Knight doing well? You bet he was. The above-detailed businesses was where my money came from. I reckon I was picking up three, three-and-a-half grand a week. Clear. All tax and national insurance contributions paid on the nail! The question I have often asked myself in latter years is: where did it all go? Then I remember that in those 'easy come' days I was an ardent disciple of the 'easy go' philosophy. A big spender. That would fairly sum up my lifestyle. I was dispensing the crinkly stuff like it had a shelf life considerably less than a cream cake under floodlights.

For someone like me, formerly of less salubrious surroundings, it was a real treat to travel through life first class. Only the best was good enough for me and mine. And having sampled the delights of the Good Life, I developed a hunger for more of where that came from. I was never happier than when going to all the best places, done up like a million dollars, mixing with all the top people. It is truly amazing how you can so quickly get used to sitting behind the wheel of a luxury limousine, after being brought up on run-down old bangers. The transition takes no time at all. I had been deprived as a kid and was I making up for it.

Sue had lots of lovely clothes and jewellery. Buying little baubles for her was one of the greatest joys my money bought me.

It had been the same with Barbara. She had been smothered with expensive rings on her fingers and finery in her dressing-room.

Call it a weakness, or an endearing quality, but whenever I have had a pound or two in my pocket I have always been generous to a fault. When I came to paying the piper I was always the one at the front of the queue. Nowadays I often reflect how so many people, many who could have bought and sold me a dozen times over, often

144

seemed to develop a case of creeping lethargy when it came to coming forward bill-wise.

Not that it really bothered me at the time. The spoils were pouring in regularly as water from a well. Most of it was in the form of crisp, negotiable readies. Only the occasional cheque filtered through the system. There was never any worry where the next few grand was coming from. There was no question. With the clubs it was one hundred per cent certain. With French Lou's Naughties, it was one hundred-plus for sure. My ship came home every night laden with enough spoils to ensure that I wanted for nothing.

Some characters of my acquaintance admitted to envying the absolute regularity of my source of income. When their funds dwindled the only way they knew of replenishing their coffers was to visit a bank or similar establishment out of hours . . . if you see what I mean.

One day I remember trying to cheer up a down-in-the-mouth customer, who took to solitary drinking; a nasty habit I always associated with a touch of the depressions. When I tried to bolster him up he told me why he was not feeling at his finest. 'It's like this Ron,' he began. 'It's been the same all my life. Every time I want something I got to go out and do a little villainy. It's the only trade I know and lately I keep getting nabbed.'

But for me money was no object. I was a real snazzy dresser. I'd order suits by the pair at prices that would be around a thousand quid apiece nowadays. I ordered silk shirts with me initials proudly emblazoned upon them. In fact I had one suit with RK stitched all the way down it. I'd have everything to match: socks, tie, shoes – everything. Real posy stuff. Sue used to pull my leg and say that all I needed to complete the ensemble was a nice little handbag.

All things considered, I think it can fairly be said that Ronnie Knight wasn't doing too badly.

But gradually it all began to pall. There comes a time when you get cheesed off with scouring through menus that all look the same. You become blasé about sitting behind the wheel of two tons of magnificent Mercedes. You begin to think that there must be more to life than the big social whirl. Familiarity breeds contempt. It's true that money can buy almost everything. But not quite everything. There's something else, beyond your wining and dining, fancy parties, toff clothes and flash cars.

At that stage in my life I wasn't really sure what it was. Only that I wanted to try and find it. And the best place to do that was in Spain with my Sue by my side.

So we sold up everything. It all added up to a tidy little sum, I don't mind admitting. Not the millions some people might think, but enough for me not to have to worry about paying the mortgage for the rest of my life. And my golden little nest egg was not the ill-gotten gains of bank robberies and other villanies, either.

The most pleasant surprise I had was bidding farewell to The Naughties. You know how emotional the Froggies can be. When I told good old French Lou that after a mere twelve months I wanted to pull out, it was all kissing and hugging and tears. He bade me 'bon voyage'. And just before I left he gave me a package that represented the selling price of my one-third stake in the game. A cool eighty grand. That was as nice a little going-away present as I ever had the good fortune to receive.

However, it posed something of a dilemma for a very well-to-do friend of mine who also happened to be my accountant. You see, as was customary in Lou's particular line of business, the £80,000 was handed to me in the form of used, mixed notes of the £1, £5 and £10 denominations. When I deposited the sizeable pile of cash on my money-man's desk he nearly had a fit. His embarrassment was that he had to pay the notes into the bank. 'I'll have to think up some explanation for having so many readies,' he mused. 'After all I can hardly put it down as "profits from the porn business".'

12

The view over the mountains took my breath away. Down in the valleys the weatherbeaten, ever-watchful goatherds tended their flocks. As the animals leaped from rock to rock the bells around their necks tinkled out little tunes.

In parts it was barren, bare, craggy rock. In some places were clumps of tough olive trees. Here and there red bougainvillaea and multi-headed hibiscus splashed blobs of colour on the landscape.

Just across the hill, a mother fox and her cubs had taken refuge in a cave. I used to watch them everyday. Until the hunters unearthed them and sent in a pack of dogs.

In the background was the shimmering, blue Mediterranean and cloudless, china sky. On a clear day you could see the mountains in North Africa, forty miles away. The Rock of Gibraltar towered from the sea like a lost island.

The first time I clapped eyes on the Costa del Sol I fell in love with the place. It was in the early '70s. I'd gone down with Barbara for a little look round.

As you know I had never been one for the delights of foreign travel, particularly after the Madeira experience. But I fell for Spain. The sun was on me back. The mountain air tasted like champagne and it drove all my niggling worries away. In fact we took to it so readily that me and my Johnny bought a 1,600 square metre plot of land up in the hills beyond Fuengirola, one of your favourite spots for British tourists, though in those days it was virtually uninhabited compared to what it's like now – almost a concrete jungle in places.

An American architect was building some beautiful villas nearby, so we got him to do one for us. He did us a smashing white-brick place, with four bedrooms, lovely big dining room and fitted kitchen. Outside was a terrace, bit lawn and veg garden and a pretty 30-foot pool. Not big, but then I wasn't practising the breast stroke for the Olympics. I kitted out a small gym to keep myself in trim and I considered that this place was probably the nearest I was going to get to my idea of heaven.

We moved into the new house around 1975, with me thinking that we had got very good value for an all-in price of just £40,000. It was all so different from the smoke and drab greyness of the London scene. A world away from Arcola Street. A big step up for an East End ragamuffin.

In that spring of 1981 when I stood there on my mountainside garden looking at the Med I felt like a King. I loved it there. I wanted Spain to be my home. The very best thing of all was that Sue was with me. That made everything perfect.

I knew that Barb quite liked the sun and the sea. She knew I loved every minute and hated going back. But the fact was that all the time she was worried sick that a big part would come up and that she would not be on the spot, in London, to accept it. I tried to reason with her, pointing to the electronic device known as a dog and bone and assuring her that if her agent had any news he might just be bright enough to dial a few digits. But my assurances didn't placate her. She was genuinely petrified that the chance of a lifetime would come along and some other cow would go and get it, all because she was sunning her backside on the Costa del Sol with her old man.

It was not use trying to reason with her. Arguments got us nowhere. Playing the heavy-handed husband was a waste of time. Barb was obsessed about getting big parts, especially on TV. Sometimes I thought she would have sold her soul to appear on the box. It would drag on for a few days with Barb sulking and pouting around. Eventually I'd suggest that maybe she would be happy if she went back. Her face would light up like a Belisha beacon, she'd pack and be off in a few hours. And I'd be left on my own as usual counting me toes.

I can scotch rumours that I used to use the villa as a little love-nest. Are you kidding? In the first place I would not have done it out of a sense of common decency. In the second, if I had Barb would have known in about two seconds flat, on account that we had dozens of friends living nearby, some of whom would undoubtedly have taken it upon themselves to call Barbara to enlighten her as to my wrongdoings. So I did no wrong.

Like most of your actors, however rich and famous they might be, Barbara was insecure. The only time she was happy was when she was working. Her greatest thrill – like them all – was to be in front of an audience and being adored by the masses. I once heard Rod Stewart spell out all entertainers' passion with performing: 'It's like making love to ten thousand people . . . all at once.'

But that was all how it had been in the past. Now I was happy to be in my Spanish idyll with my Sue. Thank the Lord Sue was as much in love with the Costa del Sol as I was. By the end of the early '80s we both knew we wanted to live in Spain and spend the rest of our lives there.

When we finally pulled up all our roots and moved to the villa I was not short of a peseta or two. I had quite a healthy bit of capital put by. In addition I had also been investing in a couple or three enterprises in Spain over the years. I had an interest in a car hire company and a restaurant. I also was half-owner of my local just round the corner, name of Wyn's bar. When I first saw Wyn's place it was half-bar, half-shop. We extended the bar and put the supermarket over the road. I had also put a bit of money to work in the booming property market, investing in a few apartments under construction. I sold at a respectable profit.

My fortunes were nowhere like what I had enjoyed as Mr Big Club Owner in the West End. But then I was hardly living the same sort of lifestyle. Dressing up on the Costa meant slipping a t-shirt above your shorts. So all my expensive suits and the like were redundant. You could have a decent meal out for next to nothing – and I was no longer interested in the social scene that involved boogalooing away in trendy and expensive night clubs. Since I am neither a gambler nor heavy drinker nor smoker (white wine and soda and the occasional lager is me lot) my needs were comparatively modest.

The three or four hundred quid per week I was pulling in in those days from the cars, restaurant and bar was more than enough to keep me and Sue in lovely style. In addition Sue went out and earned a few bob, window-dressing and bits and pieces. All in all I can honestly say that my life was about as lovely as you can get. It was Paradise found. I was so happy I used to say little prayers of a night-time. How long would it last, I sometimes wondered. No prizes for guessing.

It all started daft as you like while me and Sue were having a playful frolic in the sea.

A great big wave comes and knocks me over and we're rolling about laughing like a couple of sandboys. When the water hit me, I had felt a bit of a sharp stabbing pain in my neck, but I didn't bother too much about it. Next morning I woke up in agony. I could barely move. Every flinch brought on an electric shock in my spine, that made my legs and arms tingle and caused explosions inside my skull.

When you are suffering that much you will do anything to try and make it better. I can understand people paying fortunes to quacks, taking the herbals and nipping over to Lourdes hoping for a quick miracle. Nothing is too much trouble. No price too high to pay. When agony sears you, you would give your last quid for a bit of relief. Those quacks and sharks who prey on the sick are nasty people who should be put down.

Me, I did it all. I had your physio, natural remedies and regular medics. The Chinese pin merchants had me looking like a metallic porcupine. I kept taking the pills. None of it did any good. As my bills soared so the misery intensified. My arms went numb. My legs started to go. I could barely lift a knife and fork. My sense of balance was playing cruel tricks on me, like I was boozed out of my skull. When we went out I had to hold on to Sue as if I was crippled. We could be sitting in a restaurant, when suddenly it would strike like a bolt of lightning. It came on quick as that. The only thing I could do was lean on Sue and stagger out. It was terrible. One minute I would be all right. The next I would be crippled. I did feel a fool.

And like a fool I carried on trying to get cured in Spain when I should have swiftly nipped back to London to take advice from Harley Street's finest. There's no place like home when the chips are down. By the time I concluded that if I didn't go back to England then my future looked decidedly dodgy, I feared that I had left it too late.

There is nothing more certain than when you are down in the dumps, at the end of your tether, you tend to think the worst. I was convinced that I was riddled with cancer. Carefully considering the symptoms from which I was suffering I told myself that the boys I had consulted so far were not being entirely truthful with me. The mind can play malicious games with you. The way I saw it was that maybe the medics and fringe quacks knew damn well that I was incurable. But they wanted to get a bit of business out of me while the going was good and I was capable of signing the cheques. That is what, in my darkest moments, I honestly believed was happening to me. It's amazing what flashes through your mind when you think your days are numbered.

Sue, bless her, dismissed my cancer dread, trying to make light of it. I kept moaning and groaning. I lapsed into a daze, becoming increasingly certain that Ronnie Knight's days were most definitely numbered.

I could hear the Grim Reaper calling. I was getting to be depressed.

In the end Sue could no longer hide her concern. She phoned this lady doctor she used to work for and explained everything to her. After listening to how I had started to walk sideways with a buzzing in my head all the time the doc advised Sue to get me back as soon as possible. I went post haste. They rushed me straight into Harrow Hospital.

The specialists looked me all over from head to tail. I had all the tests, dozens of x-rays and nice long needles crunched into my spine. I had some purple coloured dye injected into my backbone. If I never have that little treat again I shan't lose any sleep. I had that little lot and everything else ever invented by the medical profession. I felt like a guinea-pig. After all that lot they could not be sure what was wrong. So they sent me to another specialist. I remember he laid me out on a table, pulled up me knees and stretched me arms. He looked at me all thoughtful. His face was a study in concentration.

Sue denies it to this day, but I distinctly remember someone telling me that this thing I'd got, well, if it ever reached up to my brain I was a goner.

Anyway it transpired that I had a choice. Either I had the knife and stood a chance of surviving. Or else it was just a question of time.

They did this operation on my spine, taking out a bit of the fourth and fifth vertebrae in what I had been warned was a long, delicate and reasonably dangerous job. Frankly, at the time I would have taken the risk with half a per cent chance of success. Had all other options failed I would have had a go at it myself. I could not have gone on living in such pain. My eternal gratitude goes out to the medical team that did the business on me, 'cos they did a brilliant bit of work.

After a few weeks the pain had virtually gone away. I began to feel there was hope for me after all. The only problem was I had to wear one of those stiff collars that make you look like a masochistic vicar. I felt a right Charlie, but I suppose it was a small price to pay for being cured of an illness that could so easily have turned me into a virtual vegetable.

Although I didn't know it, someone was about to put another rope round my neck. This time no amount of surgery would relieve the pain.

13

I have been accused of being involved in two of Britain's biggest ever robberies. Both were daring, meticulously planned and highly professional raids that resulted in a total haul of a cool £33m, give or take a half-million quid or so.

At 7 a.m. on Easter Monday 1983, six masked bandits armed with shotguns broke into the Security Express headquarters in Shoreditch, East London. They overpowered half a dozen guards and threatened to kill them unless they opened the sophisticated time locks to the strongrooms containing the loot. It was claimed that petrol was poured over one of the poor sods. He was warned that he would be torched if he did not cooperate. Then the victims were bound up wrists-to-ankles while the gang started shifting out the booty. According to all the reports the robbers must have been fit as fleas, because they shifted the five tons of paper money in less than an hour. The cash was all in used £50, £20, £10 and £5 notes, unmarked, unnumbered and untraceable. The £6m had been collected from banks supermarkets and stores.

In short, it was a robbers' dream. The job went smooth as well-oiled clockwork. Thank God, despite the wild threats, no one was hurt. The police admitted that the daylight raid had been planned like a military operation. Talk was that it had taken fifteen years to set up – by planting people as employees with the firm and waiting until they got into positions of power before hitting the place. Personally that theory always struck me as like something out of a John Le Carré spy thriller. Using defectors and moles to infiltrate secret service networks is one thing, but frankly I cannot imagine any gang sitting round for years to pull a job.

From what I saw and heard from the sidelines it seemed to me that bank robbing was a relatively short-term cancer that inevitably ended in long terms of enforced inactivity. I would have thought that villains planning big jobs would go off the boil if they had to wait half a lifetime!

Conversely, there is no denying that a dedicated firm of robbers will employ the most ingenious methods to transfer funds in their direction.

My view is that wherever a lot of money or valuables are lying about you can safely bet that loitering with intent in the background are certain persons anxious to get their hot little hands on the booty. That's the stuff criminals are made of. You can have the most expensive, space-age security devices ever developed. But they are man-made. And anything man-made has got to have a flaw. That's where the warped genius of the criminal mind comes in. The name of the game is to expose the human error, exploit it and get rich quick. Time and again engineers and designers develop systems they boast are virtually impenetrable, 'virtually' being the operative word. Because somewhere out there are experts in their own field anxious to prove them wrong. Usually at the earliest opportunity.

Both the law and Security Express's top experts were bewildered by how quickly the gang had managed to enter the building, known to all and sundry as 'Fort Knox', so easily. The company's showpiece HQ – as you might expect of a reputable organization specializing in handling millions of pounds every day – was supposed to be fire, theft and third-party proof, with all the latest in electronic surveillance and anti-robbery wizardry. The place bristled with more cameras than a television studio. The four-storey building, a virtual fortress, was surrounded by a 15-foot-high fence, with steel guarded doors and windows. There could have been a force field round the place. The bandits still got in.

There wasn't a 'professional' on either side of the law in Britain who was not amazed at the sheer, bloody cheekiness of the job, which was the country's biggest ever cash raid. Lloyd's underwriters matched it by offering a record £500,000 reward for the capture of the gang.

On June 6, 1985, after a trial lasting more than two months, four men were convicted of taking part in the robbery. Two of them were my brothers. John got twenty-two years after being found guilty of virtually masterminding the robbery. Big brother Jimmy got eight for handling stolen cash.

The story went around that a lot of the loot was taken out of the country in suitcases. It was then given the old Persil treatment by using the readies to buy businesses and apartments on foreign soil. Including Spain. Just around the corner from where I lived, as luck would have it.

My brothers had been fingered by one Allen Opiola. He told the Old Bill that he was a member of the gang bossed by my Johnny. He turned grass to escape a heavy sentence. After the case he changed his name and identity and went on his toes to another part of the country. To this day he has never been seen or heard of again. He lives quietly under an assumed name. My bet is that he still needs a change of underwear every time there's a sharp knock on his door. I have heard it said that he played extra safe by paying a few visits to a plastic surgeon.

In view of the close family connection with the crime it is not surprising that I would eventually be roped in, though it took several years before Scotland Yard finally made me an official suspect, by which time I was living happily here in Spain.

There are no doubt cynics around who might consider that I should have immediately returned to England to prove the police wrong. That's exactly what my Jimmy tried to do. And look what happened to him. Jimmy was with his family having a little holiday in Portugal, just a few hours from my place on the Costa del Sol, when we heard the news of John's arrest. When I was first told that my Johnny had been pulled in, I thought to myself: 'Soddin' hell, what's up?'

I tried to phone Jimmy at his home. His son Jimmy Jnr told me that he had spoken to his dad who was at his holiday place on the Algarve. Jimmy had told his dad that the police had been knocking on the door. Once my brother heard that he jumped on a plane and returned to see what was going on. When I discovered that upon his return my Jimmy had immediately been charged with receiving I could not believe it.

The Old Bill's case was that the supergrass had overheard Johnny say that he had to give Jimmy a hundred grand as part of the share-out. Off went a squad of officers to turn over Jimmy's home and business premises. They never found a hundred grand. They found ten grand in my Jimmy's safe, the sort of money he was taking every week from his legit scrap, restaurant and leisure businesses.

I have to admit that I didn't know anything about my Johnny. Of course, we were close. We all were. All the family. But I didn't get involved in Johnny's business affairs. Never.

The prosecution said that with Johnny they had found money here and there and everywhere. That I never knew about. I cannot comment. But to this day I am positive that my Jimmy was set up. If he had had anything to hide would he have shot back from Portugal in the belief that there was only a few minor matters to be cleared up?

He could easily have slipped over the border into Spain and sat tight till he could suss out exactly what the score was. Jimmy returned home because he was genuinely curious. He wanted to know what the police wanted to question him about.

My Jimmy was a very wealthy man. His various interests were good as little gold-mines. He was probably worth more than the six million that was nicked in the raid. My Jimmy was going so well he even had his own railway, shipping loads of scrap up to the North, with great big massive cranes lifting the gear out. There was no need for him to get in anything shady. What's he want to go and get involved in villainy for? I ask you! Ladbrokes had offered him more than £3m for his Stanmore leisure complex – he had more than thirty acres. Apart from that, and I'm sorry about this Jimmy, but he was getting on in years. Having people tied up and breaking into places just wasn't his game. I was the West End face. I was the one the police were always wanting to visit every five minutes. I was the one in their bad books.

But never, not once, did the coppers so much as send me a polite invitation asking me to join them in even an informal chat. I was in London for months after the Easter Monday caper. There. On the spot. They could have picked me up at any time. But they never did. They had done it often enough in the past. But the Old Bill never indicated the slightest interest in questioning me. Not a dicky-bird.

It wasn't until two years later when I was back in Spain that the Old Bill suddenly decided they had something on me. My initial reaction when that news came out of the blue was to go back straight away to clear my name. I wanted to. I planned to. Then I remembered what had happened to my Jimmy. I have no hesitation in confessing that that memory made me pause and think things out very carefully indeed. Everyone I knew and trusted urged me to do nothing rash, nothing that I might have plenty of time to regret. Sit tight and see what happens! That was the advice I had. That was the sound advice I needed.

During the Security Express trial Barbara, at my request, had given evidence in Johnny's defence. So you can be sure the name of Ronnie Knight got bandied about a fair bit. In fact our personal matrimonial affairs got as much coverage as the case. Barbara had given me £50,000 in cash when our Stanmore pad had been sold for around £140,000 a few years earlier, cash I paid to Johnny to pay off his share in the Spanish villa. And pay him off I had. As agents acting for the Security Express insurance company found out when they later tried to claim Johnny's half of the villa to minimize their losses.

Thank God I was able to show them the legal papers that proved that everything had been done properly otherwise they would have tried to tip me out.

In fact the wise and learned judge, Mr Richard Lowry, got so fed up with hearing 'Ronnie Knight' so frequently referred to in court that he took the unusual step of inviting the Press and counsel round the back for a private word.

I was not at that historic meeting. But I do have in front of me an official court transcript of what went on. And if you do not mind me saying so, very interesting reading it makes, too. What his worship wanted to know was: 'Why does this name Ronald Knight keep cropping up and is he going to be charged?'

That was more or less the gist of his query.

The official report from the get-together in chambers, dated April 22, 1985, quotes Judge Lowry thus:

'In the course of this trial certain names have been mentioned . . . a man called Ronald Knight who is the brother of two of the defendants, who is in Spain . . .

'The reason I have asked the Press to come into court is that two recent newspaper articles give rise to understandable anxiety that there may be prejudice in the minds of the jury about one or another defendant . . .

'I read a paragraph in *The Times* of today that stated: "Among those wanted for questioning are Mr Ronald Knight, the former husband of Barbara Windsor, the actress; John Everett, John James Mason, Frederick Foreman and Clifford Saxe.

' "Police want to see them about the £25m Brinks-Mat robbery at Heathrow in November 1983 and a £7m raid on a Security Express depot earlier that year.

' "All five men live openly near Marbella. Mr Knight has denied any involvement with the robberies." '

Judge Lowry, thankfully seeking fairness all round, went on: 'There are errors in that particular passage as follows: Ronald Knight is NOT wanted for questioning in respect of this case, the Security Express Robbery.

'Ronald Knight and the other four men are NOT wanted for the Brinks-Mat robbery.'

Despite this quite remarkable statement from the top judge, it has become almost universally accepted almost beyond question that I am guilty as sin. Certainly the Press and television seem in absolutely no doubt. They keep on branding me as a notorious gangster, with the 'Britain's Most Wanted Man' tag splashed across headlines.

Just what was Ronnie Knight's role in the raid? That precious little nugget of information has never been made clear. It has been rumoured that I was somehow involved in the planning. Some rumour-mongers suggest that I actually took part in the hold-up. The Old Bill has never approached me officially on the subject. So it is perhaps understandable that I am somewhat confused over the allegations. I gather they want to have a word 'on suspicion of handling stolen goods'. That, I take it, means helping to launder the £6,375,000 proceeds of the haul.

The gold bullion raid at Heathrow airport came on November 26, 1983, six months after the Security Express robbery. A Saturday. It was almost a carbon-copy of the Security Express caper. Again there was a team of six men wearing Balaclavas and carrying shooters. The gang had the know-how to neutralize some of the most advanced electronic security gadgetry in the world. They managed to break into a large brick and metal security warehouse at the airport, owned by Brinks-Mat, a subsidiary of the giant American Express organization.

The baddies repeated almost exactly what had happened on that previous Easter Monday . . . only this time whey were more brutal.

They gave the six security guards a tough time. One of them was stabbed in the hand, another was pistol whipped. And two were stripped, covered in petrol and callously told they would be incinerated if they did not cooperate. It was this wicked, frightening petrol-burning threat that seemed to convince some people that the gang was one and the same. They terrified the security men into opening all the necessary strong-room doors and safes. Then the gang took less than an hour to shift 6,800 gold bars weighing three tons into a couple of vans. They also grabbed £100,000 worth of diamonds. When the assessors started counting the losses they did not stop until they had reached almost £26m.

The robbery happened in the early hours of that Saturday morning. The robbers had long gone before one of the handcuffed and gagged guards managed to struggle free and raise the alarm. The audacious and ruthless raid shook everybody in the country – including Ronnie Knight.

I was just as fascinated and staggered as your average punter by the way the gang had pulled off the biggest robbery in history. My mind boggles at the way they managed to penetrate a stronghold believed to be so secure that the confident firm did not even bother employing night guards. It all goes to prove my theory about the ingenuity of the criminal mind.

But that bit of mind-blowing was nothing compared to what went on in my brainbox when I had the first sniff of rumour that I – yes, me, Ronald John Knight – was one of the crooks involved. Talk about a nasty shock to the nervous system! I could not eat, sleep or think straight.

I will never forget the date of the Brinks-Mat affair. The job was pulled on Sue's 30th birthday and we were out and about in old London town having a right old celebration. We were out with a load of old chums and did the entire rounds of the West End hot spots, unloading a good few hundred sovs en route. I'd just got out of hospital after having my neck done. I was doing my best to strut my stuff with the handicap of the uncomfortable plastic collar threatening to throttle me. I was so embarrassed about the damm thing that I tried to cover it with a polo-neck sweater. But it ruined the cut of the cashmere.

My Sue and me staggered back to base, somewhat the worse to wear, just before the milkman arrived. She noticed it first on the telly news. 'What about that, Ron?' she said. 'There's been a big gold bullion robbery at Heathrow. They say it's twenty-five million pounds.'

I was intrigued, but the merrymaking had left me pooped and tiredness triumphed. Within seconds I was in dreamland, where everything was nice and peaceful.

Later I got down to reading the nitty-gritty, totally absorbed by the audacity of the raid. I could not believe the way the robbers had pulled it off. It all seemed so impossible. But then, I reflected, that was exactly what I had thought about the Security Express number. Unless I have been in a time-warp ever since, I have never known the police to actually connect me in any way with the Brinks-Mat escapade. But if the Old Bill keeps arrest warrants up its sleeve, as they did with Sue for a year, how can you be sure of anything?

I have said it before. And at the risk of sounding a bore I will repeat it again. I was in no way connected with the robberies. Either of them. Not in any shape, form or method. Call me a convicted receiver of purloined goods, a baddie, a little chancer or what you like. But armed robbery, real villainy, is not my scene. Most definitely not. I could never go banging innocent people on the heads, threatening them or waving a gun around. Nor could I be a party to that sort of behaviour. Maybe in the past I've had inside information on one or two excursions outside the law. In my line of business – and with a certain number of wrongdoers amongst my former clubland clientele – it is obvious that the occasional word was dropped here and there. But having a nod and a wink, or even some heavy suspicion, is one thing. Actually taking part in any of the rough-stuff skulduggery is entirely another.

Sometimes when I'm worrying a bit about where my old-age pension is coming from I think to myself: 'I've been blamed enough. I wish I had had something to do with handling all that bleedin' money.' And sometimes, just sometimes, I really mean it.

My good chums in the Press have not been shy about recklessly bandying about my fair name in connection with the Great Gold Robbery. Ronnie Knight and Brinks-Mat seem to go together like con and victed. On February 3, 1985, fourteen months after the raid, I was treated to a mention in your Top People's bible, the Observer newspaper. I presume the reporter concerned, one Martin Bailey, must have carried out meticulous research because – and I quote from his article – 'Other Britons wanted for questioning over the Brinks-Mat robbery include Ronnie Knight, who lives a life of luxury on the Costa del Sol.' Very enlightening stuff. Particularly as it was all news to me.

The main body of the article was about John 'Goldfinger' Palmer, the young and wealthy jeweller, who was virtually accused by some of being the Mr Big behind the Brinks-Mat raid. At the time Palmer was on holiday in the Spanish Canary Isles with his wife and two young daughters. I am making no judgements, but Palmer was peeved because police were looking for the missing loot down on his three-acre Battlefields Estate, near Bath, which included a magnificent Georgian mansion. It also boasted a nice little thirty-foot swimming pool till the pneumatic drills got to work . . . after they had loosened the concrete floor in his lounge. The general consensus seemed to be that the three tons of gold had been smelted down somewhere . . . like in Palmer's back garden furnace. I recall he wasn't too pleased about that, claiming the unstinting search had caused around £50,000 worth of damage.

I never so much as met John Palmer, who was eventually cleared of any connection with the job. Some people get Palmer mixed up with another gentleman sought by the police at the time. He was John Fleming, the man the Old Bill travelled to Miami to bring back for questioning, who was also later acquitted. John Fleming was known to me. He came out of South London, was a regular at my club and we would often have a chinwag and drink together. Nice feller, I always found him. Never had a bad word for anyone.

It was John Fleming who bought the A and R from me and Mick. We had been negotiating the deal before I was whisked off to Brixton for the murder remand. While I was passing the time in jail I got a message from Mick that the purchase had been completed. Me and Mick were happy because after thirteen years in the club business we had both had enough and wanted to get out. I never saw John Fleming after that transaction was completed. But the two-plus-two merchants would not be denied their suspicious speculation.

14

When the truth finally sank into my unreceptive brain that people really believed I was a big-time robber I wanted to die! Die with disbelief, I tell you.

They began to point fingers. I could see them out of the corner of my eye, squinting fearfully at me like I was about to pull a gun and start shooting the place up. They would shuffle uncomfortably as I walked past, greet my cheery little 'hellos' with a nervous laugh or a sickly grin. Jesus, I began to tell myself, they really think that I was involved in those massive raids.

The whole ludicrous business induced a nasty attack of shock. When I say I nearly died, I mean it.

At first I had tried to laugh off all the suspicion and accusations. It all seemed so preposterous. Ha-ha. Ho-ho. Hoot-bloody-hoot. It never really occurred to me that anyone would take it seriously. For sure I realized it looked bad, with two of my brothers doing time for the Security Express. But just because they were convicted didn't mean that I had to be involved. The papers kept churning out the headlines about 'Knight on the Run' and all that jazz. It was all over the telly. I couldn't turn round without another allegation appearing somewhere or other. But it took a helluva long time for it to really sink in that Mr Public was taking the allegations as gospel. As my old mum always used to say: 'It's in the papers so it must be true, mustn't it?'

Some stories were painting me like a Chicago hit man. Others made out that I was a booze-swilling, womanizing playboy, night-clubbing round the clock and spending like a millionaire . . . And where did all the loot come from, hint-hint? I now know beyond any doubt that if enough mud is flung, them some – if not most – will stick.

Elsewhere I was portrayed as a ruthless, sinister Godfather figure behind practically every crime committed on the Costa del Sol. I was confronted with lunatic suggestions that I ran an underworld organization in Spain called The Office, from which I helped plan half the big robberies in Britain. It made my hair curl, I can tell you. I don't know where they got them from. I watched in spellbound fascination as the mass media created a legend.

It was me they were bloody well going on and on about. It was a funny feeling. If there's one thing the Press loves it's a colourful charismatic character to play around with. And if there doesn't happen to be one around to fit the bill, no problem. They invent one. They do it with sports heroes, like George Best, Alex Higgins and Ian Botham. They build them into superstars, then kick them so they become fallen idols. For some inexplicable reason they decided that Ronnie Knight had a certain commercial appeal. They went to town on me. I was getting more publicity than the Spanish King Juan Carlos. I worried that they might extradite me from Spain for stealing the limelight from the monarch.

Maybe it seems that I was making light of what was really a very serious matter. You bet I was, particularly in those early days. If I hadn't treated the whole affair with a degree of jocularity I'd have gone bonkers. Right off me tracks. What the papers said about me, what people began to whisper, hurt a lot. I've never publicly admitted it before, but it was sheer hell. I was being pilloried, treated like a leper with Aids. Not by my close friends, of course. But a lot of acquaintances and people I bumped into casually.

I felt terrible, so shocked that I couldn't believe it was happening to me. Naturally I tried to hide all the worries, mixed emotions and feelings of anger that bubbled up. It's easy enough to put on a brave face and outwardly laugh like the incredible tales did not matter. But inside you cannot fool yourself. All the accusations. All the lies. It was painful. They made me ill. I would get depressed. Then I'd say to myself: 'What you bleedin' well bothering about? You've got no worries. You ain't done nothing.' That hunk of personal reassurance would usually perk me up a bit. So I adopted a policy that when people started giving me the worried looks, peering over their newspapers, I'd treat them to a beautiful, beaming smile and nod affably in their direction. I managed to pull it off. But like I said, that was to outward appearances.

The full extent of the misery used to get through to me at night. I'd lie in bed, with Sue nice and cuddly by my side, and I would try to convince myself that I had nothing to fear. Nothing to worry my little brainbox about. But you cannot kid your subconscious. The nightmares came. In them I would find I was in trouble because my papers weren't in order. They were going to deport me. I'd wake up in a lather. Shake it off as another bad dream and keep repeating that I'd got nothing to worry about. I had done nothing to justify being kicked out of Spain. So go back to sleep.

Then I'd start thinking: 'Jesus Christ, they are gonna do me the same way they did Jimmy.'

That fear would bring back the repugnant memories of a stinking prison cell. The smell. The loneliness, degradation and waste of life. I'd think this was it. This was me lot. I've got to go through it all again. Last time I had been behind bars it had been those six miserable months while I was on remand for the murder. I'd been one of the lucky ones whose case had come up pretty quick. Some poor devils had sat on their backsides for eighteen months or more, waiting for the wheels of the law to grind slowly in their direction. Many of them got off, which was no consolation for the lost life. Just the thought of sitting in a poxy place like prison again made me break out in a clammy sweat. I couldn't face it.

I kept telling myself that I had nothing to fear. Even if I did get charged and was remanded in custody I knew that I would be cleared at a trial just like before. I knew I would get off. Unless . . . unless I was to be treated to another stitch-and-run job like they tried before.

Well, I'll tell you. All the worry and the uncertainty, it got me down in the end. One day my ulcer burst. It had been niggling away for a year or more. I was suffering from little, stabbing pains that came on every now and again, specially if I didn't eat properly, had a drop too much of the old vino or got into a mental state. I went to a local Spanish clinic for a check up. They took some x-rays and said there was no real problem. Just a little irritating ulcerette! I told the docs that a couple of my pals had started like this and they had ended up on their knees because it got to hurt them terrible. 'So why don't you just take it out and get rid of it, 'cos I'm not worried about operations and things like that,' I implored them.

The docs shook their heads and assured me it was not necessary. They gave me some powder. Drink plenty of milk, they said. Keep taking the pills and there will be no difficulties. So I did what I was told. Like a good little boy scout. But every time I looked at the latest Ronnie Knight saga in the papers it started the pain off again. I'd read about how I was about to be arrested and whisked back to Britain and the acid would start to eat me up inside. My stomach would do a triple somersault, tying my guts up in knots. I'd feel sick.

One bad attack came on when Sue's mum and dad were staying with us. It was Marj's birthday and of course we always go out to celebrate events like that. My Sue was all excited planning somewhere nice to visit for dinner. I was in so much pain I didn't know what to do. I didn't want to let on that I felt lousy because I knew it would spoil everybody's night. I had never told Sue that I had been passing a lot of blood. I thought that with an ulcer you brought blood up through your mouth, not at the other end. I daren't say anything about what was happening to me because I knew Sue would worry her head off. The quack had said the pills would work. It was just a question of keeping calm. But that evening I felt too rotten to go out. In the end Sue and her mum went and I stayed at home with Sue's dad, Bob.

Soon as they had gone I went straight to bed. After a while I had to get up for a pee. I slung me legs out of bed – and my head started spinning. I thought: 'Jesus what's happening to me now?'

Every time I tried to stand I fell back on the bed. By now I was desperate to reach the toilet. Me bladder was bursting. The only way I could make it was to fall on my hands and knees and crawl into the bathroom. Standing up to do a wee was impossible. So I thought to myself I'd sit down. I managed to collapse on to the seat. My head went round and round. Then bosh. I was gone.

I'll never know how long I was out for. But I came to hearing my old father-in-law, his face full of concern, asking if I was all right. By a stroke of luck I had fallen beside the toilet with my head propped up against the wall. That had stopped me rolling over – and probably suffocating myself. I looked round and saw I'd been sick. The smell was terrible. Then I knew it was my burst ulcer.

Bob was beside me then. The brave old man, who wasn't too well and had only one leg, had managed to scramble up the stairs to help me. All I could think of was getting my clothes cleaned up of the blood and vomit, so that Sue would not get upset. I threw everything into the bath and turned on the taps to soak them . . . but I was bleeding everywhere. All over the bloody place. Somehow Bob managed to get me into my bed. Once I was lying down I felt marvellous. I felt I could nod off . . . forever.

Bob was so worried that he got on the blower to the restaurant. When Sue found me she cried out in shock. I must have looked a real mess. The doc came flying round. He told me to get down the stairs and wait for the ambulance. Sue was helping me. She got me to the top of the landing. I remember saying to her: 'Oh, God Sue. I feel terrible. I ain't got hardly any blood left in me now. I'm down to my last pint.' With that I must have tumbled arse over head and collapsed at the bottom of the stairs. The doc's wife sat me up, so that what drop of lifeblood I'd got left stayed in me.

My poor old mum Nellie was also staying at the time. She suffers from that dreadful Parkinson's disease and she didn't really know what was going on. She kept saying 'My Ronnie's gone and fallen over. He's hurt himself, he has. Are you all right son?'

It is funny how you behave in certain situations. There I was thinking I was on my last legs, and I was almost chuckling thinking about what had happened to my old mum, Nell. When I'd first suggested she come over and visit us she hadn't really been able to grasp how far I was away, that I was living in a foreign country and things like that. 'Course, she had never been on an aeroplane before. When she got to Heathrow she was taken directly on to the aircraft through all those long corridors and connecting ramps. So my dear old lady sat there inside this huge flying machine, about to be whisked 1,300 miles in under three hours and she said: 'Aren't these new buses great big things.' Bless her.

Now here she was, all old and frail, suffering from this shaking illness, asking me if I was all right. I wasn't exactly at my finest. I was fifty-two years old and the chances of reaching fifty-three seemed pretty remote. But you know how it is with your old mum. You don't want to worry them, do you? So I just mumbled that I was a bit unwell and that there was nothing to get upset about.

Sue gave me some peculiar looks in the ambulance. She said I started to go an interesting shade of bluey-grey. I remember feeling irrationally irritated because she seemed unusually concerned that I should not be sick again. I kept thinking, here's me dying and all my Sue is worried about is me making a mess over the ambulance. What I didn't know was that the doctor had told her it was touch and go. He had warned that I must not be sick. To lose another drop of blood could mean the next mention I got in the papers would be in the obituary column.

Strangely enough as I lay there with the life ebbing out of me, I had a warm glow on. I felt all lovely. 'Don't worry,' I kept repeating to Sue. 'I'm all lovely.'

I heard my Sue start to yell and give somebody a mouthful. The ambulance had stopped at the time. Apparently strikers were picketing the hospital gates and were holding up the traffic. Bloody great, I thought, Ronnie Knight victim of picket protest. That should make a good headline or two. But Sue's jumping up and down act got us through. They moved real quick at the Angala transfusion clinic in Malaga, which had taken about half an hour to reach from my home. They said I'd lost a lot of blood. I could not be sure exactly how much because they were rabbiting on not only in Spanish, but in litres. But I gathered it was several pints.

All the necessary equipment was wheeled in to set up a drip to give me the life-saving transfusion. I took a good look around and felt a certain sense of unease. Almost an animal-like whiff of impending doom. My reaction was to ask whose blood I was about to receive. The nurse told me it was fresh out of the blood bank, so not to worry. But worry I most certainly did. 'No, no,' I hissed. 'Don't give me that. Please don't.' I'd heard all the stories. And despite my frail condition panic set in. I was terrified of catching Aids. The nurse was telling me that without the transfusion I would die and that I had better not cause any more fuss. I was completely torn.

Just then Sue walked in. Thank heavens, I thought, I am saved. I knew she was the same blood type as me, group A, so I said can I please have some of my Sue's blood, 'cos I knew that was nice and pure with nothing wrong. My Sue said 'Si.' Of course, she said. How much did they want?

'About eight or nine pints.'

Sue said stuff it.

A pint or two was all right. But a gallon! Sorry, she said. I was dying and my Sue was arguing about giving me a few pints of her blood. Lovely.

I said: 'Thank you very much Sue, I'll do the same for you some time.'

She loved me. But eight pints! She just didn't have it in her.

The doc was getting a bit hot under the collar. 'What wrong with you?' he asked.

I told him what was scaring the dying daylights out of me.

'Aids? You are not serious,' he responded in that cute Manuel lisp. 'There is no Aids. No trouble.'

The choice was mine. Either I had the blood or I would die within a few minutes. Eventually I became so weak that I couldn't care less about anything except that they kept me alive. I'd worry about the Aids peril at a later date. I couldn't understand how they could pump twenty pints into me when I knew your body only held around nine pints. The simple answer was that most of it was being lost just as quickly. I just thought they were thickening the stuff up a bit.

I had an emergency operation to do whatever they do to ulcers. They stitched me back up. Then I just wanted to be left alone. I felt whacked out. Drained. Like I'd been half kicked to death by a mass battalion of spiders all wearing little football boots.

*

I was well and truly down-in-the-dumps. I had to sort myself out. As I lay there in the hospital bed I told myself that the time had come for some long, hard and honest soul-searching. What had caused my illness had been worry. The constant pressure of what was likely to happen to me and my Sue. Knowing that at any time of the day or night we could be arrested, put in prison – or extradited. It was a lot to live with.

The never-ending frustration at being unable to do or say anything about all those stories had been the worst. The misery of being imprisoned in my own house every time there was some panic in Fleet Street and the reptiles descending like a plague of blood-sucking locusts had taken its toll and almost bumped me off. I suffered from an attack of wounded pride and consuming sense of injustice. I thought to myself: 'For Jesus Christ's sake accept that worry is definitely what gave you a bleedin' ulcer in the first place. It was anxiety that done it. Trying to play Jack the Lad, pretending that nothing's getting you down, when all the time it's been nibbling away like a rat trapped in a ball of Edam cheese.

'You have been bottling it all up, until something had to give. It was bound to burst.'

That's the truth of the matter, I told myself. Once I had admitted the fact I vowed that would be the end of it. I would not allow myself to get in a state like that, not ever again. I thought to myself: 'I hope and pray that they will leave me alone.' I never worried about getting another ulcer 'cos I was told that once you've had one you're not likely to suffer another, advice which I am now told was based more on hope than fact.

When I started to recover I tried to adopt a calmer and more tranquil attitude to life. 'They've done you once and you just cannot get your Y-fronts in a twist about it all again,' I kept telling myself. It wasn't the British police who were on my back. The Spanish cops had always been marvellous, even when the hordes of reporters were crawling all over the place. The British Press had done me all the time. Just as they had from the very beginning, when they decided to tie me in with the crimes because of my brothers. They kept coming out with the allegations so consistently that everybody assumed they must be true. It was only a matter of time before the Spanish newspapers and other European publications jumped on the bandwagon.

But, as I kept telling myself, I mustn't let it get me down. The way I looked at it was that if I hadn't married Barbara Windsor and got involved with the glittering showbusiness crowd nobody would have been very interested in Ronnie Knight, club-owner. As it was, through no fault of my own, I became a sort of shadow-celebrity. I never done anything to court the role – and I have never been very comfortable in it. On the other hand I must be honest and confess that when I first started having me photo in the paper and everybody seemed pleased to meet me, it did give me a certain buzz. I suppose everybody likes to be a somebody, if they are honest about it. It made me feel important. I was not just a nameless face among the East End jungle I was brought up in.

But it was that pure accident of marrying a famous sex-symbol actress that got me lumbered. There was no doubt about that. From the day I left that hospital bed I realized that I'd got to try and put all that rubbish aside and live as normal a life as possible.

So when I read the comic stories I dismissed them as of no importance. I stopped hiding myself in dark corners of restaurants, hoping that no rubber-neckers would see me. If people did recognize me I no longer hung my head and scuttled away. Instead I beamed the molars at all and sundry. Peace with good luck to everybody, was the attitude I tried to adopt. I could not let my unwanted notoriety worry me no more. Not after it almost worried me to death. I knew that unless I kept cool I could easily go under again. That was an inadvisable state to get into on account that there might not be no second chances. 'I cannot let them do it to me again.' That's what I kept repeating like an African grey every time I felt my blood pressure starting to boil.

I've just been looking through a catalogue of false allegations that were made over a period of just a few months. 'Runaway Ron Faces

Ruin . . . My Dirty Rat of a Husband . . . Strain in Spain Ruins my Sex Life . . . Ronnie Knight's Secret Son . . . Costa Ron Coming Back.' There's a pile of cuttings about a mile high. You would have to be made of cast iron not to be affected by the really wicked lies. All that baloney about me going off to Rio, buying a 'second hideaway' in Morocco. Who swallowed that? The rubbish of me and my Sue jetting into London to see a gynaecologist 'risking arrest because he is so desperate to become a father'. Ronnie Knight slipping into Gibraltar just because he fancied a pint of the old British wallop!

Getting branded as a drug dealer did not thrill me. I hate drugs. I wouldn't give a pusher the time of day. I'd push him into a hole and fill it up with cement if I had my way. Drugs ruin young lives. You hear about people jumping off the top of buildings 'cos they think they can fly. They get Aids from using needles. Drugs and anybody connected with them gives me the creeps. I loathe them. I would rather be called a bank robber than a drug merchant. I'd rather not be called either. But if they cannot live without lying and it has to be one or the other, make it bank robber. Any day.

*

Whatever you do in this world there is a price to pay. Like not seeing your son till he is twelve years old.

Walking out on your kids means that you relinquish some of the joys of being a dad, watching them grow up and go out into the world. It's true that you also miss the undoubted heartache, worry and sleepless nights that are part and parcel of being a parent. All things considered, however, I sometimes feel a bit sad that I did not see more of my children.

I reckon it all goes back to that dreadful day when my little Lorraine saw me coming and scooted off like a born sprinter. That little episode haunted me for years. The experience was a strange mixture of shame, guilt, confusion and a peppering of anger. But after I got over the shock of that brief encounter I kept thinking about them a lot. Well, it's only natural, I suppose. I had a few temptations to go and sneak a peek at them, but somehow acting like a Peeping Tom was not my style. The more I thought about it, the more it didn't seem right that I should interfere with their lives. I had made my choice. I had got to live with things the way they had turned out. You make your bed and you has to lie in it, as they say.

When the news came down the grapevine that June had gone and

169

got remarried to a nice man who used to be on the floor below us in the Highbury flat I felt really pleased for her. I remembered the guy as a nice, quiet, steady sort of individual. After the likes of me I suppose June wanted nothing more than a peaceful life. They moved out to the country, to Kent or somewhere, I recall. From what I heard they were all very happy. They took his name, of Randall. I confess that didn't over-please me at the time. But they obviously liked him, so what's in a name, I asked myself? Besides, it was comforting for me to know they were nicely settled.

I missed them, though. As the years passed I got more nostalgic and kept wondering how the children had turned out. I don't mind admitting that it got to be a real ache inside me. So one day I decided to chance my arm, prepared to accept that if I got it bitten off in the process I could not really complain. I got a message to June saying how much I would like to see the children and if she could find it in her heart I would be most grateful if she would consider a nice family reunion. Somewhat to my surprise June agreed. I knew for sure that I had hurt her a lot in the last few years of our marriage. I had not exactly bestowed her with matrimonial bliss. I had done her wrong. But gawd bless the girl, she was prepared to let bygones be bygones.

We made a meet at Harringay Station and I scurried along there like a nervous teenager on his first proper date. When I saw my little children I had this big lump in my throat. I couldn't believe it. I looked at my Lorraine. She wasn't little at all. She was nearly seventeen, almost grown up. Jesus Christ, I said to myself, she's a lovely young lady. She was like her mum, both in looks and temperament. She clung to her mother, just like June had always been hanging on to her old lady like they were joined at the sides.

Gary was shy. Big for twelve, I thought. Cor, and going to be good looking just like his dad! You could see it in him already.

June had brought her sister Rene along, for a bit of moral support, and it was all a bit stiff and strained for a few seconds. Anyway we looked each other over and hundreds of thoughts flashed through my mind, about things long said and done. It's a strange feeling seeing your ex-missus after all those years. Very peculiar indeed.

'Hello, June,' I said in a nice bouncy voice. 'It's really nice to see you. Been a long time, ennit?'

Over twelve years. Time does flash by.

June nodded and smiled sweetly.

The conversation was not exactly earth-shattering. But it broke the ice. June proceeded to introduce me to Lorraine and Gary. 'This is your father, Lorraine, Do you remember him?'

If she did she didn't let on. She continued to entwine herself round June.

Being presented to Gary like some long-lost relative was a bit of an eerie experience. But we got through it.

All I could think of was that I wanted to buy them something. June wasn't wild about me spoiling them, but she agreed to come down to Wood Green shopping centre so we could have a look around. I was bursting a gut to tell Gary that at his age I was making the grade with Tottenham Juniors. I mentioned it casually in passing, hoping that he would be suitably impressed. He seemed quite pleased, so in we nips to a sports shop. Out we came with Gary the proud possessor of a complete soccer outfit. Everything from boots to ball . . . and as you might expect in the white strip of the glorious Tottenham Hotspurs.

Lorraine and her mother somehow managed to walk together like the glue had set. I thought it would be lovely to get a nice watch for Lorraine, but I had a heck of a job getting them into a jeweller's. Eventually Lorraine saw one she fancied. Then I told June I would like to get something special for her as well.

'No, really,' she blushed. 'I don't want anything. I couldn't.'

So I bought her a watch, similar to my Lorraine's.

It turned out to be a very peculiar reunion. Like thinking you've won the pools, but not sure you posted the coupon. But if I had to make a judgement, I would say it was quite a happy day. That was the last time I saw Lorraine or June or Rene. And another good few years was to flash by before I met Gary again.

I was in the A and R one night when Mickey Regan's brother Brian says that there's a fellow with a young lady that wants to see me. Full of your natural curiosity I goes over and there stands this strapping, handsome young man.

'Hello dad, remember me?' says Gary.

'Course I recognized him straight away. With those good looks he made a fine figure of a man. How could anybody mistake him for anything other than the son of Ronnie Knight?

When I asks him what he fancies to drink he says: 'I'll have a pint of mild and bitter.'

No you won't, I told him, on account that classy joints like this don't serve pints. Especially of mild and bitter. So he settled for a lager and his young lady had a short. We got to talking father-and-son chat and we was nice and relaxed and comfortable. The years of parting seemed to melt away.

Soon Gary was regularly visiting me and Barbara up in Stanmore. Following the change in my domestic arrangements he was a welcome guest staying with me and Sue and I am pleased to say that we all got on really lovely together.

Gary's now got a lovely wife called Sharron and she is like one of my own. I love that girl. She's nice and sweet. Once the news leaked out that Gary Randall was the son of Ronnie Knight the Press, naturally, had a field day. One headline screamed out: 'My dad dumped me.' The very next week in the same rag it was: 'Ron's son dumps wife.' It's true that my boy went off the rails and got involved with another lady. He made the sort of silly mistakes that seem to be about your norm for headstrong young men. Deep down inside I somehow didn't feel qualified to lecture him on the subject of sound and good domestic behaviour. My own track record was not one to hold up as a blue-print for my Gary's future happiness.

But he's thirty now and is settling down nicely with his Sharron. They come over to see us whenever they can and we have some happy family times together. We have a good relationship. He wants everyone to know that I am his real father. And I'm proud of him.

It's a pity about never again seeing Lorraine. Last I heard she had two children. Maybe it's three by now. I'm a grandfather and I haven't seen any of them. I would love to. If my Lorraine was ever to get in touch and say she wanted to renew acquaintances I'd be trilling like a skylark. If she were ever to say to me: 'Dad, can I bring your grandchildren to see you?' I would welcome them with open arms. But the move would have to come from Lorraine. It wouldn't be right for me to interfere in the life she has made. Deep in my heart I doubt that we will ever meet again.

I have come to accept that I will never again see my daughter or my grandkids. That's the price I am paying. It saddens my little heart. But I cannot complain. Can I?

*

One thing that always surprises me is how surprised most people are when they get to know me. After about five minutes of friendly socializing they start to admit that I don't live up to their expectations of how a hard-nut villain should behave. They expect to meet a right bastard, throwing his weight around and demanding 'What about a fuckin' drink, then?' It doesn't take long for folk to change their minds about Ronnie Knight. Most of them eventually confess that they had believed all the garbage in the scandal sheets. The worst impression they take away is that I am a bit of a rascal. But a lovable one.

15

One of the villainous 'Famous Five'. That's what they say I am. All part of the firm involved in the £7m Security Express job. That is what is always put about: that I am intimately associated with four other criminals and that together we live in the lap of luxury on the Costa del Sol on our ill-gotten gains.

One article put it this way: 'They are lapping it up . . . the sun, sea, birds and booze and all on an unlimited budget.

'That's the lot of villains who have taken the money and run, too far away to get their collars felt . . . they are wanted for crimes from massive drug dealing to handling missing millions.'

In scores of newspaper and magazine articles my mug has been printed alongside a 'rogues' gallery' of known and hardened criminals. I have had the rare distinction of being called 'Britain's Most Wanted Man'. When you think about it, it is not the most flattering of descriptions. Freddie Foreman, described as 'The Mean Machine', is currently being held on bail in Britain after being extradited last summer. It is darkly hinted that I am a member of his firm. He is a well-known East End hard man, formerly associated with the Kray Twins and a long-term acquaintance of the Old Bill. He has considerable form, including being sentenced to ten years for his part in the 1969 gangland killing of Jack 'The Hat' McVitie. The Krays got life for that macabre murder. McVitie, who was supposed to have upset the Twins by defying their territorial rights, was knifed to death.

The other members of the so-called 'Five' are Ronald Everett, also frequently described as a Kray Twins henchman. He is an old pal of Foreman's and nobody denies they have done business together. John James Mason, a former company director, was cleared in 1976 of conspiracy in the £8m robbery at the Bank of America in Mayfair. Finally, Clifford Saxe. Out of Hackney, where he was landlord of The Fox in Kingsland Road, where it has frequently been claimed that both the Security Express and Brinks-Mat heists were planned.

So that's the picture. Five old lags (all in their fifties and sixties) on the run from British justice – that's what the papers say. But it is not necessarily the truth. There is absolutely no doubt whatsoever that we all have a lot in common. We are all out of the East End. We are well known to each other, We all have police records. We all, at various times, moved to the Costa del Sol, where there was no extradition treaty between Britain and Spain. We are all wanted over the Security Express robbery. I am the first to admit that for Ronnie Knight the picture looks rather black. The circumstantial evidence, on the face of it, is pretty damning. Sometimes it does not surprise me that even fair-minded people might be tempted to put two and two together and come up with your 'Famous Five'. I do not deny that it all seems very suspicious indeed, veering far beyond the realms of coincidence, even though I first discovered the Costa long before anybody had heard of multi-million pound security raids. I do not deny that I did a bit of business with one or two of them. But never business of your criminal kind. Not bank-robbing, nor raiding, nor any sort of what you might call proper villainy.

I knew Cliff Saxe for donkeys' years back, to when we were ragged-arsed youths together running round the back streets. I really got to know him when I first joined the scaffolding firm. We worked together on the same site, having a laugh and drink and that. Cliff was a good friend of my Johnny's and he became partners with him in the infamous Fox pub. He was always throwing parties there and I went to a good many of them. We chatted a lot at those do's, mostly chewing over the bad old days when we used to work our nuts off on those steel scaffolds in all winds and weathers. Me and Cliffy Saxe, we got on all right. We were pals. I go back with Fred Foreman even longer. When Fred came out after doing the ten for the McVitie killing, he took to coming round the A and R where a lot of colourful people used to gather, as aforementioned. After his bird Fred was presumably short of what you might call a regular income. He had to get into a line of business to bring in the necessary, didn't he? Something straight and simple and strictly legitimate, since the last thing he wanted was any more trouble with the law. After carefully considering the opportunities on offer Freddie decided that the answer to his dilemma was to cash in on the boom in pub pool tables. Fred knew everyone in South London, he got on well with my partner Mick, so we formed a little company and did the tables together.

Fred and me became mates. I do not deny it. We used to go out to dinner regularly. Me and Barbara and Fred and his old woman

175

Maureen. Sometimes I'd go out with them when Barbara was away, 'cos I was lonely and hated eating on my own. The pool tables lark was a good business. A very nice little earner indeed. No bones about it. We first had them in pubs, then branched out to other sites like mini-cab firms, cafes and any other places where people hung around and there was space for a six-by-four. The beauty of it was that the overheads were low and the business virtually ran itself. We used to get together once a week and in the early hours of a Thursday or Friday morning so we would go round and empty the coin boxes. They needed doing only every two weeks. So if we did twenty-five one week and twenty-five the next, it was no bother.

No one can deny it was good money. I was getting between £1,500 and £2,000 a week. It helped Fred get back on his feet after his time away. And it enabled me to carry on my growing reputation as the biggest spender in town. With being alone so much I was always inviting people out – and I was always the buyer. Blimey, I wish I had some of that sort of money now. I could use it. But in those days I thought it would never end. Hope – and the money – flowed eternal. 'Course, like all good little tickles in life, it was too good to last. Eventually the brewers and licensees began to catch on. They booted us out and installed their own tables. Still, it was good while it lasted.

That firm-footing pools table arrangement was as far as it went with Fred. We had the business and we mixed socially. We were close. Freddie's other interests – if he had any and whatever they were – had nothing to do with me. The only bother I ever got in with him was picking up a parking ticket one night he was out on the town.

Big Ronnie Everett and Johnny Mason I know only from them coming up regularly to the club. They were always there. Just good customers.

When I was working in London I suppose I often went on about my lovely little paradise down on the sunny Costa, especially when it was grey and miserable in England. I'd talk to lots of my mates about how I could get away – and within a few hours could be in a warm, airy place in Spain, swimming in me pool without a care in the world. I'd go on about how you could buy spacious villas for a song, have dinner and a night out on the town for next to nothing – and the weather was lovely all the time. You would have thought I was being paid to promote the virtues of Southern Spain, which in those early 1970s days was still virtually undeveloped. I was so much in love with the Costa Del Sol that I suppose my enthusiasm sounded like a sales pitch. A lot of people must have been impressed, because pretty soon they were buying houses close by. Among them were Messrs Foreman, Saxe, Everett and Mason.

Scores of people I knew, including showbiz folk, came and settled down on the fast developing Costa. It was inevitable that we would get together socially from time to time. Anywhere you go in the world you will find the British tend to congregate and make their own little bit of the home country. Like in the Colonial days when the fellas would sit around India and Africa dressed in tailcoats and starched collars with the temperatures soaring into the hundreds. It's the same with the ex-patriates on the Costas. There are places you can go and you would never guess you were in Spain if it wasn't for the palm trees and waiters. There are restaurants where there's only roast beef and Yorkshire pudding on the menu. With English mustard.

Down on the Costa Del Sol, as millions of holidaymakers know well, there is a little bit of old London. And in the centre of that lot is your East End crowd. They stick together, don't they? Bound to. It's only natural. You go to the same restaurants, clubs and night places. Play golf and bowls. The Costa del Sol is just like a little village and you just cannot help bumping into people you know all the time. But if I saw the so-called other 'Four' more than three or four times a year it was unusual.

When me and Sue got married I invited them all. Sure I did. I could not leave them out. It would have been rotten of me not to ask them, whatever the Press might say about it. My attitude was that they were people I had known for years, whatever they might or might not have done. We never discussed their business affairs. It is not the sort of thing you do in those circles. You do not open conversations with talk like: 'How many times you been inside then?' Or 'What they get you for?' As far as I was concerned my wedding was a big, happy celebration and I asked practically every person I knew to join in the festivities. Most of them were ordinary, decent, hard-working citizens.

I got criticized. But that's life, as they say.

16

My Sue made an honest man of me one fine Thursday morn in 1987.
June 4 is a date I always try to remember. Not just for sentimental
reasons. If I forget our anniversary Sue gives me a right rollicking.

The civil ceremony at Fuengirola Town Hall was the best kept
secret of the year.

All the Press had discovered that we were getting married, because
we had to put the banns up in the British Consulate in Malaga. They
were on the wall for three weeks, so it was obvious some nark was
going to tip them off. But everybody thought it would be on a
Saturday. Not even our vicar knew the truth, until the last minute.
We fooled everybody.

After spending the best part of twelve months cutting through all
the red tape and making all the complicated arrangements we didn't
want a thing to go wrong. So we planned the quiet, simple civil
ceremony, with just a handful of close friends. Ron Popely, one of my
oldest pals, who used to have the Bethnal Green pub, was my best
man.

If the Press boys had been there they would have had a field day
because they missed a picture scoop. It happened like this. The town
hall also leads off to the courtroom and nick. We were sitting there
waiting for the Spanish Registrar to call us in when suddenly half a
dozen handcuffed prisoners barged into the room. There we are, my
Sue and me, surrounded by a gang of cons, with a load of coppers
rounding them up. For a while it got really confusing with us mixed up
in a right little mêlée. I thought, good God, if they could see me now.
The headlines would have gone something like: 'Ronnie Knight – in
with the prisoners . . . he should be going with them not up the aisle
. . . wanted Ron in cons drama.' I went cold at he knees just thinking
about it. Can you imagine? Fortunately it was our secret. It was about
the only time we managed to organize anything without it becoming
front-page news.

Only the previous year I had arranged a great New Year celebration knees-up at one of our locals. It was a really good 'do' with champers, a seven-course nosh up, a comic and singer. That little affair was splashed all over the place. 'Auld Lang Syne' was what some bright spark came up with. Two indelible memories remain from that affair. One being that my Sue got so upset and angry she rather let herself down by giving a dramatic two-finger greeting to a pushy photographer. That picture made the front page and she has never got over the indignity of it. The other unforgettable fact was that the venture, a mixture between pleasure and business, cost me a small fortune. I charged about sixty quid a head, but it nowhere near covered the costs and I had to dig deep into my own pocket. That's one little deal I don't talk about.

Following our secret wedding, the fittest and finest of the Press was out in full force the following Saturday, when we had a blessing and reception at the El Oceano, a lovely restaurant-cum-club and sports centre right on the beach – a place favoured by boxer Frank Bruno. It was inevitable that it would be turned into a circus. But there was nothing I could do about it. There were almost as many reporters and photographers as guests. I remember thinking that with all the things happening in the big, wide world – all the tragedy, the life-and-death situations – what the hell were they doing spending so much time and money on a couple of people getting hitched? I bet it must have cost hundreds of thousands of pounds for all the newspapers and television people to send down their teams of sniffy-nosed news-hounds and snappers. One television company hired a helicopter and others a couple of boats so they could pry with their long lenses from a hundred yards out at sea.

We had originally planned to make our entrance by way of a launch, but hurriedly cancelled it when we knew that the Press had cottoned on.

In situations like that there's only one thing you can do: grin and bear it and make the best of things. That's exactly what we did. Like I said, lots of my old connections from the East End were there, though it was inevitable that other mysterious 'underworld heavies' would be invented. 'A typical gangland-style wedding' was how it was described.

Did I know I was inviting trouble by asking along people like Freddie Foreman and co.? Frankly I did not. And if I'm honest with myself I would probably not have asked them had I realized what a kerfuffle it was going to create. Some papers reported that Great

Train robber Charlie Wilson and James Hussey were there. It just so happened that they cocked it up by taking pictures of one of my chums, name of John Ashmore, who is a respectable businessman. They wrongly named him as a villain and he sued them for the mistake. My heart bled for the poor papers responsible.

The reporters were beside themselves because they could not break through the strict security we had imposed. So what facts they could not uncover they made up as usual. I am supposed to have come out with little gems like: 'It's a fair cop . . . this is one sentence I don't mind serving.' I am supposed to have jumped on the tables and started singing 'I Left My Heart in San Francisco'. According to reports the big hoot of the night was everybody joining in a chorus of 'Jailhouse Rock'. Of course, you would be bound to sing that at a wedding reception, wouldn't you?

The flow of false information was endless. According to the absent witnesses our wedding cake was created in the shape of Wandsworth Prison. That was in pretty poor taste, I thought.

But knowing that our couple of hundred guests were having a smashing time made up for most of the aggro. My Sue was beautiful. Stunning. She wore a lovely dress of ivory silk and satin and carried orchids and salmon roses. It cost around £3,000 and worth every peseta, I thought. I bought her a lovely diamond-studded wedding ring . . . and my big surprise gift was a black BMW 325i sports car. She was thrilled to bits.

The biggest pork pie spread about our nuptials was that the celebrations cost £30,000 – including a £10,000 firework display. Let me put matters in perspective: the rockets and Catherine wheels set me back about eight hundred quid. The whole affair, including both wedding parties, left me change out of ten grand. Not cheap, I'll grant you. But I took the view that it was third time lucky, so I dipped into my savings.

What never occurred to me then was that back in London my ex-wife Barbara, who was a bit down on her luck at the time, would believe all the bedtime stories she was reading. But apparently she was wound up sufficiently for her to say some unkind things about me. She never did get over that miserable, wet Monday morning when we tied the knot. It haunted her all down the years and it seemed she absolutely seethed when she compared it to the super way things went for me and Sue.

For me the biggest upset of our day was that the Anglican preacher who blessed our union, the Rev. Ronald Matheson, came in for some stick. He was heavily criticized in certain quarters for helping us out. I thought it was appropriate the way he replied: 'If someone asks for God's blessing, who am I to refuse?' That was very Christian of Rev Matheson, a very nice gentleman. He got a good reward a few weeks later when he again officiated at the wedding of another celebrity, the comic called Des O'Connor.

Sue and I had barely completed our honeymoon and got over the nastiness of some of the Press reports when I was faced with a real shock to my nervous system. Millions of readers of the *News of the World* in Britain were told that Ronnie Knight, 'The runaway playboy', had been named as 'the mastermind behind a huge Spanish drug-smuggling ring'. It claimed that a Scotland Yard informer had said that I was the brains behind an international drugs racket that had been uncovered by Spanish detectives. They said I had used stolen money to finance the operation in Morocco.

Yet again an unnamed senior detective was quoted, this time as saying: 'If we can convince the Spanish police that Knight is running drugs from the Costa del Sol they might send him back.' I doubt if that mysterious detective ever existed. If he did and said that he was either nuts or drunk as a skunk. As outrageous invention went that rotten falsehood just about took the prize. Nobody ever convinced the Spanish authorities of anything. Because like almost everything else it was a total fabrication.

17

You cannot deny the truth of those wise old sayings. Things like 'a stitch in time; a trouble shared; half a loaf; patience is a virtue; look before you leap.'

And 'hell hath no fury like a woman scorned!'. Gawd love me, were there ever truer words in the English language! If I ever had any doubts about just how far a woman would to get her revenge, twist the knife and go for the jugular I was about to find out. My ex-missus, the cheery, bubbling, happy-go-lucky Barbara Windsor was out to cook my goose.

It was in July 1987, about a month after me and my Sue had married and were settling down nice and happy. Barb had got her divorce on January 2nd a couple of years earlier on the grounds that we had been apart for two years. It was all nice and civilized. There was no fuss. No scandal. That nice man of hers, Stephen Hollings, had celebrated Barbara's freedom by romantically presenting her with a single red rose and they toasted their future happiness together in champers. I remember thinking at the time that it was a nice, theatrical touch.

They got married, took over the Plough Inn in Amersham, Bucks and I was the first to wish them 'happy ever after'.

Barb and me had had a stormy few years together. It hadn't all been sunshine and roses for us but I had some nice, warm memories. Who wants to be nasty and bear grudges? Life's too short. We had a few pleasant little chats on the phone. Every few weeks. Nothing too intimate or endearing. She told me that she was settled and happy.

I can never be sure, but I reckon it must have been me and Sue getting married that turned her. That's the only reason I can think of: the fact that I'd laid on a big celebration for my Sue and given her the motor and a diamond bracelet. As I say, Barb never did get over that wet Monday morning Register Office job of ours. She must have read all the hot air about me spending a massive fortune on a wedding firework display and her fury must have started to erupt like a Roman Candle.

Next we heard she was talking to reporters:

'For 20 years,' she was quoted, 'I've been waking up at 5.30 a.m. with a start . . . that was the time the police always called to pull Ronnie in – at least twice a year through our marriage.'

I cannot in all honesty deny that our slumbers were frequently disturbed by the uninvited arrival of the police. But that was most certainly not of my making and was due to circumstances entirely beyond my control. None the less Barbara always blamed me for it.

In the papers she expressed the considered opinion that I would be hauled back to Britain, much against my wishes, within the next six months. In interviews Barbara made it sound as though my number was well and truly up. 'Things are about to erupt for Ronnie . . .' she was opining. If there wasn't a ring of menace about that, I don't know.

Pals were soon on the dog and bone asking what it was all about. Was Barbara giving new evidence against me over the Security Express business?

While I'm still recovering from the shock of that little lot I am further informed that Barb has sold her story to the *Sun* newspaper. Exclusive. What's she gone and done that for? I asked myself. What is more she is appearing in telly adverts with lines like: 'You ain't heard nothing yet . . . I'm gonna tell all.' She also kept on about 'opening up my little diary and letting out all the secrets'. Diary? She never had no time for filling in any diary. She never had time for nothing but furthering her career.

People I'd known for years were suddenly looking me straight in the eyes and challenging: 'You sure you had nothing to do with it, Ron . . . after all your ex old woman's laying it on heavy on the telly.' One mate actually said: 'Has Barb got anything on you Ron? It looks like she's turning evidence.' I tried to laugh it off and told people to take no notice.

Then I had tapes of the telly ads Barbara was making sent over . . . I could not believe what I saw and heard. I got on the blower and I asked Barbara what she was trying to do to me. 'I'm not doing much,' she said a bit on the quiet and reserved side.

I told her she was 'cos I had seen her on the telly . . . 'You wait and see what I got to say in the paper.' That was her line.

So I asked Barbara what the hell was going on? Was she planning to do a Bradshaw on me and try to swear my life away? She told me it was nothing at all like that. Barb said: 'The police come round and took me to Leman Street. They told me to tell them everything I knew and that they would look after me when they brought you home. They said they would hide me.'

Barbara went on: 'They asked me more questions. They asked if I knew where you had been on that day. I said I didn't know. I said you came and went and I didn't know where you were.'

She was so convincing I believed her. How could anybody make a song and dance about that straightforward little routine, I asked?

'I don't know, Ronnie,' she whispered.

But what about all this 'little diary' stuff and the newspaper?

'It's nothing . . . nothing at all, Ronnie. Just a little story.'

'That's all right then,' I said calming down considerably.

A little story! Was Hiroshima a bit of a damp squib? Did Noah prepare for a heavy shower? Was Genghis Khan a social misfit?

Barbara almost destroyed me with her charming little piece. She inflicted wounds from which I will never really recover.

Whatever the reason, grave damage was done to Ronnie Knight's already dubious reputation. Fury? Next time I'll take my chances in hell.

When I saw the massive headlines I almost choked. 'My rat of a husband . . . The Two-Timer.' That was just for starters. Next day it was 'It was so easy to hate him . . .' I remember thinking that if this lot was Barb's notion of a little story, thank God she wasn't getting really upset about our lives together. Talk about an ordeal by fire. My ex-missus lit a furnace and seemed intent on roasting me alive.

'I have always painted Ronnie as a brightly-shining Knight who deserved my loyalty during his horrendous murder trial . . .' she confided in the strictest confidence to about twelve million avid readers. She said she had 'played along with his image as a Cockney rogue with a lovable charm'. But she could not go on lying about her horrid ex-hubby, she complained. She cheekily then referred to me as 'Britain's most wanted man'. She harped on about how she had paid the mortgage, hinting that I was a small-time baddie who could not even pay my way.

During our colourful marriage Barb had given me the odd meaningful ear-bashing, same as you get in most domestics. I mean marriage is not all bliss is it? But this was something different. Perish the thought, but it was almost as if someone was putting words in her mouth as she lashed into me in that article. She said I was nasty, underhand and had conned her over my marriage to Sue. I thought

184

that particular grouse was a bit rich, especially as she had already remarried and had settled down. I could also have reminded her that even before I moved in with Sue she had told me that she had found someone new in her life. I didn't drag all that up because it was in the past. What's the use of causing more distress?

The more I thought about it the more I became convinced that it must have been the wedding that got Barbara's hackles up. What else could it be but jealousy? I could think of no other explanation. Until I married Sue, Barbara hadn't had a bad thing to say about me. But as soon as me and Sue are Mr and Mrs, Barb couldn't wait to spoil our happiness. If it wasn't jealousy then you tell me what!

In her colourful article Barbara went to great lengths to say she was not (repeat not) angry about me 'running off with a beautiful younger woman'. Yeah, and the Pope don't pray on Sundays.

In the next sentence she is admitting: 'What really made my blood boil was that he sent £20,000 up in smoke with wedding day fireworks.'

Barb said I was always wailing about being broke, that she owned half me villa and that I hadn't paid her 'a penny from my promised divorce settlement'.

I've just read it again . . . and after all these years I still cannot believe how Barb could have gone along with all that rubbish. She was slagging me off as a ruthless, uncaring villain. But I could never have been as wicked as she was being. It hurt to read it. It really did. She knows that we sorted out all our financial affairs when we said our fond farewells. If Barbara had had any grouse about money she would have brought it up before. But she never complained because there was no reason for it. It wasn't until the old green-eyed monster reared his ugly head, stirring up a hornet's nest of fuss again.

Barb said people had called her a gangster's moll when we were together. Well, that was the first I knew about it. Anyway, what did she want to go calling me a gangster for? It wasn't nice. Worse, she wrote that when she gave evidence for me at the Old Bailey murder trial she had blushed as she told everybody what a marvellous man I was. Now she was slagging me off as 'an ungrateful fugitive from justice . . . everything I have ever said about him is a bundle of lies.'

Well, there's a turn-up, I pondered to myself. If everything she had sworn to on oath had been a bundle of lies, what was this stuff she was dishing out now – for what I had been reliably informed was a handsome payment? I mean, how can you tell when the lies end and the truth, the whole truth and nothing but, begins?

Once she had warmed to her meaty role of giving me a roasting

Barb really went to town. She said I was so selfish I went out boozing while her old mum lay dying; that I insisted Barb left her hospital sick-bed just so that she could come home and cook my breakfast. And that I was so insanely jealous of her that I made her confess to what she called 'a harmless affair I had before we met'.

I have never denied that I deceived her rotten when I first fell for her. True, I did not volunteer the information that her indoors was looking after our daughter Lorraine at the time. As I've confessed, I am none too proud of that little bit of deceit. It was lousy of me. But if she had felt that strongly I don't know why Barb stuck with me when she eventually found out. She was rewashing all the dirty linen that I thought had been neatly laundered and stored away years ago.

I was a typical East End chauvinist, she revealed. I was awkward and out of my depth in her showbusiness world and she had to look after me like I was a little baby. Gawd grief, did she lay it on. I was inadequate, would rant and rave if she was a few minutes late. She said that she had to go on the road with touring shows to make ends meet. All those little matters considered I am full of admiration for Barb that she managed to stick with me and my millions of faults for all those years.

'Course she harped on about our wedding – Barb's and mine that is. No, she never forgot it. I doubt if she has got over it to this very day. I sometimes wonder how things would have turned out if me and Barb had had one of your fairy-tale type of weddings. You know, with the sun shining, bluebirds singing their heads off and a massed choir of angels.

Most of the stuff she dished out in that newspaper was hard to take. When we had been together she had always told me: 'Now don't you go believing what you read in the newspapers 'cos it's all lies.' Now she had fallen for the porkie about the twenty-grand firework display and the lavish reception. I reckon she must have considered I'd done about a hundred grand, which as you know is not the case.

She told the world she thought I was a rat because I got involved with Sue. But be fair. Barbara had several little liaisons during all those years she was on the road away from home. I never ridiculed or queried her over her indiscretions. And I am pretty sure she was tasting the culinary offerings of her little chef while we were still sharing the same breakfast table. But I never blamed her for that. If it made her happy, good luck to her. I had been unfaithful. True. But I was married to her for years before I strayed.

As I read all the stuff that Barb was writing about I could see that at

186

the time she must have been all bitter and twisted. I had been told that she was down on her luck. She must have been short of a bob or two. I have always thought it hard on women, particularly the beautiful ones, how frightening it can be for them when their looks start to fade. These days, the ravages of time can be challenged by the surgeon's knife and some judicious use of a bit of silicone here and there. Look at your Joan Collins, Raquel Welch and Sophia Loren. I mean when I was a nipper women of that age were wearing shawls, and peering over their specs reading the obit columns in the local paper to see how many of their old friends had passed on. But old age comes to us all in the end. That's why I felt it for Barbara. She had earned a good living and been famous for playing the archetypal, busty blonde. She could not carry on Carrying On forever. In the end that's what I put it down to in Barbara's case.

But some of her accusations were really below the belt.

She only went and told the world and his dog that she had to teach me how to read and write. If you want to make a bloke look like a real dickhead you have only got to hint at his secret difficulties with the pen and ink. It's a sure-fire winner, that one. It's like questioning a man's inclinations by delicately suggesting he likes black suspenders . . . even if they are a tight fit. So that reading and writing jibe was really sneaky. Barbara never taught me nothing. I have never been one of your academics, that is for certain. I have never studied Shakespeare in great depth and until I got down to writing this epic, my longest literary work had been a letter to me old mum.

It is true that I left Barbara to handle most of our written and verbal business affairs. Just like Sue does now. She deals with all enquiries, speaks to the banks, negotiates contracts, deals with phone messages and things like that. Sorting out the nitty-gritty problems of life is not my strong point. A lot of my mates are the same. They leave all that to their trouble and strife. I do it with Sue, like I did with Barbara. Women are more down to earth and efficient. It's only natural.

Another allegation that really upset me was Barbara's insistence that I had sneaked Sue into our matrimonial bed at the big house in Stanmore while she was treading the boards to make a crust for me. That was really nasty and mean. She said her old mum Rose had copped me between the sheets with Sue, that Sue had cursed at being discovered in the nude and that I had begged old Rosie not to spill the beans.

Sue had her own place. That's where we used to meet. Most of the time when Barb was away, I was virtually living there. There was no need for me to take Sue to Barbara's house. Anyway, I wouldn't have done it.

But Barbara was out to nail me and you have got to admit that if you accuse your old man of having another bird in the domestic double it does tend to make him look like a no-good rat-bag.

My old Barb went right over the top when I saw the words: 'Ronnie and his wife should have it on their consciences that they contributed to my mother's death by exposing her to their lust.'

Ooch! The least said about that the soonest mended.

I was also very cut up about Barbara claiming she had another abortion when she was forty-two. She put the blame on me by saying that our marriage was on the rocks and it was not fair to bring a baby into an unhappy domestic situation. If Barbara was having a baby at that time then she certainly did not mention it to me. I mean it is not the sort of event you can easily overlook.

'Terminating my pregnancy was an awful decision to make and I regret it' Barb wrote. Well, of course, it must have been hard. But she made it without consulting me.

I hate talking about things as personal as this. But Barb has had a great deal to say on the very sensitive subject and I just want to put the facts straight. The truth is that Barb never wanted children because babies tend to tie you down. That was the last thing she wanted. When she had one or two abortions early in our relationship – when we were both very much in love – she made the decisions then. I had been over the moon and would have loved her to have a child. But it was her life. She made the decision. I respected she had the right to do as she wished. She said she did not want children at that time because it would have interfered with her career. That was the most important thing in her life. She told our friends that she didn't want to be a mother because all she wanted in life was to be a wife to me. She said a child would get in the way of her devotion to me. She said: 'Why should I have a baby when I have got Ronnie to look after?' Barbara knew how I felt. I always wanted a family and was always pleading with her to settle down. I would have preferred her to be a wife and mum first and an actress second. But there was no way she would agree to that. The first time she was pregnant with me was just before we got married. But in the same breath as she told me the good news, she announced that she had already decided to end the pregnancy straight away. I was very disappointed. It hurt me.

That part-time marriage situation was what led to me seeking pastures new in the first place. Where I came from husbands and wives stayed together, through thick and thin. The wives had the dinner on the table of a night even if it did bake up in the oven sometimes.

There was one accurate story that Barbara revealed in her kiss-and-hate exposé of our time together: about having my hooter fixed. I finally got round to getting the schnozzle shaped to size after following it around for thirty-three years. I went to see one of your top plastic surgeons in Harley Street. I told him how my beak had always been a source of embarrassment and asked what he could do about it. My concern was that the educated snifter should in no way be robbed of its renowned sensitivity. The doc certainly knew his stuff. But while he was showing me the various models available, Barbara was begging me to stay just as I was.

'Your nose is part of you Ronnie. Don't mess about with it, 'cos I like it just the way it is,' she pleaded with me.

After all those years of praying I'd get it busted in a punch-up I couldn't wait to have the old hooter seen to.

When all the bruises and swelling had gone I took a long, hard look at the new Knight snifter and decided it was the best £250 I'd ever spent.

Time heals. Both re-shaped noses and emotional pain. I've got to admit that all the anger and resentment I felt for Barbara at the time has subsided a lot.

I spoke to her after that story appeared. I asked her why, because I had never done anything to her. But she never did say she was sorry.

My relationship is a lot better with Barbara now. She phoned up after me and Sue were arrested and spent the night in Malaga jail. Like always Sue answered the phone and Barbara said to her: 'I am just calling to say I care.' That was the first time she had said anything civil to Sue. She told me she was very sorry about what had happened to us. We had a little chat. I try to forgive her for everything. I would like us all to be friends again. Maybe we will all get together one day. Me and Sue and Barb and her bloke Stephen. Perhaps have a bit of dinner. That would be nice.

18

Some well-known television faces have knocked – and kicked – on my front door. Two of them are so-called intrepid reporters Brent Sadler, who works for ITN, and beefy Roger Cook, who fronts the Cook Report show, in which he appears as a champion of truth and integrity. Intrepid, did I say? More like insipid. Both of them. I hope that one day I have the pleasure of meeting them on what you might neutral territory. I'd really like to give them a piece of my mind. Or something similar.

Sadler staggered into my life like a walking casualty case. He was so pathetic I almost took pity on him. One night there's a helluva banging at the door. It was a fists and feet job and got me worried. Sue always answers the door, for obvious reasons, but this time I was so concerned I stood behind her, fearing it was a nut case on the other side. The door swings open and there he stands: Brent Sadler, the roving hero I had seen and admired on the telly scores of times acting like a goody two-shoes and a paragon of virtue. He had climbed over a fence into my garden where our Alsatian was supposed to be doing his fierce guard-dog bit. Now I knew that R.J. was about as dangerous as a mouse in a trap. But he is still a big, strapping animal, with a bark to match.

There was no way Sadler could have been absolutely sure that my boy wasn't just as ferocious as he appeared to be.

There Sadler stood at the door, with my guard dog licking at his hand like it was flavoured with best beef dripping. Sadler couldn't see me. But I had him in full view as he started to give Sue the line in patter that came out so smoothly it must have worked a hundred times before. He began with the bit about having no cameras, no tape recorder, no nothing. Not even a piece of paper on which he could record our encounter. He just wanted a little chat with Ronnie Knight to set the record straight. He wasn't like all the others who had done the dirty on me. He was a decent sort, who only wanted to get at the truth of the story. Sue is so impressed by this well-rehearsed twaddle that she tells him what he can do with his microphone. Thank you and good night.

She closes the door, politely as possible under the circumstances. Sadler seems to take this rebuff as a personal slight. He starts kicking again. Being a lady of some spirit Sue opens up again ready to have another quiet word in his ear on the merits of damaging other people's property. Before she can speak, Sadler is in fast as a cobra's tongue. This time it's the sob-story act. He starts blubbering. He's giving it to Sue about how his personal life is in turmoil. He's out of his mind with worry 'cos his missus or girlfriend was giving him the elbow. He was having so much trouble with her it was driving him out of his mind. In addition to which, he sobbed, he would get the sack if he didn't get an exclusive interview to send to the folks back home.

He was doing absolutely nothing for me with this load of bull droppings. Nothing at all. I was about to reveal myself when Sue interrupted him in full spate. It seems she was equally unimpressed with his drivel. She told him to pipe down.

'My husband has not the slightest desire to see you, speak to you or bid you good evening. So kindly clear off before I call the police,' she smiled sweetly.

She slams the door.

Then Sadler starts screaming and shouting enough to wake the dead.

'I know he's in there . . . tell him to fucking well come out and face me like a man,' he yelped.

This was not the Mr Cool Brent Sadler I had seen and admired on the box. I feared that maybe he had caught something nasty on one of his foreign assignments. Like rabies, or something. He was a demented nut-case. It occurred to me that a broken bone might give him some real cause to scream like a stuck pig. But Sue, bless her, in her wisdom suggested letting him get on with it. He eventually staggered away after exhausting himself with a torrent of abuse that seemed to somehow sober him up a bit. It crossed my mind what a stinking rat he was. Rotten as a six-month egg.

I wasn't too pleased with that guard dog of mine either. He cost me a fortune in keep, with his liking for a kilo or two of fresh meat.

And he had repaid me by fraternizing with intruders. I made a mental note to consider sending R.J. back to training school.

Next morning I made a bad mistake. An error as embarrassing as a Scotsman doing the Highland Fling suddenly remembering he has forgotten to don his undershorts. I ventured outside at lunchtime to barbecue a couple of sausages for my Sue's dad. He loves his bangers, does Bob. So there I am turning the four porkies over when a glint of sunlight on glass attracted my attention. Over on the craggy rock, not a hundred yards from my back door, I espied a camera crew, with a long lens pointing in my direction. That was the only film they ever got of me at my house. Now they use it every time they do me again, trying to make out it is new as mown hay. But it's years old. But I swear it's the same. Stop the film and you will see the living proof: four little sausages sizzling on the grill.

Roger Cook used that same bit of ancient footage when he blundered down in an attempt to turn me over at the time of our wedding. Of all the dirty tricks we have suffered over the years the tactics used by Cook took the prize for a new low in lying, cheating treachery. I had good advance warning that Cook, who had recently switched from radio to television, was planning an invasion of me and mine. He turned up with a massive crew of reporters, camera and sound men, producers, directors and local reporters to run around after him. Blimey, I thought, the famous director David Lean shot *Lawrence of Arabia* just up the coast in Almeria with a smaller team than Cook had trailing behind him. The enterprise must have cost them a hundred thousand quid or so, I reckon. All to get a few feet of me on film. If I hadn't been so pissed off I might have been flattered. Naturally Cooky had to have a helicopter to transport his elephantine frame out and about.

I know he is snooping around, since several people have already kept me posted on his activities, from where he is staying, who's with him and what he is planning to do. My little moles were right on the ball. So it is not exactly a bolt out of the blue when Cooky phones up and asks for an exclusive interview. Sue told him I was not interested. I had watched Cook and knew his technique. He always tried to stir people up, getting them to the pitch where they did something daft – like poke him one. Then he plays the hurt little hero, staring sorrowfully into the lens like he was suffering for the glory or mankind. There is no question that he is a convincing little performer. But I prefer my actors to be in plays. I wasn't falling for that. I knew that if Cook got me in front of the camera he would not be interested in finding out the truth. He would try to engineer a situation that would make him look brave and daring. He would taunt me, hoping I would lose my rag. That's the way he does it. You watch him on television. He always seems to be projecting himself.

Anyway, no sooner had Sue rejected Cook's clumsy advances than the peace of the neighbourhood was completely shattered. A great big helicopter swooped round the mountain, hovering only a few feet from our rooftop. At first I thought it was a coastguard patrol chopper off course. But when I looked up I could see Cook's great face peering down like a full moon in August; he could not see me because I was watching from a window. The noise and air disturbance created by the whirring blades had a devastating effect. Our friends and neighbours were out in their gardens, waving angrily at the vandals. The air was blue with their curses. All the petrified pets and animals on the mountain were howling, barking and running round in circles. Window panes shook fit to shatter. Our garden furniture, tables, chairs and loungers, were whisked into the pool and over the cliff. Our lovely plant pots and flowers were smashed and destroyed.

If I could have got my hands on two-ton Cooky he'd have got what he wanted all right. And what he deserved: a punch on his smirking mush. Thank God, I couldn't get at him. I was so furious I might have done something rash.

Then the infernal machine put down on top of a craggy hilltop about thirty yards away. Our long-suffering neighbours, mostly Americans, were beside themselves with fury at the outrageous intrusion. They were screaming and shouting at the people in the helicopter. I thought that Cook and Co. were behaving like loutish bully boys, prepared to go to any lengths and to upset anybody to get what they wanted. Their uncaring vandalism caused hundreds of pounds of damage.

I saw Cook clambering out of the helicopter on the rocks, obviously playing his hero bit to the cameras. While he was showing off I took Sue by the arm, walked up the garden path, jumped in our car and drove quietly off down the back streets. When I reached the coast 2,000 feet below I could see the helicopter still hovering above my house trying to sneak shots of me. Your clever super-sleuth had been so intent on getting his own pictures taken he hadn't even noticed that we had flown the coop.

Later I apologized to my long-suffering neighbours. God bless 'em, they were right behind me and didn't blame us for Cook's outlandish reign of terror. The Spanish police were furious. Flying the helicopter so close to a residential area had been stupid and dangerous. They broke all sorts of safety regulations and local by-laws. The cops were keen to arrest them. They wanted me to officially denounce him so they could throw him in jail.

As it happened I knew exactly where Cook and his crew were staying – at the Mijas hotel a few miles away. For a few seconds I was tempted to turn them in. The idea of smarty-pants Cook languishing in a Spanish nick for a few days gave me a sudden rush of joy. But again Sue was right. Whatever happened Cook would turn it all to his advantage. He would emerge as the shining hero, risking life and limb in his public duty to track down the villainous Ronnie Knight. He was the one who needed the publicity, not me. Having him picked up would have been just the sort of little drama he would have feasted on to glorify himself. Far as I was concerned he was just a big yob, who needed a lesson in good manners.

Later, from an inside source, I heard that he had recorded a piece saying that he was terrified that I might have a gun and shoot at him. What a berk! At least I don't think he had the gall to broadcast such a corny line. All I can say is that Cook's Central Television employers did not get very good value for the fortune they spent on his expedition. They even hired a boat to try and gate-crash my wedding reception. But all Cooky got for his trouble was a few feet of film showing houses and mountains and sea. He was so crooked that he used the same old footage of me out in the garden with the sausages, passing it off as new material he had shot.

Made a good pair did those two. Sadler and Cook. Like Laurel and Hardy. Or Little and Large. I have mentally recorded them as lovely people. Real stars.

*

Now and again in moments of weakness I have talked to journalists and television people believing I might get a fair crack of the whip. At least I hoped that my side of the story would get an airing. Soon after I was first invaded I agreed to face the cameras for a big television programme. They said their research showed that I owned lots of apartments, bars and villas, the innuendo being that they had all been bought with dirty money.

So I said to them, all right. Let's go and check it out. I took them to every address they had on their list. The real owners were not too happy when I told them that according to the television people I was supposed to hold the title deeds. The cameras whirred faithfully recording the events.

I answered other questions. I looked into the camera and didn't shirk. I spent a day with them going into all the little ins-and-outs they wanted to know about. You know what happened? When the programme came out they carried all the same accusations and rumours, without my denials. They gave me about twelve seconds, saying something completely unimportant.

So how could I trust any TV company after that little lot?

One or two journalists have written stories that got somewhere near the truth – but it's been like spitting into a blizzard. Some have really betrayed my trust and courtesy. They have come into our home, eaten with us and promised that this time everything would be strictly honest, accurate and truthful. Then they have made it up. They unashamedly tell the world I've asked them to turn me in to Scotland Yard. They've made it seem that I like nothing better than to sit here twisting the tail of the Old Bill, taking the rise out of the police. I do not deny that I've passed the occasional witty remark about the law, but most of the outlandish statements attributed to me have been made up.

Yeah, they've pulled some really slick tricks. Some journalists have made hundreds of thousands of pounds writing their fictionalized tales about me and what I was supposed to be doing/saying/thinking/planning. Not so long ago there was a big exclusive in your *The News of the World* claiming that Det. Supt. Peter Wilton, the Scotland Yard chief who had led the Security Express enquiry, had invited me and Sue to his wedding. 'Cop Invites Fugitive Ron to Wedding' screamed the headlines. The story said that Mr Wilton, who had retired, had sent a printed invitation to 'his old adversary, the fugitive Ronnie Knight'. On the back of the invitation, we all read, Wilton had impishly written 'My boys came to your wedding – can you come to mine?' To prove it was absolutely genuine the paper printed a copy of the invite. It looked a bit funny because the 'Ronnie and Sue' were written in one hand with the 'Knight' in another. I wonder if the readers noticed that little slip up. I can only assume that Mr Wilton, who turned publican when he hung up his truncheon, must have been tired and emotional when he entered into the jolly jape. If he ever did.

The reported involved, one David Bromfield who I had earlier invited to my home, quoted me as cheekily saying: 'Very nice of him . . . but Sue and I are fully booked.' Lovely, especially as I had never received any invitation in the first place. And I didn't consider it all that side-splitting anyway. Ages later the card did drop through my letter-box. It bore no resemblance to the invite printed in the *News of the World.*

*

Making it all up. Fabricating quotes. Distorting facts. Intrusion. I get it all. We have also been the victims of downright crooked deception. Sue had gone back to the flat in Hendon, sorting out some business matters, and her mum and dad had come down to join her. Sue had experienced a tough time at the customs because she had brought back my passport for renewal. The immigration boys had seemed excited at the prospect of yours truly walking through the door at any minute.

Anyway, Sue was taking a bath next morning when the door-bell rang. She picked up the intercom and the caller introduced himself as an 'Inspector Wilton'. Sue told him it was a bit inconvenient and asked him to come back. But the caller was most insistent, stressing it was a certain matter of great importance that could not possibly wait. Whereupon my Sue gets herself decent in double-quick and lets them in. On reflection she often kicked herself for not thinking to ask for their identification. But then, she's a trusting sort of lady.

They were two big heavy gentlemen who came a-calling, looking every inch like your genuine Old Bill and Ben. The obvious boss of the dynamic duo said he was Inspector Wilton and did my Sue know she was being followed? By this time Sue's parents had come into the room and they heard all that was going on. They told her that I was under observation concerning £100,000 worth of traveller's cheques. Sue said she didn't know what they was talking about. Sue began to get a bit suspicious because one of the men began to look around the house, poking his nose where it wasn't invited. So eventually she asked them for their warrant cards. Upon this request our heroes began to look a bit flustered. Did they hear correctly? Warrant cards, did madam say? But only the cops carried warrant cards. Not people like them, who were working for the *News of the World.* They could not conceive how such an unfortunate misunderstanding could have arisen.

Sue was furious and threw them out. Our lawyers said we could sue them, particularly as Sue's parents were witnesses to all that happened. But there was no point in getting involved in court cases. There was no way we could do that without returning to Britain to contest the case. That was not really a brilliant idea. I suppose the papers are fully aware of that situation and count on that fact when they give us the run around. I have been advised by experts that if I can clear up this little matter to a satisfactory conclusion I can sue the backsides off half of the tabloids in the country. I'd really love to do that . . . give them a taste of their own medicine.

After Sue had been conned by the fake coppers, it all came out in the papers. The headlines said Sue was back in London laundering Ronnie Knight's dough.

Probably the sickest the hacks got was trying to bribe members of Sue's family, who are all decent, straightforward people. It got so bad that her parents had to take out an injunction to stop being harassed and hounded. Reporters were camping outside their home making their lives a misery.

The reporters even followed our young nieces and nephews to school. They knocked on the doors of family and friends offering a nice few quid to anyone who would tittle-tattle about me and my Sue. One woman reporter, who worked on a local paper, wrote a vicious piece claiming inside information 'cos she went to school with Sue. That was a load of cobblers. They may have been in the same school building. But Sue never even knew her.

Many a time I've been tempted to belt those lovely people who think they have every right to intrude on my life, hiding behind rocks and getting us out of bed in the middle of the night. I know they have got a job to do. I don't mind a decent, straightforward approach. But they won't take no for an answer. And I know that if I give 'em what for they will get a better story and more money. So why should I do them any favours?

The law in Spain says that if somebody comes into my house I can do anything I want to show them the error of their ways. But I restrain myself. One of my golden rules is never to answer the door – or step outside. If you do they've got you in their little clickety-click boxes.

They have tried every approach in the book.

Like on the day I was looking out of my bathroom window when I sees this funny-looking character a-dithering by my garden gates, like he was dying to take a leak, but couldn't find anywhere to go. The dogs started barking and Sue goes out to investigate. This guy is beaming like Santa Claus and saying he's new around these parts and does she know where Mr Knight lives. Cheeky as you like he walks down the garden to the front door, arms held about his head like he's surrendering. Then I notice what his game is. In his hand he's got this

197

tiny little camera and he's shooting away like a big-game hunter on safari.

Suddenly, I shouted out: 'Sue hold him!'

I thought the bloke was going to soil his pants. He stares up and saw me glaring down at him only a few feet away.

When she's roused my Sue can be a demon. So by the time I fly down the stairs faster than a speeding right hook, she's got this little weasel up against the wall. He's whining and wailing so much you would think he was for the high jump. I quickly relieved Sue of her task and gently suggested that the intruder might care to hand over his sneaky box of tricks to my Sue. He complied with a speed that suggested the camera was about to explode. I asked Sue to take the film out, but she was so worried I was going to bash him she got over-excited and could not open the back.

Reluctantly I let him free and tried to remove the offending film. I was getting mad because I could not sort out how it worked. Sue's pleading with me not to hit him. I tell the bastard that he's trespassed on my property now and that under the very sensible Spanish laws I can fucking well kill him if the mood takes me. Suddenly the intruder pipes up in his reedy little voice: 'Please give it to me, Ronnie. Don't do nothing to me, don't get mad or give me one . . . and I'll open it up for you.'

He pulls out the film, holds it up and hands it to me, a look of impending doom on his chalky face.

'It's not my fault,' he bleated. 'It's the first time I've ever done anything like this. Only the office sent me out and they said I'd got to get some pictures . . . or else.'

My soft old heart slipped into gear again. Suddenly I felt sorry for this pathetic runt who had probably spent a lifetime having people kick sand in his face. So, without more ado, I kicked his tail and told him to hop it.

A few days later we found he had been virtually camping out under a rock at the bottom of the garden. He started shaking soon as we copped him. Without so much as a polite request he started to hand his camera over again, promising he hadn't got any pictures. I knew he hadn't. He was shaking so much the poor sod could hardly breathe. I felt sorry for him after that, and in a moment of total weakness I looked at the camera in his hand and hung on just long enough for him to snatch a shot. It wasn't the sort of photo you would stick in the family album, but he couldn't have been more pleased if he'd got the scoop of the year.

Other more persistent and pestering Press people are not so easy to deal with. We've been tailed in car chases, tracked down at friend's homes and hounded in restaurants. One night we threw off a couple of paparazzi types. First I drove along a winding, narrow mountain road, then hid my car in a back street in Fuengirola before walking through a hotel, leaving by the staff quarters. But the bloodhounds managed to stay on our trail. I was walking back to our BMW when a car pulls up next to it. Suddenly this bloke jumps out, leaps over the bonnet and starts firing away with his motorized camera. The way he was shooting them off it was obvious he was getting free film.

'Ha-ha, I've got you now Ronnie Knight and there's nothing you can do about it.' He cackled like a witch.

Well, I couldn't have that, could I?

He stood there grinning at me like some schoolkid.

'You've got me have you? Very clever. But you are wrong. I can do something about it.'

So I pushed out an arm, casual as you like, and suddenly this cocky cameraman is flying over the bonnet of the motor. Behind me Sue's crying 'Oh, Ron, don't do it, don't do it!' In front of me this individual is squealing: 'Ronnie, don't do it, don't do it.' It was like hearing it in stereo. I turns to Sue and tells her it's all right. I tell him he's a waste of fresh air and he's going to get some. His cameras are lying across the street. The guy who I take it was the writer of the duo nips up to me and pleads: 'Don't get mad, Ronnie. We're just doing our job. Please don't.'

I suggest he kindly removes himself; and jumps in my car. As we are about to roar off up he jumps, this cameraman, grabs his Nikon and tries again to snatch some snaps. So I slammed the car in forward, drove straight towards him – and back over the bonnet of the parked car he goes.

*

It's not just the Press that have hounded us. One or two other tricksters have pulled sweet little strokes. And made a nice bit of the green stuff out of selling me down the river. A greedy, sneaky little toe-rag did the dirty on us, pretending to be a long-lost friend and relative. Sometimes I wonder how I fall for them. I must be a soft mug at heart. This bloke turns up at our wedding, bluffs his way in saying he's a mate of Terry Downes.

'Course I knew Terry, the ex-world boxing champ. Well, I'm in a good mood 'cos it's my wedding and all. So I says hello.

'They all send their regards Ron. Here, don't I get a drink to celebrate then?' the cheeky beggar enquires.

I feel a bit mean, so I let him into the company. Before you know it he's the life and soul, popping up all over the place having his picture taken with everybody. Next thing there's a big picture of me and Sue on the front page of a tabloid newspaper with this bloke's arms round us. I know the picture was doctored. But it looked convincing enough.

This bloke claims he is my secret cousin and he has a little story to tell – like how me and my Sue keep popping in and out of London in a tiny, private airplane. Every few weeks I buzz in and out, he revealed. Last Saturday at 7 p.m., I'd jetted in for a night on the town. Another time they said Sue and I were dropping in to see doctors and get fertility treatment.

I know the newspapers pay these jokers thousands of pounds for their lying little tit-bits. I know the editors cannot believe them, because it don't take an intellectual to deduce that things like that are impossible. What I wonder most is: do they really expect the readers to swallow all the fantasy. Or don't they give a damn?

*

Then there was the time eight burly Welsh rugby players hatched up a plot to kidnap me. Someone had kidded the boyos that there was a £60,000 reward on my head. So they decided to come get me. They drove all the way through France in a clapped-out van, carrying an inflatable dinghy, ropes, chains and all the other paraphernalia a kidnap gang is likely to need.

Then they checked in at a backstreet apartment down in town and worked it all out. They were going to abseil down the mountain over my house, grab me, bundle me into a van, drive down to the beach, put me in the dinghy and whisk me the 60-odd miles to Gibraltar. If that failed they were either going to ambush me in my car, or grab me as I left a restaurant. The Welsh Wonders reckon they took three weeks working on their infallible plan, carefully rehearsing the routine, trying to spot any pitfalls.

What they did not take into account was their own drinking habits. On the night of the planned snatch, they dropped into a bar for a glass of Dutch courage and a final points-check. The lads were so thrilled at the thought of making £60,000 for a night's work that one or two of them burst into song . . . as you might expect. One or two locals were not particular music-lovers and politely enquired where the pain hurt most. Sadly it all developed into a bar-room brawl that left them too bruised and battered to carry out any kidnapping.

I think they really lost the heart for it when the police towed away their van for illegal parking. And someone told them that the £60,000 reward was just a hoax. They were nuts. But harmless enough.

19

We all have them. They make us squirm. We want to forget it ever happened. I'm talking about . . . Embarrassing Moments.

My biggest blush came when I went with Sue to hospital for her to have some fertility tests. And I ended up being asked to have a sperm count! I soon found out that this particular method of counting had nothing to do with adding up. And when I got the message of what exactly was expected of me I could have hidden out for a week in a row of beetroots.

We both want to have a baby. Okay, so I'm getting on a bit. I've got two grown-up children and I make no claims to being a model dad. But I know Sue would love to be a first-time mother. And what Sue wants is fine by me. A child would make our happiness complete. We'd be a lovely little family and we would both be contented. Heaven knows we've tried hard enough. The Lord loves a trier, but so far we have not been blessed.

We always enjoy it when Sue's sister Sal comes over with her four little 'uns. They stay for weeks on end and when they go back the house seems a bit empty and somehow lacking.

Anyway, Sue had lots of tests trying to find out what was wrong. She's been going to the famous Familia Sagrada Clinic in Barcelona. I slept there a couple of nights while she had all the exploratory probings they do. What never occurred to me was that there was any question about the well tried and tested Knight equipment. After all I had fathered a healthy son and daughter. There was definitely no failure in my engine room. I was firing on all cylinders and I've never been one for wasting an opportunity to make Sue's dream of a baby come true.

So I must confess it came as a bit of a stunner when the docs said they wanted to check me out. At first I thought that meant an intimate examination of the old job and tackle. That very thought brought a blush to my cheeks. Then the medics explained that fertility is all a question of the potency of the sperm. The merest suggestion that my produce was not up to scratch dented my pride. I was quick to point out that the supply had never been more fruitful in that direction. Aha, they explained. What they were talking about was not so much your quantity as your quality.

Oh, that's all right then. Thank you for the information.

If I hadn't loved Sue so much I don't think I could have agreed to even go along to the Malaga hospital. After we had talked to the docs about my situation, thought to be the result of one of my illnesses, they took me into a little cubicle. A young nurse walks in, whispers in Sue's ear and smiles knowingly at me. Sue gives me a tender, loving look and leaves. This sweet young nurse produces a little glass bottle and cool as a cucumber asks me: 'Please, put the sperm specimen in there.' As she closed the door I got an encouraging little wink and was left to get on with it.

Well, I just couldn't. No matter how I tried it was no good. It was as simple as that. I lay back and thought of Sue. In fact I tried to think of a lot of things to get me in the mood. But try though I might I could not rise to the occasion. I felt like a naughty little schoolboy. And I remembered all those terrifying stories about your hair falling out and going shortsighted. Poor Sue, I thought. She had been through so much pulling and poking about. It was the least I could do to suffer a bit of embarrassment and produce the goods.

But I couldn't. Once, when I had a slight surge of hope that I could manage it, a couple of nurses started chattering away behind the door . . . and I was fumbling and on my feet in a twinkling. I did me best to get down to it again. But I heard a typewriter clattering away. Then mumbled voices. It was no good. In the end I smartened myself up and bit and tip-toed to the door. I gingerly opened it and looked out.

There was my Sue, sitting quietly, wringing her little hands, looking for all the world like an expectant father.

'Pssst . . .' I hissed. Sue came over.

'It's no good, Sue. I just cannot do it.'

What I really needed was a helping hand!

The doctors grinned. They understood. But not in the cubicle, I insisted. It was useless even trying. This caused some concern. Apparently the old spermatozoa's lifespan is pretty limited and dies by the millions if it's outside body temperature. So there was no question of us popping 20 miles back home and dropping a sample by at our leisure, like you can do with urine.

Trust Sue to come up with the perfect solution. We checked into a hotel near the hospital. We went up to our room. We did the necessary. The receptionist gave us some funny looks when we dashed out after only a few minutes. Then we got a taxi back to the hospital. Sue kept the little sample bottle at the perfect temperature by storing it under her arm.

Tests showed that my count is a bit below par. Sue's got a blocked tube or something, which makes it difficult to conceive. But personally I reckon that the biggest problem is the constant pressure we are under. Nature has a wonderful way of sorting things out. Maybe it's a way of telling us that now, with all the uncertainty, is not the time to have a baby.

So although we would like to be parents, we aren't getting obsessed about it. If one comes along, then great. If not, we still have each other.

My Sue is a very sexy lady. She's a lovely looker with a figure like a model. In fact after studying at an all-girls' school she went to the London Academy of Modelling but packed it in because her folks didn't consider modelling a career for 'nice girls'.

If there is one thing that I love about Sue it's her laughter. In some of my darkest hours, and gawd knows I've had my sprinkling, she has raised my flagging spirits with her unfailing sense of humour. Remember how I said it was her laughter that first attracted me to her on that first day at my club? Well it still feels the same.

On one of those occasions when we were surrounded by the Press and I was feeling like a caged bear with a sore head, Sue suddenly says: 'You watch this.'

She strolled out into the garden, like she didn't have a care in the world, turned on the hose and started watering the garden. Hello, funny, I thought, 'cos the gardener usually did that at night. Suddenly Sue turns with the hose on full blast and gives the gang of reporters huddled round the gate a really good washing down. To be fair, they took it in relatively good spirits and it eased my tension no end.

Another time I felt really needled was when I lay in the surgery after an acupuncturist had spent hours sticking hundreds of pins in me to treat my bad back. They had put little electric wires round the pins. 'Whatever happens, don't move.' That's what they told me. My little bed is surrounded by a screen. Suddenly I hears a lot of scuffling about and the scraping of bedlegs. Hello, I think, they're giving somebody else the works. I'm lying face-down when the screen suddenly opens. I see this white-coated figure and a stethoscope swinging from the neck. A soft, velvety hand tickles down to where it didn't ought to and I hear: 'Can I do anything for you, Sir?'

Sue starts to giggle. I have to bite my tongue to stop myself hooting with laughter.

'Please don't make me laugh Sue, 'cos they'll go stark, raving mad if the needles come out,' I pleaded.

The biggest stroke Sue ever pulled on me left me looking like a prize idiot. As an inner-city boy, I must confess that I've never thought much about your gardening. Tilling the soil and greening the fingers was not my line of country. When I was a nipper I used to think they made fruit and vegetables down at the market. But when I had my bit of Spanish land and time on my hands I decided to get into spirit of The Good Life and grow my own. I planted a few radishes and a row of spring onions. When the little seedlings pushed their heads through the soil I was beside myself with happiness. It was a little miracle, that's what it was. Encouraged by my outstanding success I put in a couple of sweetcorn, marrows, cauliflowers and beetroots. Every morning at the crack of dawn, before the hot sun came up, I'd be down at my little plot watering the plants and pulling the weeds. I'll tell you everything grows like wildfire in the rich Andalusian soil. Conditions are absolutely perfect.

One morning, up with the lark, I walked down to inspect my plot and I couldn't believe my eyes. My harvest had come in all at once. Overnight at that. I had king-sized caulies . . . giant marrows . . . beets . . . and a lovely bunch of carrots. I'd already whooped for joy and was running down the path shouting for Sue when I suddenly realized something funny was going on. I hadn't planted no carrots. And the cauli was nicely trimmed.

Sue was beside herself with laughter at how I had fallen for that one. I tried to laugh it off and say that of course I knew, but she was right. For a few delightful minutes I did think it was all my own work.

Sometimes, though, Sue's little fun and games back-fire on her.

One night we came home after dinner. It was in the middle of a tropical downpour with raindrops big as ice-cubes splattering down. I ran down the path to get the kitchen door open so's Sue could rush straight in. After a few minutes I hear her crying out 'Ronnie, Ronnie, help me'. Knowing she's got some fiendish trick in mind I shouts back 'Yeah, yeah, I'm coming.' I pokes my nose outside the door expecting a wet sponge in my face or a bucket of water over me. Then I hear her cry again and see her legs sticking in the air halfway down the side of the mountain.

'What you bleedin' well doing down there?' I wanted to know.

Sue explains she thought she'd heard some animal in trouble, had gone to investigate and tipped arse over head.

I scrambled down the hillside, with water cascading down, did a double-somersault and crashed beside her in a thicket. We were both covered in mud, scratched to pieces – and chortling our heads off.

Sue is the most important thing in my life. She does everything for me. She gives me so much love. Anything I want she makes sure I get it. Like when we are going out. I'll wonder what to wear, then go upstairs and find everything laid out for me on the bed. She matches my shoes, shirts, socks and trousers. Everything.

Sometimes I look at this poor little country girl and think what did she ever do to end up with me? I mean, she has gone through it, hasn't she? She's been pestered and hounded, called a tart, gangster's moll – and even faces arrest if she goes back home to see her old mum and dad.

I love that girl, sure enough. Despite all the misery, doubts and fears, we have lots of fun times. Sue has the gift of making people happy and gets them all going. We are blessed, we know it and we are thankful. We share the same dreams – to first get over all the trouble that plagues us, then settle down to a nice, simple and quiet lifestyle.

Both of us are potty about animals. We have our dogs that are almost as close as a couple of children. We've also got a cat . . . and if I didn't put my foot down I reckon our house would look like Noah's Ark. Sue found a wild kitten living under a rock up in the hills recently. Every morning and night Sue was trotting up there taking it milk and little tit-bits. She got to love the little thing. It broke her heart when our alsation R.J. tried to eat it. Sue nearly lost a finger, trapped in the chain, getting R.J. off the kitten. It died soon afterwards and Sue was really cut up.

Our dream is to buy a little finca up in the mountains. A few acres of our own where we can run a smallholding, grow our own grub and have as many animals as we want. I have no idea why I want a farm. I am a city boy. I've always favoured flash cars and I cannot really see myself perched on a clapped-out old tractor. But that's what I want. There will be no matching the expensive suits and shirts if we take to the hills, just a pair of wellies and old shorts.

Despite all the talk of me being a rich man (some jokers claim I'm a millionaire) I still have to earn a living. Like I said, when we first came out here we had a nice few quid stashed away and all legit. But when you draw on your capital, it tends to dwindle like an icecream cone in August. So I have to carry on working to pay the bills.

I don't suppose I'd ever make Chancellor of the Exchequer, but by using the business sense I've got I have managed to get by and earn a reasonable lifestyle. When me and Sue first came out here we were in comparative clover. We had our nest egg, put some down on a couple of apartments and had a weekly income from the car hire and Wyn's bar. A lot of local people play the flats game. You pick out a nice new block you fancy that's getting built and make an initial payment. Then you pay in stages until the apartments are completed. By that time they have gone up at least five or ten grand, so you unload them at a decent little profit.

When we got out of the car and bar business I opened the Indian restaurant down in Fuengirola, for no other reason than I've always liked a nice bit of curry and fancied my own place. I called it The Mumtaz . . . the same name as the place in swanky Puerto Banus, your millionaire's yachting harbour in Marbella. On one of our rare excursions into the expensive jet-setters' paradise we went for an Indian. I liked the meal, chatted to one of the managers and before you could say takeaway-tikka we had decided to go into partnership.

However, I soon found out it is one thing liking a curry. It's an entirely different proposition owning a friggin' restaurant. I'd got an Indian partner and Indian staff. when I am on the premises I stick out like a vicar in the front row at a strip show. I didn't fancy sitting there all night with my turban on. The restaurant game's not for me.

Anybody who thinks I'm just a rich little playboy filling in his time should cop me three nights a week helping to run an all-night club on the beach front in Fuengirola. It's called 'The Roxy', has a mixed clientele of Brits, Scandinavians and local Spaniards – and it's packed every night. The takings are fair. But I promise you that sitting through eight or nine hours of your new acid rock music is not my idea of a little sinecure. It's bloody hard work and there are times when I'd give anything not to have to spend the night getting my eardrums blasted. But we all have to make an honest quid or two.

Once or twice I've toyed with the idea of opening a friendly sports centre not far from where I'm currently residing. Bowls is one of my favourite games. I know, I've heard all the rubbish about it being a pensioner's pastime. But that's a load of bowls. I'm not one of your golfing set, because as I mentioned I get shy if people start watching me. When I used to have a dabble I was always waving on the people behind me. It got so that I hardly got past the second tee.

Sue and me work out in our little gym keeping ourselves in good condition, 'cos we both like to keep fit. We take long walks with our dogs, wandering for miles over the mountainside. It's nice and peaceful up there. You can get away from the work and worries . . . of what might or might not happen. Live for today. And enjoy every minute. That is all you can do.

Will I be extradited from Spain? Will I be booted back to Britain and end up behind bars again? God knows. I don't.

All things considered – and despite the uncertainties – I am content with my lot. My biggest joy in life is helping round the house, preparing meals and doing a bit of cooking myself. I am not too proud to get my hands stuck in the washing-up water. Now there's one in the eye for them that say I'm a chauvinistic piglet.

Most mornings I'm first up, taking Sue a nice cuppa tea. Sometimes I take her a red rose to wish her a happy day. Then it's out to scour the garden to shovel up the dogs' naughties before giving them their cornflakes. We zip into town, do a bit of shopping, come home and get a spot of lunch. Most nights we either have friends round or go out for a dinner. We watch videos a lot and telly – anything but 'EastEnders' which we cannot stand at any price.

The Press are always making out I'm a hard man. I've always been able to look after myself, but I am nothing like the gangland character they love to paint me. If they followed me around for a couple of days they would die a slow death . . . from boredom. But then, nobody wants to ruin the carefully created legend by revealing the truth, do they?

Sometimes of an evening I get a bit nostalgic and think about going back home. We both miss our families, though it's not so bad for Sue 'cos her mum and dad and sister's family come over regularly. But we are happy in Spain and have learned to live with the sword of uncertainty hanging over us. We hope and pray that we can live out our lives here, following our dream to farm that little bit of land. Time is getting short. I want to do those things while I can. The future is in the lap of the gods.

What terrifies me more than anything is the dread that my Sue dies before me. I don't want to be left alone. I could not live without her.

*

In the spring of 1989 Sue and I were arrested on some technicality. We spent a couple of nights and days in Malaga jail. It was not exactly the Ritz, especially for Sue.

It was early one morning. I'd had to put my stiff collar back on 'cos my neck had been giving me some stick and Sue had gone into town to do the shopping. The gate bell rings and as is my custom I have a sudden attack of deafness and keep quiet as a churchmouse. The ringing continues and when I look out I see four Spaniards standing there. Now a few days earlier, my faithful four-legged friend R.J., who normally found it an effort to bite into a juicy steak, had been involved in a tiny altercation with the postie, a really smashing guy.

While we had been out the previous day the police had turned up with a local vet, just to make sure that my dog was not a dangerous beast on the loose. They just wanted to check him over. Since I had absolutely no doubt that it was a mere formality I had no objection whatsoever.

So I assume, reasonably enough, that the four-man visiting party is on the dog inspection patrol and I happily invites them into my garden. I am opening the dog's mouth and telling them what a good, soft boy he is, and patting him on the back when they ask to go inside the house. What do they wanno go in the house for? The question rushes through my mind as R.J. behaves impeccably, making me very proud of him. 'He's a good boy, isn't he?' Good as gold. No trouble to anyone. Up jumps Miss Ellie, my newly acquired alsation companion for R.J., whose interest in her is purely friendship seeing as how he's had the snip. I begin to tell my visitors that Miss Ellie is so gentle she should be a sheepdog.

These people still want to go inside the house. Then it was dumb, dumb me. These are not the people about the dog. It had taken a long time dawning, but as they pulled out their impressive identity cards I realized that they were not in the veterinary business. It was not R.J. they wanted to inspect. It was R.J.K. What's this about, I wondered? Discovering the facts was not easy for two reasons. Their English wasn't up to much and they were not very talkative anyway. They managed to convey the message that what they wanted was my passport. Luckily, as events turned out, I did not have it. Sue takes care of that sort of thing.

I was not allowed to make a phone call. They took me off in a private car, just giving me time to tell my neighbours 'They are taking me away'. Then I had a brilliant idea. I told the officers that my passport was with my solicitor. They drove down to his office and two of the agents went inside. They came back saying my lawyer did not have the passport. I breathed a sigh of relief. I was not worried. At least my solicitor now knew about my predicament. Without much more ado they whisked me off to Malaga. They took me to the police station. They put me in a room and quizzed me. Again it was a bit difficult since we were speaking in different languages, neither understanding much of the other.

After they got tired of talking to me I had a visit. I believe it was Mr Thomas Tuite, himself, the British Consul in Malaga. We had a little natter. Next day all the Press knew. Back home, Sue had returned and could not understand where I was, especially as there was no note. So she starts to panic, nips to see friends nearby and is very confused because they, too, are in the dark. Not until later did Sue see our American neighbours who informed her that they had taken me away. Before she can do a thing another car arrives – and they bring Sue into the prison.

When I first glimpsed her down the corridor my heart lit up. Hello, I told myself. It's my Sue. She's brought the passports, probably got our lawyer with her. I was looking forward to a celebration lunch. Only Sue didn't get me out. She came in. Any sense of fun and frivolity that might have kept my spirits buoyant up to that time now totally deserted me. We were put in a cell – after they had taken everything off us. Sue was stripped of all her jewellery, even her lovely wedding ring. They searched her. Sue nearly died because it was all men there. One of them had a white coat on and Sue was terrified she was going to have an internal search.

Then they took us downstairs. We had the whole rigmarole of photographs and fingerprints. Everything. Back to the cells. I stood aside to let Sue in, then started to follow her. They stopped me. But we are married, I protested. We want to be together. All they would let me do for Sue was to get a mattress for her. The dirty, unkempt bed-covers were thrown out in a yard. They were covered in bird droppings. I managed to scrape off as much as I could for my Sue and took it back to her cell. Naturally I was worried sick about her. What they want to go and do this to her for? If they wanted me OK. But why do this to Sue?

They put me in a cell a couple of doors away. They were tiny and dirty. Absolutely filthy. There was a hole in the floor where you had to go to the toilet. Clunk, click. They locked us up all right. I was eating my heart out because I knew my Sue must be suffering something terrible. All day we had been there, without so much as a drink of water. I had asked for a drink. 'Mañana' was what I got for my trouble.

That was a terrible night. Not knowing was the worst. Not knowing how Sue was coping. Not knowing what was going to happen.

Next morning they came and got us to appear in court. I will never know why they did it, but they handcuffed my wrists behind my back. I nearly cried when I saw my Sue was also in the police bracelets. They had fastened hers in front.

'Thank God, Sue,' I says, when we are standing there waiting.

'Thank God, for what?' she replies because she does not like what is happening one little bit.

'Thank God,' I comes back, 'that they've done you at the front . . . 'cos my nose is itching something chronic, so do me a favour and give us a good scratch.'

She had to have a little smile at that.

In court it was all about us being aliens with no passport. I honestly didn't understand exactly what was happening. Then it was back to the cells. By then some friends had brought us a change of clothes. I just wanted my toothbrush and a bit of deodorant to kill the smell a bit.

I could not get to the sink because somebody had their stinking socks and underwear soaking away. There was some crazy in the cell. A head case from Denmark. He had no teeth. He was obviously as high as a kite on booze or drugs or something.

In the afternoon they had us in court again. This time we were told it was all taken care of. There was no problem. We could go home.

The attitude of the officials changed immediately. The police chief was all smiles and asked us if we would like to join him for a coffee. We said no thanks. All we wanted was to get back to our home. To take a long, cleansing bath. To change into fresh clothes. Just to sit quietly and let the nightmare melt away. To have a good sleep in our comfy bed.

But immediately we walked out into the street it all started. Hordes of cameramen and reporters were waiting outside the prison. They started to hound us and snapped at our heels everywhere we went. By the time we got home the place was already besieged. We pushed our way inside. We were trapped like prisoners inside our own four walls. We could not even step into the garden, take a swim or go for a walk. It went on for days. The pack was getting more frustrated, restless and aggressive.

What they did not know was that I had a hidden television camera and microphone trained on them. So we could tell exactly what was going on and what was being said. The verbal that was coming out was diabolical. We'd had the builders in laying a new patio. I heard one reporter point to a pile of cement and joke: 'I wonder whose fucking body's going in that?'

I heard them plotting: 'What the hell can we tell our offices? There's fuck all new. They're going to love us.'

'Look, why don't we all say we had a word with Ronnie. He told us that he's back in court on Monday and it looks as if he's gotta go back to face the music. Who's going to know the difference?'

While the scribes were plotting their lines a couple of enterprising snappers were poking sticks at my dogs, trying to get them to snarl and look fierce. Some nice person eventually spotted my security camera and bent it.

The tension built up on both sides until something had to explode. It was me that finally went bang. Hundreds of times my thoughts flashed back to that hospital bed when I was recovering from the ulcer . . . when I had vowed never to let them get me down again. Despite all my promises to myself, no matter how hard I tried to contain the anger and frustration, I eventually cracked.

I've got two security systems in my house, covering alarms, safety locks, sirens and lights. There's two emergency systems. Panic buttons they are called, for when you want help quickly and urgently.

I pressed both emergency buttons at once. Again and again and again. Within minutes the place was surrounded by armed guards, police and security men. They even sent an ambulance.

I had sent for help to get rid of the media hacks. But naturally they turned it round. What the papers said next day was that the police had paid a little call on Ronnie Knight. I ask you: is there any justice?

20

The question has been thrust at me a thousand times. 'If you are innocent why the hell don't you go back home and clear your name?' Let me say this loud and clear so there is absolutely no doubt. I know I am innocent. I had nothing to do with that Security Express robbery. Or any other skulduggery. Nothing. And yes, I do want to clear my name. Very much so. I want to wipe away the smears and lies that have almost wrecked my life. I want it all off my back. I want to be free.

Living under the constant threat of being evicted from Spain is a nightmare. Just thinking about it makes my skin itch. Spain is our home, our little paradise. We have a nice villa, little pool and a breath-taking view across the mountains and Mediterranean . . . a vision that will surely flash before my eyes the day I die. Many of our friends from back in England have come to live down here. We have got to know lots of other people who have become special. Thankfully most of Sue's family can get out to see us regularly, like one or two other really old mates of mine.

We lead a good, active social life, visiting restaurants, having barbecues and little outings. The biggest plus, of course, is the lovely weather. It's the best in Europe, where you can sit out 350 mornings a year nibbling your cornflakes and pondering on the joys of life. It's true that there is not much in the way of culture. We miss going to see a good musical comedy, a play or top-class cabaret. The nightclubs here are not exactly our flute of champagne – and we rarely visit the cinemas that have the occasional English version. But we can live without those few luxuries in life.

I hope we can stay here for ever. But I still want to have the freedom to choose to return to dear old London when I wish, to look up my relatives. My old mum Nell is in her mid-80s, crippled with the dreadful Parkinson's, and I love her. She's in a nursing home in England, where I know she is well-looked after and she's happy enough. But I'd give anything to be able to pop down and visit her now and again. I can't.

I also miss the British seasons. The lovely countryside. It's the lush, hundred shades of green fields, hedges and trees that I remember most. A sprinkling of snow at Christmas. Sometimes I get to feeling really low with homesickness. So does my Sue. Every once in a while it gets us down.

As you might have gathered by now I have reasons enough for wanting the slate wiped clean. But most important is that I don't want people to keep thinking I'm a bloody bank robber. I am fed up with having grubby little fingers of suspicion pointed in my direction. And gawd am I up to here with being hunted and hounded by the media. There are times when I feel like a trapped animal, caged and chained and unable to fight back. I never again want those bastards on my doorstep. Every time somebody goes on the missing list they come to visit me. It don't matter a tinker's cuss who it is. It might be some villain I never heard of. But it seems they have to tie me in with whatever is happening. It's my little world they come and disrupt, blundering about like rampant young bulls in a field of fresh heifers. I want to get rid of all this stigma so perhaps the Press will say something nice about us for a change, instead of being nasty about me all the time, like I was Public Enemy Numero Uno.

Okay, then. So that being the case, why don't I hop on a plane and do the business to put the record straight. I would do it tomorrow. I would be prepared to go back and stand trial on whatever charge the police care to bring against me. Before qualifying that very serious statement let me point out a few salient facts.

It has been seven years since the Security Express raid. Not once in that time have detectives questioned me, either during the several months I was in England after the robbery or over here. I would happily cooperate tomorrow if a team of policemen care to knock on my door to clear up any misunderstandings. I would welcome them with open arms. They have taken the trouble to visit several other 'wanted' people in Spain. I have never really understood why – if they are so desperate to have a word with me – they have never so much as suggested a meet. In all those years the Old Bill has produced not a single shred of evidence against me. They waited for five years before they issued a warrant saying I was wanted for questioning 'on suspicion of handling stolen goods'. On suspicion. Nothing stronger than that. That vividly brings back the memory of the time they tried to send me down over the little matter of a miserable £5. They tried to do me on that. And but for the grace of God and dear old Betty Cronk they might well have succeeded.

My firm belief is that the police do not have enough evidence to bring a charge against me. But for some perverse reason they seem to get a kick out of the cat-and-mouse game they play with me. I concede that you can never be sure of anything in this life. Maybe the Old Bill do feel they have a case. Perchance they have been wound up by some aspiring supergrass telling a pack of porky pies . . . perhaps snivelling ratbags like your Messrs Bradshaw and Knight, who tried to stitch me up on the murder charge. You see, these things do happen. In real life, not just the story books. If they believe they have something on me I would be prepared to return to England and stand trial because I have every confidence that I would be acquitted. I would stake my life on it. When you think about it, I damn well would be staking my life on it.

One of the supposed, intriguing big mysteries about me has always been where my money came from, not that it was anywhere near the fortunes bandied about in such cavalier fashion. I have come completely clean on that score. I have told all. Had anyone suggested not so long ago that I would ever reveal the truth about my involvement with The Dirties I would have burst another ulcer at the very idea. But I've done it. It's something I never wanted nor intended to talk about. It's more embarrassing than anything else I have ever had to discuss. I squirm just thinking about it.

Ronnie Knight has bared his soul. You cannot say fairer than that, now can you? Of course, I am plagued by the nagging fear that I might be stitched up again – just like I so very nearly was over the murder and other matters. They tried it before. Could it, would it ever happen again? I cannot believe they would chance their arm a second time. There's got to be a limit on how far they will go. Especially after the blagging the British police force have had over the Guildford Four scandal. And the disbanding of Birmingham's Serious Crime Squad for similar evidence-rigging scandals. With all those allegations of framing suspects hanging over them I would imagine that even the boldest of crooked coppers will be extra careful about their behaviour in future.

But I do not underrate the danger. It's a risk I'd have to take. Even with that possibility staring me in the face I would be prepared to go back, stand up and be counted. This time the case would really be in the spotlight. The world and his missus would be watching the proceedings through a microscope. I do not think they would dare try to fix me again.

So we keep coming back to the million-dollar question. Why don't I do it? The answer is: because I am scared to death. Terrified is a better word. I don't want to go to prison any more. I am not sure I could stand another six months like the time I spent on remand waiting for the murder trial. Six months for something I did not do. Six months that I can never get back.

That's the terror that haunts me: that it could be a case of history repeating itself over this current Security Express business. That's the nightmare that keeps me tossing and turning of a night. I often wake up in a cold sweat with the sound of clanging doors and tin mugs rattling in my ears. Jesus . . . and that smell soiling my nostrils. Make no mistake about it. If I did turn myself in tomorrow I would immediately be locked away. The Old Bill has made it perfectly clear that they want me behind bars. They would oppose any application for bail. The chances are that a court would almost certainly have me remanded in custody, just like before. I could so easily find myself back in the cooler for three . . . six . . . nine months. Who knows? And all for nothing. That I do not want, under any circumstances.

The only deal indicated to me through a backdoor Old Bill source goes something like this: if I care to go back under my own steam they will get me in a remand prison near my family. If I don't and they welcome me under different circumstances then they will make it their business to scour the length and breadth of Britain searching for the sort of place that would not make the Good Guide book. Well thank you very much. But I am not interested in that sort of offer. Why should I be?

I am gambling with what is probably the last few years of my natural. I cannot sacrifice my freedom. I do not enter into the challenge I am about to make with any sense of frivolity. What I am about to say is a very carefully considered and heartfelt proposition. It is a matter that I have spent hours pondering and discussing with my Sue . . . and much that it would break her heart for us to run even the tiniest risk, she backs any decision I make. All the way. That's another reason I adore her.

This is what I am prepared to do to once and for all to end the highly publicized conviction that I am guilty. I will return to Britain if I am given an absolute guarantee that I will be allowed bail pending any hearing or trial. I want a written undertaking that I will not be locked away and left to stew for months while the police 'continue their enquiries'. They have already had seven years to prepare any prosecution against me. If that is not time enough to sort things out at their end, then what do you think?

The fact that I had turned myself in would surely be proof enough that I had no intention of skipping the country again. If I was going to do that I would hardly give myself up in the first place. Well, would I now? So what other reason could there be for them wanting to see me behind bars for as long as possible. What other reason? I can think of none, other than that of sheer bloody-mindedness: that they believe I am implicated but cannot prove it and would just love to see me have a tough time for as long as possible.

I described my relationship with the law as a bit of a cat-and-mouse game. Well, I am not a mouse. It's not really a game. It's far too serious for that. My life depends on it. So does my Sue's happiness. I have spelled out my case as clearly and openly as I can. I sincerely hope that it knocks on the head all the lies and fabricated rumours about my intentions.

As for the cynics out there who are nodding wisely and whispering that I make this offer only because I fear I'm about to be kicked out of Spain, let me say this: my suggestion is not new. I have been making it for years. So far I have had no response from the British police. As for being extradited from Spain, who knows! Had I wanted to I could years ago have fled to other so-called sunshine sanctuaries. I could have taken the Road to Rio. I have not done so. Why?.

If I am kicked out then there is only one place for me to go. Back home. But as matters stand there is no way I will go back unless I get the reasonable guarantee I am asking. If I was daft enough to do that they should book me in at some happy farm for immediate attention.

So there it is. I rest my case.

I must admit that there is one other very important reason why I want to clear the fair name of Ronnie Knight. It would enable me to hit back at all those people who have tried and sentenced me, believing I could never do anything about it. I would become 'Booty Knight' again.

This time the boot would be on a good foot. And I would use it to kick some well-deserving arses.